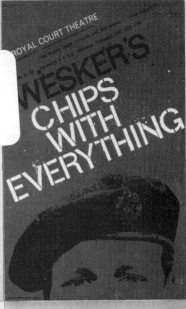

Council of The English Stage Company 1956–1981

Dame Peggy Ashcroft
The Earl of Bessborough
J. E. Blacksell
Neville Blond
* Elaine Blond
* J. R. S. Boas
Isador Caplan
Michael Codron
Lord Cohen of Birkenhead
Norman Collins
Sir Reginald Kennedy-Cox
* Harriet Cruickshank
* Constance Cummings CBE
Ronald Duncan
Alfred Esdaile
* Richard Findlater
Robin Fox
* William Gaskill
* Mrs Henny Gestetner OBE
John Golfar
* Derek Granger
Sir Hugh Greene
* David Hare
The Earl of Harewood
* Jocelyn Herbert
Sir Frederick Hooper
Richard Imison
Oscar Lewenstein
Alistair McAlpine
* Lady Melchett
O. B. Miller
John Montgomerie
* P. H. Newby CBE
* John Osborne
* Greville Poke
* Joan Plowright
* Jack Raby
Tony Richardson
* Rob Ritchie
Lord Sainsbury
* Nicholas Scott MP
Mrs J. E. Sieff
* Lord Snowdon
Julian Thompson
Michael White
* Sir Hugh Willatt
Councillor John Yeoman

* Denotes present Council Members

The English Stage Company at the Royal Court Theatre Sept 1980

Permanent Staff

Accounts

Financial Administrator	Les Michaelson
Assistant	Cleo Hall
Wages Clerk	Eileen Copsey

Administration

General Manager	Anne Jenkins
Secretaries	Fiona McRae
	Susan Needleman
Membership Secretary	Judy Matsumoto

Direction

Artistic Director	Max Stafford-Clark
Director for the Theatre Upstairs	Les Waters
Literary Manager	Rob Ritchie
Assistant Directors	Antonia Bird
	Danny Boyle
Resident Playwrights	Alan Brown
	Gilly Fraser

Front-of-House

House Manager	Richard Masterman
Box Office	Stephen Evans
	Nick Espinosa
	Kim Ringsell
Bars Manager	Douglas Soper
Housekeeper	Phil Allen
Stage Door/Telephonist	Julie McMahon

Press and Publicity

Press Officer	Harriet Cruickshank
Press Assistant	Fiona Waters

Production

Production Manager	David Jones
Chief Electrician	Jack Raby
Assistant Electricians	Duncan M. Scott
	Dick Johnson
Sound	Charles Wright
Master Carpenter	Adrian Cook-Radmore
Assistant Carpenter	Alex Fedorec
Wardrobe	Amanda Kime
Technical Director for The Theatre Upstairs	Matthew Richardson

Young People's Theatre Scheme

Director	David Sulkin
Youth Worker	Catherine McCall
Writers' Tutor	Caryl Churchill

At the Royal Court

Waiting for an audience: the Royal
Court auditorium in 1977. When full it
holds 401 people – 50% less than in the
historic 1904–07 regime of Harley
Granville Barker and J.E. Vedrenne.
(*Photograph: John Haynes*)

At the Royal Court

25 Years of the English Stage Company

Edited by Richard Findlater

Amber Lane Press

Published in 1981 by
Amber Lane Press Limited
9a Newbridge Road
Ambergate
Derbyshire DE5 2GR

British Library Cataloguing in
Publication Data
At the Royal Court.
  1. English Stage Company – History
  I. Findlater, Richard
  792'.09421'34   PN2596.L7R5

ISBN 0 906399 22 X (cloth)

Designed by Pat Ariss ARCA

Printed and bound in Great Britain by
William Clowes (Beccles) Limited,
Beccles and London

Contents

Acknowledgements

Our gratitude is due to all those who have helped in the compilation and illustration of this book, and in the research required to complete its documentation, in particular, to Lindsay Anderson, Athol Fugard, John Haynes, Jocelyn Herbert, Oscar Lewenstein, John Osborne, Greville Poke and Nicholas Wright. We are also grateful to the staff of the Royal Court; and to the Royal Court Theatre Society for their generous financial contribution.

The editor would like to record his appreciation of the help given by Edward Blacksell, Elaine Blond, Stuart Burge, John Dexter, Peter Gill, the Earl of Harewood, Anthony Page and Sir Hugh Willatt. His especial thanks go to Anne Jenkins for her labours on the appendices; to Les Michaelson, for organizing the financial statistics and bringing up to date the tables published in Terry Browne's *Playwrights' Theatre* (Pitman, 1975); to Harriet Cruickshank, who has played an indispensable part in launching this project and keeping it afloat on its voyage to the printers; to Bill Gaskill, who has pursued with unshakable zeal his invaluable research into our illustrations, and has master-minded their selection from many thousands of photographs; and to our publishers, Brian Clark and Judith Scott of Amber Lane Press, for their courage in venturing on this book and their cooperation in the problems of producing it.

For permission to quote from copyright material we are grateful to Irving Wardle and Jonathan Cape, publishers of *The Theatres of George Devine*; to Martin Bax, editor of *Ambit*, which published the full text of Ann Jellicoe's article in its Theatre number in 1976; and to John Osborne and Faber & Faber, publishers of *Look Back in Anger*.

Richard Findlater

Preface

For the greater part of the past quarter-century the most persistently seminal, significantly productive and stubbornly controversial place in the British – perhaps in the Western – theatre has been a small Victorian playhouse in south-west London known as the Royal Court.

On 2 April 1981 the English Stage Company will have completed 25 years at this much-loved, much-reviled and much-repaired showplace in Sloane Square. With extreme precariousness, through one touch-and-go crisis after another, the Royal Court has survived uniquely as a writers' theatre ever since the ESC's first discovery, John Osborne, changed the course of theatrical history with *Look Back in Anger*, staged five weeks after the opening production in 1956.

More than 450 plays have been produced and re-produced on its stages: scores have been transferred to West End playhouses and have reached theatre audiences throughout the world, while many have been screened and televized. The Court has also introduced to the theatre – and, frequently, to the performing arts at large – many leading actors, designers, directors and other theatre workers, serving as a kind of special school for the stage. It has changed the life and work of many established artists, from Laurence Olivier to Max Wall, by giving them opportunities for new directions and fresh growth. It has been a major factor in the development of the National Theatre and also in the evolution of the alternative stage. It has had a widespread influence, still reverberating, upon attitudes to the theatre as an art, a trade and a social activity among politicians, educators, journalists, broadcasters, art apparatchiks and the intelligentsia, and among theatre workers, too. Through some of its more versatile graduates its influence has percolated into television, opera and (most crucially) films. It has attempted to build bridges between theatre and other contemporary arts. It has been a champion of theatrical freedoms, playing a decisive role in the abolition of censorship as exercised (until 1968) by the Lord Chamberlain. It has been a test-bench of stage theory, a personal laboratory for exploring the connections between social and theatrical conscience, prompting the theatre to reflect more closely the social and political contexts of its time. It has been a cockpit of battling egos, and its dazzlingly eclectic range of talent and work defies all pigeonholing and labelling by academics and journalists, including this one. It has been a home for clowns, as well as a workshop for social realists; a platform for stars, as well as ensembliers; a place of fun and games, as well as shocks and sermons. It has set standards in direction, design, lighting, acting, with an insistent respect for the integrity of the text – and it has also set standards in survival. It has been a catalyst of change, a centre of experiment, a nursery of excellence and the focus of a legend.

This book is a celebration in words and pictures of those astonishing 25 years at the Royal Court, supplemented by a factual commentary, a list of productions and other documentary material. The celebrants are some of the people who have worked there at different phases in the past quarter-century. Although they were invited to look on the brighter side of their experiences for such a jubilee occasion, their contributions do not compose – we are happy to acknowledge – a totally unanimous and full-throated hosanna: that would scarcely be compatible with the Court tradition of mutual criticism and dissenting iconoclasm. A different cast might well, at a different time, present a darker and more disenchanted picture of life inside the old theatre in Sloane Square. But to create a comprehensive dossier of unfettered autobiographical testimony by the key talents in the performing history of the English Stage Company, in order to do justice to that history inside its wider social and theatrical contexts, clearly demands a book of a very different kind and size from this one, enlarging and updating Terry Browne's valuable *Playwrights' Theatre* (Pitman, 1975); and that task probably requires for its achievement a safer distance from the past decade. What we have attempted to do here is to reflect, through the contributions of our distinguished cast, some of the reasons why the Court has been so special a place to work in and watch in; and to record, through our selection of photographs, a few of the people and productions from the throng of 25 years.

In the prologue that follows I have sketched the background to this rare jubilee; and in the commentaries which briefly introduce each chronological section I have selected and summarized some of the main events and trends in each period, indicating a few distinctive aspects of the Royal Court's problems and achievements, as I see them.

The book has been compiled at the invitation of the English Stage Company, but they bear no responsibility for any errors of fact or interpretation in my own contributions. This is not a critical survey or an analysis of Royal Court theatricals: the plays, productions and performances are not described (that would double the size of the book) and few are commended. We ask forgiveness from the many for such involuntary superlatives. Our personal experiences of Royal Court productions have included a far wider range of far greater pleasures than we have been able to indicate in a selective documentary chronicle of this kind. We regret, especially, that while we have had to omit from our commentaries the names of many plays, we have been obliged to pass over most of the players. But some may be seen in our choice of photographs, and every one (we hope) is recorded in our tables in the last section of the book.

Richard Findlater

Curtain-raiser

When people talk about the Royal Court, in the world of the arts, they don't just mean a playhouse in London, on the eastern side of Sloane Square. The Royal Court is more than a building. It is an attitude, a discipline, an inheritance, a global constituency whose members are scattered throughout the performing arts. It is shorthand for the complex calligraphy of 25 years' experience in the life of the English Stage Company. But if you want to find the place itself, take the tube to Sloane Square and turn right as you go out of the station. The theatre is there beside it, with a pub on the other side. It has been there since 1888.

The birthplace of Jimmy Porter, Archie Rice and *The Rocky Horror Show* looks, from the outside, like many other decaying Victorian playhouses with facades approximating, seedily, to the French Renaissance style once thought appropriate to the architecture of pleasure. Inside, there are no fingerprints of the past, although for older playgoers the place is thronged with ghosts. From the foyer, a few steps up from the Square, you go into the dress circle, and downstairs to the stalls, where the seats – installed in 1980 after an intensive fund-raising campaign – are labelled with the names of their donors. The bar at the back dates from the mid-1960's; so does the lighting box in what used to be part of the upper circle. Here the working lights shake when the trains rattle audibly underground – a traditional Court sound-effect which is, for addicts, part of its indestructible charm. Up one flight of stairs from the foyer is the circle bar; up two more flights are the theatre's tiny offices; and higher still, at the top of the building, is the infinitely flexible room known since 1969 as the Theatre Upstairs.

If you go backstage downstairs you may find it hard to believe that it was here, in these cramped spaces, that so many outstanding productions of the past quarter-century were created. As you stand on the historic stage, where so many brilliant novices, now internationally famous, first faced a London audience in that traditionally tiered, challenging intimacy, you may strain in vain for intimations of immortality. You have to go round the corner into Holbein Place, past the garage headquarters of the Young People's Theatre auxiliary of the Court, and up a rickety wooden staircase into the leaky-roofed press office, to find the evidence of past glories and disasters, in dozens of files crammed with cuttings, photographs and programmes. Reading through them you may come to feel that, although the Court is more than a building, the building has made 'the Court' what it is.

The uniqueness of that phenomenon may well be unknown to many of the office workers, King's Road shoppers, Sloane Rangers, and tourists who pass the theatre daily, and those rainbow-haired punks who decorate the theatre steps in sudden staccato friezes. The Royal Court has seldom made the headlines in recent years, and it has rarely been a popular theatre, in the widest sense, although it has housed many smash hits and many public favourites. Even when it held some 200 seats more than it does today, before the advent of the English Stage Company, it was frequently hard to make money there and to build a regular audience. As a somewhat precarious outpost of the entertainment industry, it aimed to find long-runners and occasionally succeeded. But the Court has served more often as a platform for rebel professionals, adventurous amateurs, pioneering managers and others struggling to demonstrate that the theatre can be not only a more serious art (or unity of arts) than show business can usually tolerate, but may offer a more exalting, improving, aesthetically enriching and socially valuable experience than Shaftesbury Avenue can ever hope to provide. Behind the English Stage Company a visionary pedigree stretches back to the early champions of an exemplary theatre who believed (like so many of the Court people since 1956) that this was an essential part of society, a major educative force, a potential agent of political change, a temple of ideas and a cultural necessity. The most celebrated of these Sloane Square experiments – and, perhaps, the most influential venture in 20th-century British theatre before the ESC – was the 1904–07 regime of the actor-author-director Harley Granville Barker and his businessman colleague John Vedrenne, whose short-run productions included work by Galsworthy, St John Hankin, Ibsen, Maeterlinck and, most conspicuously, Shaw (eleven of the 32 plays staged), and who succeeded in mobilizing an audience for the 'intellectual drama' (until they moved to the West End). But after a chequered life, financially, in the 1920's, the Royal Court closed down in 1932, was damaged during the war, and did not reopen as a theatre until 20 years later.

Before describing how the English Stage Company came to Sloane Square, let us take a summary look at the state of the British theatre in the mid-1950's. There was no Royal Shakespeare Company or National Theatre (still no more than a foundation stone). There was no fringe. No new theatre had been built in Britain since the war. Many towns had been without a professional playhouse for a generation. Theatrical architecture perpetuated old class divisions and artistic conventions, preserving the picture-frame stage as the only platform for drama. The censorship of the Lord Chamberlain still paralysed the freedom of the dramatist. To many people the theatre, already weakened by competition from television, seemed to be an anachronism, appealing to a tiny and decreasing section of

George Devine, the English Stage Company's first artistic director, photographed backstage before the opening production in April 1956 – Angus Wilson's *The Mulberry Bush*. 'Board-room tactics and visions of the new drama never distracted Devine from the physical essentials of running a playhouse,' says Irving Wardle. 'He loved the fabric of the building...'

the middle-aged and elderly middle class. The London stage, dominated by the long-run system, was moving closer to the hit-or-bust pattern of Broadway, where a play had to be an instant box office success or it would be an instant casualty, probably never to be seen again.

In most buildings there was no continuity of artistic policy and personal direction. Constricted by rising costs and the conservatism of theatre owners, many managers attempted to play safe with musicals, farces, thrillers, light comedies, Broadway successes and adaptations of French successes. The theatre of comfort, the theatre of nostalgia and the theatre of classical revivalism, served by stars and decorated by clappable scenery and glamorous costumes, were the glories of the West End. Many fine artists were at work there, off and on; there was great acting to be seen, at times, as well as great entertainment; high standards of production and casting were maintained by Hugh ('Binkie') Beaumont of H.M. Tennent, who

The writers' stage, seen from the auditorium of the writers' theatre, 1977. The proscenium opening is 21′ 4″ wide and 17′ 9″ high, compared with, for example, the Haymarket's 27′ and 25′ and the Aldwych's 31′ and 19′ 6″. 'I think you can do *anything* on that kind of stage,' says John Osborne. (*Photograph: John Haynes*)

dominated the West End scene for many years, and did much to advance the prestige of the British stage and the careers of many theatre workers. But the drama seemed to be in decline, insulated from contemporary realities and the other arts: 'hermetically sealed off from life', as Arthur Miller put it, famously, in 1956. And at the same time London's 'other theatre' was apparently foundering under the weight of economic pressures: the minority clubs, play-producing societies and other idealistic ventures which had helped to keep alive the arts of the stage (and to feed the industry with talent). Arts Council aid did not, as yet, make a decisive difference, except in the provinces.

In the early 1950's George Devine and Tony Richardson embarked together on an attempt to revitalize this decaying landscape. Devine, who had begun his stage career 20 years earlier as an actor, had been producer and manager of the pre-war London Theatre Studio and director of the post-war Young Vic, two short-lived but seminal ventures. Richardson, 18 years his junior, was a television producer and, like Devine, a former President of the OUDS (Oxford University Dramatic Society). They set out to lease a London theatre for staging the work of neglected writers, with a small permanent company and a permanent setting. Most of the writers on their list were French: only two of 21 were British. They also aimed to search for 'a truly contemporary style'. More immediately, they searched for patrons and a building. They 'explored' the possibilities of two near West End theatres – the Royalty and the Kingsway – and in 1953 negotiated for a three-year lease of the Royal Court.

The Court had been reopened in 1952 by Alfred Esdaile, pioneer of non-stop variety, inventor of the microphone that comes up out of the floor, and builder in 1937 of the Prince of Wales Theatre in Coventry Street. With the London Theatre Guild Ltd. he had acquired both the Court's lease and that of the Kingsway, also damaged in the war. That this retired music-hall comedian, among the sharpest of commercial managers, should be a foster-parent of

12

The Royal Court style, 1961: Jocelyn Herbert's spare, austere set for Arnold Wesker's *The Kitchen*. The shape of the lighting rig follows the shape of the design, in a way then seldom seen elsewhere in Britain. (*Photograph: Peter Smith – Scaioni's Studio*)

events at the Court in the last 25 years is one of the earliest and more entertaining incongruities in the history of the English Stage Company. Esdaile's manager at that time was a Marxist impresario-in-the-making, Oscar Lewenstein, whose theatrical training had started at the age of 30 as business manager of a Scottish left-wing group, Glasgow Unity. Lewenstein, later to become a pillar of the English Stage Company and one of the most enterprising new-model West End managers, met Devine and Richardson and discussed their plans. The Arts Council smiled upon a scheme linking them with the Stratford Memorial Theatre, then run by Anthony Quayle, who was looking for a London base (established eight years later by Peter Hall). But negotiations collapsed, either because Esdaile had lost interest, having found that the current show *Airs on a Shoestring* had turned into a long-runner, or because Devine and Richardson hadn't enough money.

At about this time the English Stage Company began to be hatched in Devon. There are conflicting stories about the time, place and cast but undoubtedly the main begetter was the dramatic author Ronald Duncan, librettist of Benjamin Britten's *The Rape of Lucretia* and standard-bearer of the seemingly renascent poetic drama with *This Way to the Tomb* (1945) and *The Eagle has Two Heads* (1946), adapted from Cocteau.

13

Duncan had launched in 1953 the Taw and Torridge Festival (later known as the Devon Festival) with three friends: Britten, J. E. Blacksell, a Barnstaple schoolmaster, inventor and visionary; and the Earl of Harewood, a royal musicologist (cousin of the Queen) with two conspicuously un-Hanoverian traits – a tendency to leftish sympathies (in contrast with Duncan's rightish, high church ideals) and a zeal not only for enjoying the arts but for working hard to help them by improving their administration and organization. These remarkable Devon allies found it difficult to persuade theatre managers to stage plays for a festival week or two, so Duncan resolved to establish a management to produce non-commercial plays, including his own, and to tour them around British arts festivals, with perhaps a brief season in London. He consulted Oscar Lewenstein, with whom he had become friendly, when Lewenstein brought Joan Littlewood's Theatre Workshop company to play *Mother Courage* at the Taw and Torridge Festival. (Brecht's name is a persistent *leitmotiv* in the ESC story.) Together they formed a Council on which Harewood and Blacksell were joined by three more theatrical enthusiasts – Sir Reginald Kennedy-Cox (chairman of the Salisbury Arts Theatre); Viscount Duncannon, later Earl of Bessborough, himself an author of several plays not yet (or later) widely staged; and an old Cambridge friend of Duncan, Greville

Poke, who had recently resigned as editor of *Everybody's*, and who agreed to act as secretary. At Lewenstein's suggestion Esdaile, too, was invited to join the Council, although at that time there was apparently no plan to take the Royal Court or any other theatre as a permanent base.

More decisively, Duncan enlisted – through Edward Blacksell – the support of Neville Blond, a wealthy Manchester textile magnate who combined business and financial flair with political, bureaucratic and diplomatic experience as a long-time Government advisor on transatlantic trade. Blond was not a theatre enthusiast and did not pretend to be, but he was looking for a fresh interest in life, he was impressed by the ESC's case and status, and the lunch that Duncan and Poke gave him transformed the English Stage Company, in the words of Irving Wardle, who wrote the admirable *Theatres of George Devine*, 'from a provincial festival service to a continuous metropolitan management.' Won over by Duncan's argument, Blond agreed to come in as chairman but only on the condition that the company leased a London theatre; leaving his hosts flabbergasted, he went out to get one. This was the derelict, blitzed Kingsway, which was also under the control of Alfred Esdaile. When Blond set about raising the money, according to Wardle, he characteristically breezed into Esdaile's office and informed him that, as a member of the ESC Council, he would be expected to guarantee £1,000 towards the purchase of his own premises.

The ESC now had a chairman and a building. What they needed was an experienced but also sympathetic man of the theatre to run the company. Lewenstein remembered Devine's approaches, and was asked to approach him in turn. At lunch, says Wardle, Devine 'gave Duncan the impression of being wholly in sympathy with all his theatrical attitudes and plans for the company.' He was not, although both men admired Beckett and Brecht. For one thing, Devine despised the poetic drama which Duncan championed. But that did not emerge until the English Stage Company was in full swing with Devine as artistic director, a post he accepted on condition that Tony Richardson was his associate. He started in March 1955, at a salary of £1,560 p.a. On 7 July he publicly announced the creation of the ESC at a reception in the shell of the Kingsway.

There were unforeseen difficulties with the Kingsway, and the estimates for renovation rapidly trebled in cost. Esdaile, who may already have – as Irving Wardle suggests – 'decided to sell out', had an alternative. At a Council meeting Blond passed a note to Poke: 'Alfred says, would we like the Royal Court?' Poke wrote, 'Not 'arf', and passed the note back. Devine, too, was excited by the offer. When he went round the theatre at Blond's request he found, he told

On the march, 1959. *Left:* George Devine carries the banner on the Aldermaston March, when this annual protest against nuclear arms was still a popular demonstration imbued with festival fervour. *Right:* Left to right: Arnold Wesker, Dusty Wesker, Peter Gill, Wole Soyinka, Miriam Brickman, Ann Jellicoe, Keith Johnstone, Daphne Hunter, Anthony Page. (*Photographs: Lindsay Anderson*)

a later interviewer, that 'the place was in a frightful mess. It was very poorly re-installed. Esdaile kept saying, "It's a lovely theatre, beautiful condition, the switchboard." Well, you couldn't touch the switchboard without getting a 1000 volt shock! There was water pouring through the roof. Then Blond said to me, "What sort of a state is the place in?" I said, "It's perfect, Neville, let's take it." I wasn't really going to be fool enough to tell them what it was going to cost.' Neville soon knew.

The news was released in November. The unexpired 35 years of Esdaile's lease were bought for £25,000, of which £20,000 was to be repaid over ten years (nearly half the price of the Kingsway). The rent was £5,000 p.a. plus nearly £1,000 p.a. for rates and insurance. By West End standards these were bargain figures, but the ESC had very little money. Neville Blond advanced £8,000; guarantees of £1,000 each came from Harewood, Esdaile and Poke; £2,000 from the John Lewis Partnership, owners of the Court's Sloane Square neighbour, the Peter Jones store; the Arts Council gave £2,500 as a pre-production grant and £7,000 as a subsidy for the first year. Without that state aid the ESC could have had no hope of enduring. Without its expectation it would probably never have started.

The house curtain and proscenium borders were removed, giving greater height to the stage. The interior was repainted. A permanent surround, designed by Margaret ('Percy') Harris of Motley, was installed – not only for aesthetic reasons (simplifying the scenic context and giving more light and space to the text and the actors) but also for reasons of financial economy: productions were budgeted at no more than £2,000 each, for *all* costs, no matter how small. When the team began moving into the Court in January there was no money in the bank.

Apart from financial problems the English Stage Company faced other difficulties. The Royal Court was not built for repertory: it had no workshops, inadequate dressing-room and office accommodation, shallow wing-space, rudimentary storage, no green room. In this

On the steps, 1961: the writers' theatre protests against the jailing of writers. Arnold Wesker and Robert Bolt had been sent to prison with other members of the Committee of 100, headed by Bertrand Russell, which attempted to organize resistance to nuclear armament. Left to right: Keith Johnstone, Bill Gaskill, Miriam Brickman, Pauline Melville, Anthony Page, Derek Goldby. (*Photograph: Lindsay Anderson*)

respect it was like most other London theatres; but now it was being used as the home of the capital's first venture into big-scale modern repertoire since Vedrenne and Barker had used the same building nearly 50 years earlier. The seating had been reduced since then; and the top floor rehearsal-room was occupied by a night-club restaurant run by Clement Freud, an unwelcome but obdurate fellow-tenant. It was discovered, after the Company moved in, that the theatre's dome was condemned by the London County Council: until it was replastered, the upper circle had to be closed (a potential loss of £100 weekly). The drains, too, were obtrusively imperfect; and on several occasions the stalls were flooded.

The choice of plays for the first season posed further problems. The novelists whom Devine had solicited for plays, and on whom he counted at the start, had not yet fulfilled his hopes that the Court would bridge the gap between contemporary literature and the stage. Contemporary literature, it seemed, did not want to know about such bridges. By contrast, when Devine put an advertisement in the *Stage* appealing for new plays, he received between 675 and 750 of them (estimates vary) but only one was considered to be worth production. That was *Look Back in Anger*, by an unknown young actor, John Osborne, a play for which Ronald Duncan shared the admiration of Devine and Richardson.

It had long been understood that two of Duncan's plays would be staged in the first season; but there was a scarcity of other new English work. The minutes record an abortive project for the dramatization by Osborne of a novel by an author called Kingslake Amys. The artistic committee of the ESC thought, at one time, of starting the venture with Sartre's *Le Diable et le Bon Dieu* (*Lucifer and the Lord*), and including Lorca, Ionesco, Yeats and, of course, Brecht. Oscar Lewenstein had obtained the rights to stage *The Threepenny Opera*; but the ESC decided that they could not afford to present it, handed back the rights to Lewenstein, and leased the Court to his company on condition that they received a small percentage of the

The first reading of David Storey's *Home*, 1970, on the Court stage. Left to right: Ralph Richardson, Warren Clarke, Mona Washbourne, Dandy Nichols, John Gielgud. 'Halfway through the writing,' says Storey, 'I discovered it was taking place in a lunatic asylum.' (*Photograph: Lindsay Anderson*)

gross. It was for the sake of *The Threepenny Opera* that a forestage was installed at the Court: Brecht again! This production opened in Sloane Square on 9 February 1956. It transferred to the West End two days before Angus Wilson's first play, *The Mulberry Bush*, opened the era of the English Stage Company on 2 April 1956. That had been staged in an earlier version by the Bristol Old Vic. So had the second play, Arthur Miller's *The Crucible*. The Court's explosive discovery, John Osborne, was kept in reserve for the third production, on 8 May.

Richard Findlater

John Osborne*

John Osborne in Moscow, 1957. *Look Back in Anger* – the first Court play to win international acclaim – was taken to the USSR, as part of the World Youth Festival, by Wolf Mankowitz and Oscar Lewenstein. Osborne's work led the way, as in other directions, by mobilizing a new world audience for contemporary British drama.
(Photograph: Lindsay Anderson)

On the Writer's Side

Nobody else but George Devine would ever have put on that old play of mine: that's the absolute truth. It had already been sent back by about 25 managers and agents when I answered the advertisement in the *Stage* and posted it to the English Stage Company. And nobody else but George would have supported it, to the hilt, in spite of a lukewarm reception by most critics; in spite of a slow box office; and in spite of being attacked – and hurt – by a lot of people he respected in the conventional theatre, including personal friends. History very soon began to be rewritten, and nowadays it isn't realized how much hostility George had to face in 1956. Ten years later, I remember, Binkie Beaumont said to my face, '*I* was the only one who really liked *Look Back in Anger. I* thought it was the most marvellous play.' But I knew – everyone knew – that he had walked out of it. Terry Rattigan was vaguely hostile, but so was the entire West End Mafia. So was Larry Olivier, the first time he saw it, although he did a characteristically intuitive U-turn-about later – not exactly about the play but what was afoot. But George was the only one who responded to it, right from the start.

When George and I first met in 1955 he didn't say a great deal but he did make me feel immediately that something very special was about to happen and that *I* was going to take part in it. That may sound now like a bit of ridiculous hindsight but it was true. I had no money, no job, nothing; and he hadn't even got a theatre. But I just felt, I really did, 'This is it. It's all right.' And I lived from then on, for about nine months, on the idea of something that hadn't yet arrived. I already felt looked after. He gave me plays to read – I'd take 40 of them home at a time – and got me to stage-manage auditions (at ten bob a time) to keep me going until we actually got into a theatre. I don't believe that anyone, not even George, had a very clear idea of what, exactly, was going to happen. But he had a *feeling* about it, almost Moses-like, and he managed to communicate that feeling to other people. I've never known anybody else who could do this, as he did it. With Tony Richardson he created a remarkable sense of

19

*In conversation with Richard Findlater

John Osborne and Tony Richardson, in the Royal Court's first *annus mirabilis* of 1956–57. Ten years later, before their ways parted, Richardson said of Osborne: 'He is unique and alone in his ability to put on the stage the quick of himself, his pain, his squalor, his nobility – terrifyingly alone.' (*Photograph: Julie Hamilton*)

Look Back in Anger, 1956. *Below:* Kenneth Haigh as the first Jimmy Porter, with Mary Ure. *Right:* Mary Ure (Alison) and Alan Bates (Cliff). *(Photographs: Julie Hamilton) Below left:* Alan Bates, Kenneth Haigh and Mary Ure. *(Photograph: Houston Rogers Collection – Theatre Museum)* The key speech that made George Devine resolve to stage the play was Jimmy Porter's outburst in the last act: 'It's no good trying to fool yourself about love. You can't fall into it like a soft job without dirtying your hands. It takes muscle and guts. And if you can't bear the thought of messing up your nice clean soul you'd better give up the whole idea of life and become a saint because you'll never make it as a human being. It's either this world or the next.'

excitement, apprehension, as well as a sense of security, for a lot of insecure people. I don't know *how* he managed to do this, operating as he was on such an uncertain basis.

Both George and Tony were completely unknown quantities to me and, of course, I was to them. We were all out there in an unknown world. Nobody knew at all what anyone's real intentions were. For them to support people like myself, as they did, was a great act of faith, and they both expressed that faith openly. This was very rare indeed at that time. The first time that I met Tony, an exotic-seeming, loping creature who looked about seven feet tall, he said, 'I think

you've written the best play since the war.' Immediately, just like that. He was unequivocal about it, and so was George. It gave you an amazing sense of creative trust.

We disagreed about many things, after we'd started at the Royal Court. George knew, for instance, that I despised the Writers' Group (see page 55). I thought it was committee wanking and refused to take part. George went along with it because he thought there was some value in it, but he also went along with my opposition to it. We used to have running skirmishes about Ionesco's plays and other French work. I used to say, 'George, we're not going to do *another* of those, are we?' And he'd say, 'Yes, dear friend, I'm afraid we *are*.' He thought they were good. I couldn't abide them. But he could contain my reaction patiently, even though he was not a patient man. He could contain and comprehend many different things: that was one of his strengths. It wasn't that he was weak and compromising; he could be brutal and dismissive, and he went for what he wanted. But he had a special kind of tolerance. He suffered talent gladly.

We certainly didn't always laugh at the same things, or have the same sense of humour. I remember that at the preview of *Look Back in Anger*, on the night before it officially opened, there was a packed house – unlike the premiere – with a lot of students, and people laughed all the way through. Both George and Tony said, 'Why are they laughing?' And I said, to both of them, 'Because it's supposed to be funny.' There was, in fact, a great gap between Tony and George, and a great gap between George and me. And yet there was this web of trust, a feeling that it's now so hard to recapture.

One splendid thing about George was that he gave you the impression that whatever you did, whatever seemed to go wrong, didn't really matter. He said, in effect, 'This is what we've decided to do. It's right and it's good and we're going ahead.' *You always knew he was on the writer's side.* No one gave you that feeling before, and I've seldom had it since. It wasn't indulgent. It was inspirational support. You didn't know what he thought of your work, in any kind of detail, what his reservations about it might be, but you did know that ultimately you had his complete backing and support. This was – and is, I'm sure – absolutely unique. It might have looked over-protective from the outside, but I don't think it was. He had a really passionate concern for certain people and what they were doing, but it wasn't a blind loyalty. He followed his instinct, and it was a very sure one. He made up his mind, I think, at a certain point whether to support somebody or something, and that was that. His decision had nothing to do with what the newspapers might say, or what might happen at the box office. Above all he hated anything that was merely modish. He could be Calvinist in what he dismissed, but he could have

Later productions of *Look Back in Anger*.
Left: Richard Pasco and Heather Sears,
1957. *Right:* Touring version, 1957.
Jocelyn Britton, Michael Bryant and
Alan Dobie. (*Photographs: David Sim*)
Above: Third revival, 1957. Alec
McCowen, Gary Raymond and Clare
Austin. (*Photograph: Peter Waugh*) *Above
right:* Fourth revival, 1968. Jane Asher
and Victor Henry. This production
transferred to the West End – the first
time, astonishingly, that the play had
been seen there. (*Photograph: Zoë
Dominic*)

the expectation of a small boy at the circus.

I directed a play at the Court by Charles Wood in 1965 called *Meals on Wheels*. It wasn't half bad as a play, but it was a box office disaster. On the first night, about two thirds of the way through, George suddenly appeared – he was always there, somewhere in the theatre, or you always *felt* he was – and he said to me, 'They're *hating* it, aren't they?' And he didn't say this at all despondently; he was delighted because they were hating it for the right reasons, responding as we had anticipated. He enjoyed the irony of it. He had known what was going to happen, and he also knew the limited but particular worth of the play, which no one would be able to recognize or acknowledge. He had a wonderful realism in this way about what the Court was doing. He didn't try to convince himself that everything we did there was necessarily the best play or the most marvellous production, but what mattered was that he thought it was basically authentic in itself and worth doing in the first place. George was capable of a *just* enthusiasm, and it's such a rare quality that this is the only way I can describe it. He could demonstrate that enthusiasm to people and inspire them with it, not only for the business of putting on plays. He humanized the whole process. Can you imagine a commercial manager – a Codron or a White, say – taking the kind of real day-to-day interest in a writer that George took? If George thinks I've had a bad week – I still talk about him sometimes as though he's alive – he would worry about it, really worry. But he always used to say, 'My dear boy, all problems are technical ones.' Even now I repeat that consolation endlessly to other people, and myself.

George never harassed writers in the way that agents – or indeed managements – do. 'What are you doing *next*, dear? How many pages have you written?' That sort of thing. He would just ask you out for lunch or dinner. It was like meeting a friend: that's all. And he probably was my closest friend, but in a reticent, almost removed way. Obviously he was thinking, 'Is the old boy writing something?' or 'Is he all right?' but he never made you feel that he was probing. It's difficult to describe how welcome that was, or how unusual it is. But he did ring me up after *Look Back* and said, 'I know you're doing something at the moment. How far have you got?' I said, 'About the end of the second act,' or something absurd like that. And George asked me, 'Have you got a part in it for Laurence?' 'Laurence?' I asked. 'Olivier,' said George. I really hadn't known who he meant, because I thought of Olivier as Larry – it was actors of George's generation, I think, who called him Laurence. I can't remember what I answered but George asked me to send along what I'd written, even though I hadn't finished the play. I would never have done that for anyone else, but he asked me with such a power of tact. When Larry

Above: John Osborne and Kenneth Haigh outside the Royal Court in 1956. (*Photograph: BBC Hulton Picture Library*)

Right: Two decades on: John Osborne and Nicol Williamson at a rehearsal of the second production of *Inadmissible Evidence*, 1978. (*Photograph: John Haynes*)

read it he decided he wanted to play Billie Rice, not Archie. When I finished it he changed his mind. Just as well – for both of us.

The Entertainer wasn't any better at the Palace, with 1,400 seats, than it was at the Court with a third of that number. The Court is a marvellous building. I know every inch of it. I don't think that any play of mine could have been done better anywhere else. I don't believe that there are any ideal theatrical circumstances, and I don't care what the constraints of the old proscenium arch are, that people go on about so much, because I think you can do *anything* on that kind of stage. I have never seen anything that seems to me to be all that much of an improvement on it.

For ten years, thanks to George, I had a professional life there that I'd most certainly never had before and haven't since. You were part of a family, which accepted all your frailties and imperfections, a family that most of us don't have any longer. Everyone in that little building knew each other – even if they were at odds. And they were. Almost everyone was involved emotionally in what happened, and it helped to power the works. I knew that particular life was over, as far as I was concerned, when George left the Court in 1965. Bill Gaskill continued the tradition more than honourably, but naturally the succession had to change – personality alone made it inevitable.

At the last ghastly annual Savoy lunch for the critics in 1965, when George announced that he was going to resign, the resounding indifference of the silence was really stunning. I didn't believe it. I *couldn't* believe it. Lindsay Anderson, at least, to his eternal credit, broke that silence and spoke for England and tried to point out to an uncomprehending mob of cigar-smoking hacks the significance of what had happened.

One knows now what George had done in those ten years, not just in day-to-day physical hard labour but, what was really important, the emotional and imaginative effort of it all. But hardly anyone in the theatre or outside realized then just how much he was doing, how he hated the administrative load, how much it was weighing him down. He was picking people up the whole time and putting them on their feet again. He had this terrible phrase, 'I wish everyone would just stop swinging on my tits, day after day.' But they did. 'I never want to talk to another actor's agent or draw up another contract,' he would say. But he did. He had to.

I still miss George Devine, every day. How can you really say anything adequate about someone you loved and knew some part of, however small, 15 years after he died?

1956–1957

The Mulberry Bush, 1956. Christopher Fettes, Helena Hughes and Kenneth Haigh in Angus Wilson's first – and last – play. Like the second English Stage Company production, Arthur Miller's *The Crucible*, it had already been staged at the Bristol Old Vic. (*Photograph: Julie Hamilton*)

The English Stage Company began its regime at the Royal Court on 2 April 1956 with a permanent company, a permanent setting and a policy of 'true' repertory. Within a year it was obliged to discard two of these planks in its platform, and the permanent set was finally abandoned a year after that. In order to survive – six months after starting, the Company was in danger of collapse – it had to subsidize itself by mixing new work with classic revivals, and it had to get productions transferred to the West End. It could not look for salvation to state aid or the philanthropy (however generous) of its chairman and other private patrons. It had to help itself, so it had to change its policy. Moreover, although it had set out to attract novelists to the stage (and did so, from time to time) its first new major author came from *inside* the theatre. John Osborne's success, and persistent fertility, helped to ensure (as Irving Wardle says) that although the Court might be a writers' theatre it was certainly not going to be a *literary* theatre. And although it aimed to locate and stage new writing, its revival of classical work proved, from the beginning, essential not only to its finances but also to its productive creativity. These were illustrations, at the start, of how flexible this supposedly doctrinaire group could be.

The ESC's programme for the first twelve months included the first plays of two British novelists, Angus Wilson and Nigel Dennis (commissioned to adapt his *Cards of Identity* for the stage); the British premiere of Brecht's *The Good Woman of Setzuan*; and plays by two celebrated Americans, Arthur Miller and Carson McCullers. But it was the starrily cast revival of an English classic from the 17th century, *The Country Wife*, which, by achieving a transfer to the West End, helped to keep the English Stage Company alive. What clinched that survival, within six months, was *Look Back in Anger*. When it was first produced on 8 May, Osborne's play did not score an immediate hit with the public or the press: several derisive reviewers attempted to give it an instant burial. Business improved after the eruption of the 'angry young man' publicity, sparked by a phrase from the Court press officer, George Fearon. But it was not until the BBC was persuaded to televize a twenty-minute excerpt on 16 October (introduced by Lord Harewood) that the success of *Look Back in Anger* was established; and then, characteristically, the ESC could not enjoy the direct benefit of the box office bonanza because within three weeks the play had to be ejected to make way for *The Good Woman of Setzuan*. *Look Back in Anger* was transferred to the Lyric, Hammersmith; not until 1968, after a further Court revival, was it staged in the West End. But the ESC's profits from the sale of *Look Back in Anger*'s film rights and the leasing of its stage rights saved it from following so many previous experiments into a prematurely early grave.

27

The first year did not turn out as George Devine and Tony Richardson had expected. They believed that the unknown Osborne would be nursed along in the repertory by the box office success of the established names; but *The Mulberry Bush*, *The Crucible* and *The Member of the Wedding* all failed to half-fill the theatre. (Although the Carson McCullers play was given the treatment that had transformed the fortunes of John Osborne, a TV excerpt made no difference. It was replaced in a month by the first revival of *Look Back in Anger*.) Neither *Cards of Identity* nor *The Good Woman of Setzuan* met their sponsors' great expectations.

Nor did the inaugural year of the English Stage Company satisfy the hopes of its prime founder, Ronald Duncan. One principal reason why he had put so much hard work into getting it started was to create a platform for his own work. Two of his plays were in fact staged in 1956 – *Don Juan* and *The Death of Satan* – but at Devine's insistence they were cut down to make a double bill, and they were

28

The Crucible, 1956. This photograph shows Stephen Doncaster's set and the 'permanent' surround (designed by Motley) which was discarded at the end of the first season. Left to right: Josée Richard, Helena Hughes, Mary Ure, Stephen Dartnell, George Devine, Christopher Fettes, Kenneth Haigh, John Welsh, Joan Plowright, Michael Gwynn. (*Photograph: Julie Hamilton*)

produced by Devine with such unsuccessful effect (withdrawn after only eight performances) that Duncan believed him to have deliberately sabotaged his work. From then on Duncan regarded him as an enemy.

None of them could have predicted the way in which the Court – thanks largely to Osborne and his anti-hero, Jimmy Porter – became identified as a symbolic centre of rebellion and dissent among young artists, intellectuals and theatre workers. It was the time of Suez, Hungary and the Campaign for Nuclear Disarmament, when a surge of feeling against the political and cultural Establishment, the social system, the traditional theatre and all authority and institutions swept a flock of brilliant, oddly assorted malcontents into the embrace of a surprised George Devine. It was also the time of Beckett's debut in the West End with *Waiting for Godot*, and the Berliner Ensemble's first visit to Britain; and, whatever the political allegiances of the Court may have been, there was no doubting its bifocal loyalty to both Brecht and Beckett, poles apart though they are. That was to endure: its allure as a temple of revolt did not. But its iconoclastic reputation helped to generate the electricity that crackled inside the old theatre, over its steps where people argued and demonstrated, and into the pub next door where political debate sometimes dissolved into physical combat. And it helped to keep the box office going. That was topped up by a mixture of public and private subsidy. For its first year the ESC had £7,000 in grants and guarantees from the Arts Council and about the same amount in loans and donations from members of its Council, £5,000 of it from Neville Blond. It was hoped that this would bridge the gap between an

The Good Woman of Setzuan, 1956. Peggy Ashcroft made her debut in Brecht as Shen Te, the golden-hearted tart who disguised herself at Shui Ta, a ruthless male cousin. Dame Peggy joined the Council of the ESC in the following year. (*Photograph: Julie Hamilton*)

estimated box office gross of about £1,000 (half the theatre's capacity: 455 seats, from five to fifteen shillings). The Company, in fact, ended in the black, thanks to unexpected additional revenue from William Wycherley and John Osborne. This was to prove, in the next quarter-century, an untypical annual consummation.

Major acting talents to emerge in this first year included Alan Bates, Nigel Davenport, Kenneth Haigh, Joan Plowright and Robert Stephens. Other members of the repertory company included Helena Hughes, Michael Gwynn, Rachel Kempson, John Moffatt, Esmé Percy, Mary Ure and John Welsh. Among the guests were Peggy Ashcroft, Diana Churchill, Moyra Fraser, Gwen Ffrangcon-Davies, Joan Greenwood, Laurence Harvey, Geraldine McEwan and Keith Michell. But it was not only the actors and the authors who were at the root of the Court's success. As Irving Wardle says, 'Devine's method of running his theatre with a small technical and artistic team was then new to Britain. . . . He had done all the jobs himself. He knew what it was to put on a thimble and stitch all night; and he knew what could be expected of people and when the reasonable limits had been reached. Also he took care that the technical staff never formed a ghetto.' At the start the team was led by Michael Halifax, stage director; Kevin Maybury, master carpenter; the resident workshop unit of Jocelyn Herbert, Stephen Doncaster, and Clare Jeffery; Alan Tagg, Richard Negri, Margaret Harris and her sister Sophie Devine (two of the Motley team). In this brief celebration let their names stand for all their successors in backstage miracle-working at the Court in the next 25 years.

This is the place, too, to celebrate the role of the Council of the English Stage Company. It has battled with successive artistic directors and their advisors; it has seemed, at times, remote from the spirit as well as the substance of what came to be identified as 'the Court'; and it has been frequently pilloried in recent years for conservatism, bureaucracy, timidity, philistinism and other sins of omission and commission. Yet, at the least, it has been a necessary evil: an essential instrument of continuity, as holder of the Court lease, recipient of public funds, inspector of theatre budgets, channel to society, as well as buffer between the Establishment and the theatre. And, especially in the first decade of the ESC, the Council proved itself to be a great deal more: thanks to its chairman, Neville Blond, and to such members as Lord Harewood, it stood firmly behind the artistic direction through many political, financial and artistic dangers. It was indispensable to the ESC's survival.

Joan Plowright

A Special Place for Actors

Though it is not a true impression I always have the feeling that my life in the theatre did not begin until I went to the Royal Court in 1956. Before that I had had a two-year classical training at the Old Vic Theatre School, spent a year with the Old Vic company, played at the Bristol Old Vic and in two West End theatres. I was doing a season at Nottingham Rep when George Devine asked me to join the newly formed English Stage Company.

For the first time, at the Court, I felt totally at home in a theatre. I was in touch with people who cared, as I cared, about creating theatre which was to do with the 20th century. I found my own voice as an actress, and an exhilarating sense of purpose which had been sadly lacking elsewhere.

Though primarily a writers' theatre, the Court became a special place for actors too. Until then I had been mostly concerned with the work of dead authors, so it was enormously stimulating to be living alongside live ones, talking to them in rehearsals, arguing with them

The Country Wife, 1956 – the first Royal Court production to be transferred to the West End. 'The contemporary theatre,' said George Devine, 'was saved by a classical revival.' Left to right: Alan Bates, George Devine, Joan Plowright, Laurence Harvey, Robert Stephens. (*Photograph: Angus McBean*)

Above: George Devine and Joan Plowright in *The Chairs*, 1957 – Jocelyn Herbert's debut as a designer at the Royal Court. Ionesco's play was revived twice in the following year, and was also staged in New York, with Eli Wallach in Devine's role. (*Photograph: David Sim*)

Above right: *Cards of Identity*, 1956. Agnes Lauchlan, Joan Plowright and Peter Duguid. Nigel Dennis was commissioned by the Court to adapt his successful novel of the same name, published the previous year. (*Photograph: Julie Hamilton*)

in the pub afterwards and even acting with one or two occasionally. There was literally no other place in existence where I could have become involved with such diverse talents as Arthur Miller, John Osborne, Nigel Dennis, Arnold Wesker, Ionesco and Beckett. I was getting a very broad education and also getting paid for it.

It was an unpredictable theatre for the actors, who were just as diverse in their talents as the writers. We were not a permanent company, though there was a nucleus of promising young people, chosen by Devine and Tony Richardson, who could hopefully encompass a large variety of styles. The style, after all, was going to be determined by the authors, not the actors.

It was shortsighted of people to label us 'kitchen sink' or 'angry young men' (and women) but we were all irretrievably identified with that image after *Look Back in Anger* – whether we had played in it or not. I only played in it once, when the author, George Devine and I presented a potted version of the ESC's work at a gala evening in Rome. Nevertheless the label 'angry young woman' stuck firmly to me throughout my first visit to America with the Ionesco double bill. It had little to do with the old woman in *The Chairs* or the pupil in *The Lesson* but it was indicative of the forceful impression which the Royal Court had made on people in a relatively short time. It had little to do with Nigel Dennis, either, whose first play, *Cards of Identity*, I appeared in by accident. I was playing Mary Warren in *The Crucible* and had not, initially, been cast in the next play. Quite suddenly one night, shortly before rehearsals were due to start, Tony Richardson said, 'We've all decided that we want you to do Miss Tray in Nigel's play.' I admired his writing and liked him enormously. His approval of me as an actress manifested itself in such oblique statements as 'I'd like to lock you away in a cupboard and feed you saucers of milk from time to time.' Presumably until he had written another play in which I could appear. He did write his second play, *The Making of Moo*, with three specific actors in mind – George Devine, John Osborne and me; though I am not sure if the experiment was ever repeated. Anyway,

The Making of Moo, 1957. Left to right:
Martin Miller, George Devine, Joan
Plowright, Robert Stephens, John
Wood. Nigel Dennis's second play was
subtitled 'A History of Religion in
Three Acts.' (Photograph: David Sim)

we loved it for its wit and inventiveness and enjoyed rehearsals tremendously. I was quite shocked after the first night to see my photograph in an evening newspaper under a thick, black headline, BLASPHEMY.

I cannot remember whether it was on the first night of *The Making of Moo* or *The Chairs* when George broke his own golden rule and decided to make a curtain speech. (Both plays aroused a vociferous and not entirely pleasant response from the audience.) Whichever play it was, the speech was a mistake. It is possible to pretend that boos are indistinguishable from cheers when bowing and taking very fast curtain calls. When George stepped forward, however, and indicated that he wished to speak, it was only the friendly, cheering part of the audience who stopped abruptly and the field was left wide open for those shouting 'Boo', 'Rubbish' and 'Disgraceful'. After a gallant attempt to make his reasons for doing the play heard above the din, he finally retired defeated and the stage management thankfully brought the curtain down.

Some time later I was justifiably slotted into the 'kitchen sink' category after the first night of *Roots*. I say 'justifiably' only because there was a real sink on stage, not to mention a real stove, on which real liver and onions were cooked. The play itself, however, was concerned with a great many other and more weighty matters. I, personally, am eternally indebted to Arnold Wesker, who provided for the contemporary actress what Osborne had provided for the actor – a character who spoke to and for our own generation and who had never before been seen on an English stage.

Roots in rehearsal, 1959. Joan Plowright as Beatie Bryant, in exultation, discovering her own voice. Premiered at the Belgrade Theatre, Coventry, like its predecessor *Chicken Soup With Barley*, Wesker's play was transferred from the Court to the Duke of York's, and was revived at the Court the following year as part of the author's trilogy, newly completed by *I'm Talking About Jerusalem*. (*Photograph: Sandra Lousada*)

Four months before *Roots* I had been lured away to the West End by Robert Morley. He had worn down my initial resistance to his play *Hook, Line and Sinker* by remarking how dreadfully pale and overworked everybody looked at the Royal Court. Not to mention underpaid. He said it would do me the world of good to get away, and offered to conduct rehearsals on the beach at Cannes. I was acting in a return engagement of the Ionesco double bill at night and rehearsing *Major Barbara* during the day, and I am sure that I did look pale. The policy at the Court was wide enough to include a classical revival every now and again, either because someone had thought of an exciting new way of doing it, or because it was necessary from a box office point of view. (It was always possible that it would score on both counts, in the way that Jonathan Pryce's Hamlet did recently.) We did not, however, have the same success with *Major Barbara* that we had enjoyed with *The Country Wife*, and by the time the play had finished its six weeks' run Mr Morley's offer had begun to look extremely inviting. Though the sojourn in the South of France put colour back in my cheeks, the play itself gave little satisfaction to anybody. One night Robert wandered into my dressing room and asked plaintively, 'Should we do something worthwhile together at the Royal Court in the spring?' On hearing this, Bill Gaskill promptly offered him *The Man of Mode* (which he unfortunately did not accept) and John Dexter turned up with the script of *Roots* for me. I have acknowledged my debt to Wesker; I need only add that he, John Dexter and I had a marvellous, though argumentative, time during rehearsals at the Belgrade, Coventry and were given a warm welcome home when we opened at the Court. It was the beginning of my long association with Dexter as a director, which continued through the first years at the National Theatre, one of many similar working relationships which were first established in Sloane Square.

I am finally, and above all, indebted to the man who gave his life to the Royal Court, George Devine. Apart from having trained me at the Old Vic School, he proceeded during my time with the English Stage Company to transform me from an actress contracted to play as cast into a leading player with a choice of scripts. To many of us who started with him he is now, quite rightly, a legendary figure. He is sorely missed by us all.

The Entertainer, 1957. Laurence Olivier as Archie Rice. 'He had,' says Bill Gaskill, 'a complete understanding of the role. In an odd way he knew it was about him. His qualities as an actor were seen at their best.' (*Photographs: Snowdon*)

Laurence Olivier

The Court and I

When I was nine I was sent to a prep school in Cliveden Place called Mr Gladstone's School. It was, I think, the first of the houses on the left on the way from Sloane Square towards the garden wall of Buckingham Palace. I believe that my mother must have picked this place because it was only a penny bus fare from Pimlico, where we lived. Mr Gladstone's was a much soncier school inside than it looked from the outside and it was attended by a far higher class of young gentlemen than I had ever found myself amongst before. I think my mother must have had a horrid shock when she got the first term's bill because I was whipped out of the place pretty smartly and sent somewhere else.

When I was still there, however, I was coming out of Sloane Square tube station one day and I glanced up a passage beside it that I had never taken much notice of before. To my astonishment I saw, gathered round what I later knew to be a stage door, a group of men and women with paint on their faces. But what truly amazed me was the extraordinary clothes they were wearing. I stared and stared at them, dumbfounded. I simply could not believe my eyes, that people could get themselves up in such a fashion. I rushed into school and told a couple of boys, 'There are some of the weirdest looking people you ever saw in your life up that passage.' They laughed uproariously at me. 'Why, you stupid fool, that's a theatre,' one said. 'They must have been just actors – they wear those sorts of things – just out for a breath of fresh air. It's hellish hot in those places, I believe.'

And so I became aware of the Royal Court. The next time that it was given to me to be aware of it was when my choir school thought of a charming reward to me for passing my Common Entrance exam – I was given a splendid seat in the dress circle to see *Henry IV Part 2*. There can hardly be a more felicitous choice for a first visit to a Shakespeare play: it has everything of the best that ever could be found in almost any of the works – a wonderfully fascinating story, scenes of great humour and humanity, all the most noble passions and the most stirringly emotional experiences on top of all. The speeches,

too, which I had dreaded might be too complicated to understand, were wonderfully simple and easy to follow, apart from their extreme beauty.

The production, one among four such by J. B. Fagan, was delicate and exquisitely elegant, beautifully contrived, most tastefully romantic and lit with a marvellous suggestion of atmosphere. The cast seemed to me to be superb. I remember Frank Cellier showing no vestige of his youth as Henry IV; a devastatingly attractive Doll Tearsheet, whose name I have remembered ever since – Leah Bateman; and Prince Hal. Oh, that magical Prince Hal, the most

The Entertainer, 1957. Dorothy Tutin and George Relph, as Archie Rice's daughter and father. Dorothy Tutin was followed in the role by Joan Plowright and Geraldine McEwan. (*Photograph: Snowdon*)

George Devine and Laurence Olivier in 1964, looking at the new grid installed during the Royal Court's temporary closure. When Olivier knew that he was going to run the National Theatre he had urged Devine to join him. In Devine's place, with his blessing, Olivier recruited Bill Gaskill and John Dexter. (*Photograph: Zoë Dominic*)

beautiful male I have ever laid eyes upon. His profile was that of a god, his figure pure Olympiad, his voice the most beautiful instrument I had yet heard, and even his name suggested the utmost in glamorous masculinity – Basil Rathbone. To me he had it all, and more, and represented a collation of theatrical virtues that I could never hope to attain.

I had no reason to think again of the Court for a few years after that experience until I enjoyed the enviable fortune of belonging to the Birmingham Rep, in the late 1920's with, among others, a really excellent all-round actress, Dorothy Turner, who was never given her due and was, unhappily, known only for having had a lengthy affair with a very eminent leading man. A wonderful artist she most certainly was but I doubt if anyone now remembers her or if there is any record of her work. She suffered a fate that must have happened thousands upon thousands of times in this profession of so many lost people. Liverpool, our special rival, had, for the most part, better known actors; but Birmingham had a very particular advantage over any other repertory company. Sir Barry Jackson, who built, led and sustained the theatre, was a man of means as well as brains and he leased, at various times, three theatres in London – the Kingsway, the Regent and the Royal Court – which gave his Birmingham actors the perennial hope of being shunted, at some moment, into the capital. And so it was for me.

At first I was quite unable to believe my luck; but gradually, as parts began to be announced and notices to be formally pinned on to the board at the Rep, I had perforce to believe that I was to appear in each of the five productions that were to be presented for a shortish season of six months, from January 1928, at the theatre where I had seen my first actors – and my first Shakespeare. I played a tiny (nameless) part in the graveyard scene in Elmer Rice's *The Adding Machine*; Malcolm in *Macbeth* (in modern dress); Martellus in *Back to Methuselah*; then – a tremendous step forward for me – Harold in Tennyson's imitation Shakespeare play of that name ('Oh! Tostig!

39

Tostig! What art thou doing here?'). Finally, and this was quaintly typical of the management, they offered me – obviously and merely to test how conceited I might have become with all the recent promises of glory – the miserable part of the Lord in the prologue of *The Taming of the Shrew*. Of course, I saw the trick a mile off, and took it like a lamb. That was the end of the Royal Court for me, for nearly 30 years.

When my most dear George Devine started his thrilling new policy there in 1956 I became immediately fascinated by the work that was being done. I followed it avidly and, I should confess, enviously. After seeing *Look Back* for the second time I took pains to express my admiration to John Osborne, daring to hope that perhaps it just might occur to him to think of me for some future possibilities. His modest reception of this idea and his obviously brimming enthusiasm for it delighted me in the extreme. But I noticed George prick up his ears in a way that I at once recognized meant business. Up to then there had been no expressions of interest by any of the box office names in joining his company, and with his canny sense and wide experience he perceived possibilities for quite a new turn of events.

I was about to go off to New York for a small job, directing something, and George and I promised to keep in touch. True to his word, within ten days an envelope arrived. I opened it with some apprehension, sensing it was something of importance; and there it was – the first act of *The Entertainer*. I read it right away, without regard for anything else I ought to have been doing, and then I telephoned George at once, telling him that I would accept the part on that act alone. I could be run over and killed at the beginning of Act 2 for all I cared. Of course I would be intensely interested in whatever was to follow, I told him, but I was his if he wanted me and he could stop any slight feelings of anxiety – would he please send the rest immediately, whatever amounts at a time came from the author.

One thing was soon clear to me: my most fervent prayers might be favoured with a kindly answer. At that time I had reached a stage in my life that I was getting profoundly sick of – not just tired – sick. Consequently the public were, likely enough, beginning to agree with me. My rhythm of work had become a bit deadly: a classical or semi-classical film; a play or two at Stratford, or a nine-month run in the West End, etc, etc. I was going mad, desperately searching for something suddenly fresh and thrillingly exciting. What I felt to be my image was boring me to death. I really felt that death might be quite exciting, compared with the amorphous, purgatorial *Nothing* that was my existence. And now, suddenly, this miracle was happening. I began to feel already the promise of a new, vitally changed, entirely unfamiliar *Me*. In many ways it showed the worst

Rhinoceros, 1960. Laurence Olivier as Berenger – 'the last exemplar of individualism', resisting rhinocerization – with Joan Plowright. When Ionesco's fable transferred to the Strand Theatre her role was taken by Maggie Smith. (*Photograph: John Timbers*)

side of me, and that felt good too: something like a confession, a welcome and beneficial expulsion of filth. I could feel in this opportunity a great sea-change, transforming me into something strange. I felt, in fact, that I was starting a new life. We all pray for that constantly, and here, with *The Entertainer*, I could sense it already within my grasp.

I have owed a great deal to the rep system; but to George and his Royal Court I owe a special debt, not only for the magnificent opportunity they gave me, with John Osborne's play, but for a real conviction that I now belonged to an entirely different generation. I feel that this debt *must* be in excess of those of the splendidly generous people writing alongside me now, eulogizing the wondrous gifts and experiences that are theirs from the greatly all-providing theatre we love so much and wish so well.

1957-1960

The identity of the English Stage Company took shape in this period with the efflorescence of new talent not only in writing but also in direction, design and acting. Of prime importance was the introduction of Sunday night 'productions without decor'. Sponsored by the English Stage Society, which had been formed as a supporters' club in the autumn of 1956, at the suggestion of Lord Bessborough, they were plays 'rehearsed up to dress rehearsal point, but performed with only indications of scenery and costumes.' Compared with the £5,000 that a full-scale production might cost, a Sunday-nighter could be staged for as little as £100. Authors were paid only £5, actors accepted a couple of guineas. The first of these, on 26 May 1957, was Charles Robinson's *The Correspondence Course*, directed by Peter Coe. Neither author nor director (then unknown) worked again at the Court; but their Sunday night was followed by the first plays of John Arden (*Waters of Babylon*, 1957), N. F. Simpson (*A Resounding Tinkle*, 1957), Doris Lessing (*Each His Own Wilderness*, 1958), Keith Johnstone (*Brixham Regatta*, 1958), Donald Howarth (*Lady on the Barometer*, 1958), and Wole Soyinka (*The Invention*, 1959). Six out of 22 Sunday plays in this period were later given full-scale productions. But the main objective was not to score a bull; it was to let the author see his work in performance – and at such low costs, with such subsidies from its artists, the Court could then afford this educational bonus.

These Sunday night shows were also used by George Devine to try out new directors, who were in desperately short supply (Richardson and he directed all the first year's plays between them) and for whom there were few opportunities of professional training and apprenticeship. Four key figures in ESC history got their first directing jobs at the Royal Court through Sunday work. Three came in the summer of 1957: John Dexter (Michael Hastings's *Yes – and After*) was introduced by John Osborne, a friend with whom he had worked in rep: he was the only non-university man in the group, and felt the difference keenly. Lindsay Anderson (Kathleen Sully's *The Waiting of Lester Abbs*) was invited by Tony Richardson, a friend and associate in Free Cinema. William Gaskill (N. F. Simpson's *A Resounding Tinkle*) was an Oxford contemporary of Richardson, whom he had known since schooldays in their Yorkshire home town. Anthony Page, who arrived in 1958 (co-director, with George Devine, of John Arden's *Live Like Pigs*) was another Oxford man recruited by Richardson, from an actors' workshop in New York. From 1957 onwards dozens of directors gained invaluable experience of many kinds at the Court but none in the following 20 years, with the exception of Peter Gill, matched the prestige and power of this brilliant, fissile quartet of talents. George Devine set his junior

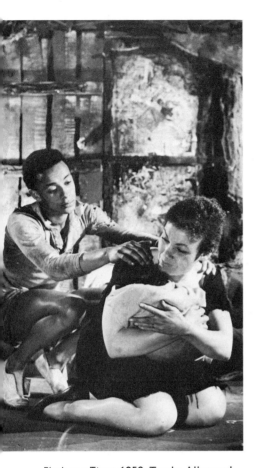

Flesh to a Tiger, 1958. Tamba Allen and Cleo Laine, making her debut in a straight play, the first by a West Indian writer to be seen in London. Originally entitled *Della*, it was written by Barry Reckord while he was at Cambridge. (*Photograph: David Sim*)

recruits to work for a time as assistants to him, spending time in the office and the workshops, getting to know about both stage management and theatre business, but also keeping in touch with the other arts, 'Not just,' as he said, 'to live inside the theatre.' Within a year or two he usually encouraged them to work outside his theatre. Gaskill, Anderson and Page were to return frequently, and to play major roles in the Court's later history. The last productions there by Dexter, Page and Anderson were in, respectively, 1972, 1973 and 1975. Gaskill's connection with the theatre persists, and in 1979 he became a member of the ESC Council.

Marrying an author and a director – Osborne/Richardson, Simpson/Gaskill, Logue/Anderson (and, much later, Bond/Gaskill, Hampton/Kidd and Storey/Anderson) – was one of the ways in which the Court achieved a special identity as a writers' theatre. Pursuing his ambition of involving authors Devine issued in the autumn of 1957 a writers' pass, admitting them to rehearsals and free seats at Court performances. The following year he set up the Writers' Group (see page 52). He commissioned authors to work on translations and adaptations (e.g. Ann Jellicoe on *Rosmersholm*.) He set other authors to read incoming manuscripts (as he had done with Osborne). He gave them, as Osborne says, a sense that he was *on their side*: that they were welcome to his theatre.

In 1957 Osborne followed *Look Back in Anger* – brought back three times into the bill that year, and toured extensively – with *The Entertainer*. In spite of Olivier's eagerness to appear in the play, the artistic committee of the English Stage Company originally voted against its production. Ronald Duncan and Oscar Lewenstein outnumbered George Harewood, and that – under the ESC's constitution – was supposed to be that. Harewood, however, went to see the Blonds the next morning at their Portman Square flat. The dissenting members of the Committee were then asked there for lunch, and opposition to *The Entertainer* was withdrawn. (Neville Blond said, 'We owe it to the boy', and Elaine Blond said, 'You must be barmy to turn down the play, with Olivier wanting to act in it.') Ten days after the news was announced, every evening seat had been sold throughout the four-week run. When Tony Richardson's production opened it was a smash hit for the author, the star and the Court. Long queues formed outside. It was transferred to the Palace Theatre (more than three times the size of the Court). It went to Broadway. It was turned into a film, another Court triumph, also directed by Richardson. *The Entertainer* made the Court a star theatre, and it represents another turning point in the history of the ESC. Osborne's third play to be staged, *Epitaph for George Dillon* (1958) – written four years earlier with Anthony Creighton – could

John Arden. Trained as an architect, his first play to be staged at the Court was *The Waters of Babylon*, as a Sunday night production without decor in 1957. Although Arden later became recognized as one of the major writers of the English Stage Company's first decade, he was, at the time, among the most conspicuously unsuccessful at the box office. (*Photograph: Snowdon*)

not hope to match *The Entertainer's* success at the Court (it played to less than 50% of box office capacity); but the Court's profits from its transfer to the West End, sale of film rights, etc. also helped the ESC to risk the work of less immediately successful writers and those with no prospect of long runs or screen deals. When Ann Jellicoe's *The Sport of My Mad Mother* had to be withdrawn after only fourteen performances 'Dillon' was brought back into the programme. *Look Back in Anger* came to the rescue when other plays had to be taken off. Neville Blond even suggested that there should be a permanent company available to play *Look Back* at a moment's notice. In the Court's first five years Osborne's plays brought the ESC a subsidy of £50,000 compared with the Arts Council's £30,000.

Of the newcomers who were to become identified as Court authors, Arnold Wesker was the most successful at the box office. Yet his first play, *Chicken Soup With Barley*, was originally rejected and was, in effect, farmed out to the Belgrade Theatre, Coventry, with John Dexter as director. This production was staged at the Court as part of a four-company repertory season, to mark the 50th anniversary of the repertory movement. Business then was poor: only 26% of box office capacity. But when the play came into the Court programme the following year, it did more than 82%. This was after the success of *Roots*, with a triumphant performance of Beatie Bryant by Joan Plowright, which transferred to the West End. Neither Devine nor Richardson had thought this, originally, suitable for the Court; it too was sent to Coventry.

The only other new writer who, for a time, scored a box office success comparable to Osborne, Wesker and the Court revivals was N. F. Simpson, whose *One Way Pendulum* played to 87%. Christopher Logue's debut, *Trials by Logue* (1960) did no better than 22%; Barry Reckord's *Flesh to a Tiger* (1958) – the first West Indian play professionally staged in London – managed only 15%; in the 18 performances of *The Naming of Murderer's Rock* (promoted to a run from a Sunday night), it achieved only 8%. John Arden's three plays were all box office disasters: *Live Like Pigs* (1958) filled 25% of box office capacity, *Serjeant Musgrave's Dance* (1959) 21%, and *The Happy Haven* only 12%. This made no difference to Devine's support for the author. As he wrote to Neville Blond, 'We must support the people we believe in, *especially* if they don't have critical appeal.' And Arden didn't. Few did. Many Court authors who became internationally famous were, at best, damned with faint praise by many reviewers at first acquaintance. Very early on, Devine established what Tony Richardson described as 'the right to fail': now a cliché but then – in a theatre still in servitude to the bitch-goddess of commercial success – a necessary and useful affirmation.

Live Like Pigs, 1958. John Arden's play about culture-clashes on a housing estate, when an anarchic family of travelling people, the Sawneys, are shoehorned into co-existence with conventional neighbours. *Right*, Wilfrid Lawson (the idol of Albert Finney and Peter O'Toole) grapples with Anna Manahan in the kind of Sawney family encounter that shocks and enrages the community they have invaded. *Below*, the set by Alan Tagg. (*Photographs: Snowdon*)

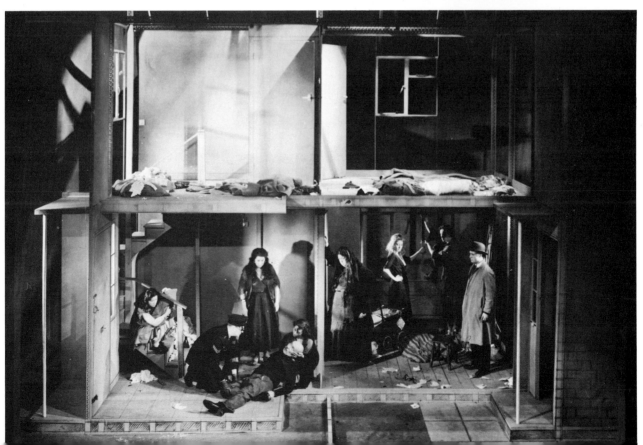

Other new English plays staged in this period included Nigel Dennis's second Court commission, *The Making of Moo* (1957); Alun Owen's debut, *Progress to the Park* (1959); a double bill by Harold Pinter, *The Room* and *The Dumb Waiter* (1959); Shelagh Delaney's second play, *The Lion in Love* (1960); and Willis Hall's long runner *The Long and the Short and the Tall* (with Robert Shaw and Peter O'Toole in the cast). Errol John's *Moon on a Rainbow Shawl* (1958), with *Flesh to a Tiger*, were the first in a long line of 'ethnic' plays at the Court, which has given opportunities to African and West Indian authors and actors unequalled by any other British theatre. Although it also, in the 1960's, gave unequalled opportunities to authors censored by the Lord Chamberlain by turning itself temporarily into a 'club' theatre, George Devine was reluctant to do this in 1958 when Ronald Duncan's *The Catalyst* was banned (because it portrayed a lesbian relationship). Instead, the ESC staged it at the Arts Theatre Club, which had served before as a haven for censored dramatists.

Trouble of a different kind was expected from the authorities over one conspicuous Court innovation, *Eleven Men Dead at Hola Camp* (1959), a largely improvised, highly controversial documentary by Bill Gaskill and Keith Johnstone about the treatment of African detainees during the Mau Mau guerilla campaign in Kenya. This was so instant a reaction to public events (then generally ignored by the theatre) that the Court consulted a leading QC over its possible infringement of current restrictions on Parliamentary debate; and there were murmurings in the Council (not infrequently vexed, as well as perplexed, by the activities of what Neville Blond called 'the artistic boys') about its political content. But the Council remained loyally supportive to the Company (as it indispensably continued, by and large, to do); the authorities did not intervene; and the Sunday night performance passed without a battle – and without any follow-up at the Court, although the event was the forerunner of many fringe productions in the next decade. In the same year Devine showed that his concept of the Court as a writers' theatre was not limited to young writers by directing *Cock-A-Doodle-Dandy*, which Sean O'Casey, then 79, had written eleven years earlier and which had not yet been given a professional performance.

In April 1958 the ESC presented the world premiere of Samuel Beckett's *Fin de Partie* (in French), inaugurating a still unbroken connection between Beckett and the Court, and a close friendship between Beckett and Devine, to whom the author gave control over all English-speaking productions of his plays. In October 1958 Devine directed (and acted in) the English version of *Endgame*, after a long tussle with the Lord Chamberlain over Hamm's reference to God: 'The bastard! He doesn't exist!' Six months of negotiation ended in Beckett's agreement to 'swine' as a substitute for 'bastard'. Devine's persistent attachment to French drama was reflected by productions of Giraudoux's *The Apollo de Bellac* (translated by Ronald Duncan); Sartre's *Nekrassov*, with a miscast Robert Helpmann in the lead (the first ESC production to be staged at the Edinburgh Festival); Ionesco's *The Chairs*, *The Lesson* and *Rhinoceros*. The latter, directed by Orson Welles, had Olivier in the lead and nearly matched the box office success of *The Entertainer* at the Court (playing to 99%). Noël Coward's version of Feydeau, *Look After Lulu* (1959) – with a starry cast led by Vivien Leigh – was deliberately chosen, against the grain of ESC policy and considerable criticism, as a money-maker; but in fact, although it packed the Court (nearly 94%), its West End transfer made a loss for the ESC. Two more distinguished revivals were Ibsen's *Rosmersholm*, with Peggy Ashcroft, and Chekhov's *Platonov*, with Rex Harrison, both major critical and box office successes.

The dissension over *The Entertainer* in 1957 led, in due course, to an

Serjeant Musgrave's Dance, 1959. It is under this improvised gibbet in the market-place, from which Musgrave and his men suspend the skeleton of a dead comrade in his uniform, that the Serjeant 'dances' and sings. (*Photograph: Snowdon*)

enlargement of the Court's artistic committee, which was joined by Peggy Ashcroft and John Osborne, and by 1959 to its neutralization as an arbiter of plays, which Devine was now permitted to stage without authorization. This added to Ronald Duncan's growing list of charges against the artistic director. In January 1960 he complained to the Council, in a statement on artistic policy, that the original aims of the English Stage Company had been betrayed by George Devine, who had favoured left-wing and social-realist second-raters at the expense of established writers with different styles and political views. He requested Devine's dismissal. But in May the Council

Serjeant Musgrave's Dance, 1959. Ian Bannen, right, as the avenging Musgrave, a supposed recruiting sergeant who turns out to be a deserter with an evangelizing mission. Alan Dobie (left) as one of the soldiers he leads. (*Photograph: Snowdon*)

issued a statement reaffirming their complete support for the current policy and their 'complete confidence' in Devine. He remained as artistic director, and Duncan remained on the Council.

In search of a bigger theatre, where it could reach a wider audience and make the best of its successes, the ESC pursued in 1960 the possibility of taking over the old Metropolitan music hall in the Edgware Road, in partnership with Laurence Olivier (L.O.P. Productions Ltd), Oscar Lewenstein Ltd, and Granada. But the scheme collapsed because the site was scheduled for redevelopment: a road was driven through it. The Court was already, however, on the point of reaching a far greater audience through the medium of the British cinema, on which it exerted a decisive, revivifying influence during its first decade through many of its writers, directors and actors and the naturalistic authenticity, imaginative depth and freshness, artistic discipline and living-in-the moment immediacy of their work. This process started, once again, with John Osborne and Tony Richardson, who, after the theatrical success of *Look Back in Anger*, established Woodfall Productions. Having filmed *Look Back in Anger* and *The Entertainer*, they went on to make *Saturday Night and Sunday Morning*. This, as Lindsay Anderson says, 'changed the face of the British cinema overnight'; and with its combination of a new director, Karel Reisz, new writer, Alan Sillitoe, and new star, Albert

Finney, it 'opened doors that had been nailed fast for 50 years.' Other Woodfall productions included Tony Richardson's *A Taste of Honey*, *The Loneliness of the Long Distance Runner*, and the immensely successful *Tom Jones* (scripted by Osborne). Oscar Lewenstein, too, went into films with Woodfall, of which he was a director from 1961: he produced the screen versions of two Royal Court successes, *One Way Pendulum* (directed by Peter Yates) and *The Knack* (directed by Dick Lester). Miriam Brickman, the Court's influential casting director for several years, also moved into films and became, according to Lindsay Anderson, 'responsible for a whole new style

Look after Lulu, 1959. Vivien Leigh as the heroine of Noël Coward's period frolic, based on Georges Feydeau's *Occupe toi d'Amélie*, as revived, 50 years after its first production by the Renaud-Barrault company. This was staged in order to stave off one of the Royal Court's perennial financial catastrophes, but its Sloane Square success was not repeated in the West End. (*Photograph: David Sim*)

and class of actor' in such films as Karel Reisz's *Morgan*, Anderson's own *This Sporting Life* and John Schlesinger's *A Kind of Loving* and *Darling*. For a time Woodfall was the most creative force in British films. Tony Richardson devoted an increasing amount of his time to film-making and from 1964 onwards he effectively turned his back on the British theatre, never to work again at the Royal Court, although he served for some years on the Council of the ESC in the following decade.

One major event of the 1957–60 period at the Court was the emergence as a leading designer of Jocelyn Herbert, who had worked there as a scene-painter from the start: she made her debut with *The Chairs*. Actors and actresses who made their debuts on the London stage here at this time include Colin Blakely, James Bolam, Richard Briers, Patsy Byrne, Zoe Caldwell, Donal Donnelly, Avril Elgar, Susan Engel, Frank Finlay, Michael Gambon, Alan Howard, Jeanne Hepple, Charles Kay and Margaret Tyzack. Cast-spotters looking for early and/or unexpected appearances of household names and celebrities in other media will find Ronnie Barker, John Wood, Michael Caine, Wilfrid Lawson, Diane Cilento, Cleo Laine, Edward Fox, Anton Rodgers, Joan Greenwood, Isla Cameron, Ronald Fraser, Fulton Mackay, Tom Bell, Shani Wallis, Bessie Love, Richard Goolden, Georgia Brown, Shirley Ann Field and Peter Bowles. Royal Court enthusiasts will note the acting appearances of directors John Dexter, Peter Gill and Anthony Page, and authors Edward Bond, Donald Howarth and John Osborne. Among those giving special poetry recitals on Sunday evenings in 1958/59, under the auspices of the English Stage Society, were Dame Edith Evans and Christopher Hassall, Louise MacNeice, and Dame Sybil Thorndike and Sir Lewis Casson.

Economic note: During 1957/58 audiences were as low, on occasion, as £19 for the gross takings of an evening performance (and £6 for a mid-week matinee). 'This does not indicate much of a following,' say the ESC Council minutes. Neville Blond warned in 1958 that he had grave doubts about the Company's future if the losses of the past year were repeated. In the autumn there was a deficit approaching £30,000.

Ann Jellicoe[*]

The Writers' Group

George Devine cherished writers: it is really as simple as that. Devine was a modest man, never a charismatic personality, and I think he had a fair idea of his own talent as solid rather than sensational. His faith in himself came from the immense love and respect he had for those who had faith in him – Peggy Ashcroft, Glen Byam Shaw, Michel St Denis, Tony Richardson – if *they* thought he was all right, then he must be ... but what if they were wrong? This insecurity gave him sympathy and insight into the paranoiac insecurity of writers and their constant need for reassurance.

When the idea arose of forming a Writers' Group I think Devine welcomed it as a means of creating a more formal structure to which young and promising writers could be invited and where they would come to know other writers and members of the Court staff. I don't suppose he actually thought it would help people to write: to him rehearsal and performance were the best teachers. What he wanted from the Writers' Group was to make people feel that the Court was interested in them and thought them worthy of effort and attention.

The first meetings were tentative and a little stiff. There was no suitable space at the Court and we met in the old paint shop in Flood Street, Chelsea, now demolished. It was romantic but dirty. We sat on boxes, creaking chairs, anything to hand, in a strict circle surrounded by debris and draughts. Devine himself was there, and his friend Michel St Denis. I think Tony Richardson was away in America, but William Gaskill and Lindsay Anderson were there. Lindsay chose to sit on a throne, which those who know him will recognize as entirely in character. There was also John Dexter and Miriam Brickman, the casting director. The writers I remember included John Arden, Arnold Wesker, Keith Johnstone; about 15 people in all. In these formal and uncomfortable circumstances contact did not flourish. But something had been started: the key members of the group had met. It was a time when we felt that things were about to happen and that we would be part of them. Historically that first meeting took place in January 1958, about a

   *Summarized from an article in the special theatre number of 'Ambit' 1976.

The Sport of My Mad Mother, 1958. *Above,* Ann Jellicoe rehearsing. *Above right*, left to right: Philip Locke, Sheila Ballantine, Jerry Stovin, Avril Elgar. This play about a London street gang had been awarded third prize, jointly with N.F. Simpson's *A Resounding Tinkle*, in the 1957 competition for new plays run by the *Observer*. In his preface to the volume of *Observer Plays*, Kenneth Tynan described it as 'a *tour de force* that belongs to no known category of drama.' (*Photographs: Roger Mayne*)

month before the first production of *The Sport of My Mad Mother*. John Arden's *The Waters of Babylon* had been given a Sunday production about three months previously. *Chicken Soup With Barley* had probably been delivered (which would be why Arnold was invited to the Writers' Group) but would not be seen until August. Keith Johnstone's plays were given Sunday performances and at Aldeburgh in June.

Very quickly Devine withdrew. He probably felt, rightly, that he overawed us. Dexter dropped out: it was not his scene. William Gaskill took over: he had just arrived from television and had directed N. F. Simpson's *A Resounding Tinkle*, soon to go into the main bill. Gaskill is a man in whom masculine and feminine meet violently and this conflict makes him a difficult friend and a brilliant talent. He has a capacity for flashing and original judgements: critical insight which transcends intellect and becomes intuitive and creative. He was a good man to run the group. Deeply distrusting anything established, even if he himself has built it up, he doesn't actually destroy: simply turns his back and starts something new. He once said, 'If we can understand it, we're not interested.' This catches the tone of his occasional flippancies, but there was the spirit of the time in it. It's a measure of the group that Gaskill did not dominate it.

Another influence was Keith Johnstone. He was discovered by

The Knack, 1962. Philip Locke (in the carrier bag) and Rita Tushingham. In contrast with *The Sport of My Mad Mother*, which was withdrawn after fourteen performances, Ann Jellicoe's second play became a box office success (later filmed). (*Photograph: Roger Mayne*)

Tony Richardson in documentary films: Richardson was immediately struck by the teeming, passionate originality of Johnstone's ideas, his air of uncorrupted idealism and his sweetness of nature. Since he was virtually penniless the Court gave Johnstone a job as playreader, ten shillings a script in those days, and he proved an acute judge of a written text. Johnstone had a great contempt for intellectuals: he believed that things should be shown happening in the theatre, not analysed and talked about. It is hard now to remember how fresh this idea was in 1958, but it chimed in with my own thinking and had great influence in the way the group began to operate.

Some writers in it, like Evelyn Ford and Alison MacLeod, had had Sunday productions. Anne Piper and Maureen Duffy had submitted interesting scripts. Others were Ronald Hayman and Michael Geliot. Edward Bond was a particularly fortunate example of George's approach. It was probably Keith Johnstone who first spotted Edward's plays coming in around 1958. These were *Klaxon in Atreus Place* and *The Fiery Tree*: neither was performed but Bond was invited to join the Writers' Group. His first Sunday production, *The Pope's Wedding*, was in December 1962. *Saved*, by which he became known, was not produced until November 1965. Thus the Court maintained a close contact with Edward Bond over seven years (a biblical interval) and, apart from any definite effort George himself may have

Shelley, 1965. Ronald Pickup as the poet and Kika Markham as Harriet Westbrook, in the Ann Jellicoe play (subtitled *The Idealist*) which opened Bill Gaskill's first season as artistic director of the English Stage Company. (*Photograph: Roger Mayne*)

made, it was a natural contact kept up by the close friendships Edward Bond made within the Writers' Group.

There were some obvious absences: N. F. Simpson, a personal friend of Gaskill, Johnstone and myself, would have been welcome. Harold Pinter always kept aloof from the Court, though they did two of his plays in 1960. Both probably disliked the idea of 'groups', and I know what they mean. John Osborne never came – was probably never invited – maybe he was too grand for us: we were on the brink of acceptance, but had not yet arrived.

The group had strength and cohesion because we were all much of an age, of the same calibre of personality and at the same time not too egotistical. We recognized each other's talent and supported it. This is said to be rare among writers. We were extremely careful whom we invited into the group – not from exclusiveness, but because we were aware that anyone too argumentative or destructive would upset the balance. Unsympathetic people would sometimes come in for a few meetings, but they tended to fall away: the central core was probably too strong for them.

We began to meet at 7 Lower Mall in Hammersmith, the home of David and Anne Piper, two doors up from George Devine himself. Although he seldom came to meetings, George's proximity probably helped the general sense of belonging. The drawing room of No 7 overlooked the river and was large, warm and informal. We met once a fortnight to improvise. We tried to explore the nature of theatre. Believing as we did in theatre depending on action and images rather than words, we hardly ever analysed or discussed what we were doing, or each other's plays, or theories of playwriting. Sometimes we improvised around a set theme, sometimes from a spontaneous idea. Improvisation also gave writers some taste of what it was like to act: this doing, rather than sitting and talking, was refreshing for them. Curiously the best writers were also the better actors. John Arden had a good line in brisk army officers and headmasters.

Although we almost never talked about our plays we sometimes used the group to help us through a block. I was in the middle of *The Knack*, and stuck. I dislike talking about work in progress, so with some caution I set up an improvisation in which a group of people came to buy a bed off an old man in a junk yard. As the improvisation developed the old man refused to sell and the others began to tease and confuse him. Suddenly William Gaskill said: 'That's not a bed, it's a piano,' and the scene took off.

Improvisations were not always so positive. I remember rather boring scenes at bus stops: we tried to make this more interesting by increasing the difficulties so that Miriam Brickman first became a nun, then a drunken nun. We did Living Newspapers, mock TV interviews, borrowing money. Someone stole a rare bird's egg from a museum, hid it in his mouth and then tried to talk casually to a suspicious keeper. One disastrous evening George Devine came to talk about comic style and began by mentioning Shaw and Congreve. This was too much for Keith Johnstone, who couldn't abide Shaw and interrupted so much that he destroyed the evening. It was interesting that George was depressed rather than angry.

But George did give a remarkable series of evenings when he taught us the use of masks, particularly comic masks. He had learned an extraordinarily pure and mystical technique from the Compagnie des Quinze, by which the mask releases or creates a totally free and distinct personality, to which the actor is merely host, and hardly in control: a concept which has close parallels in writing. The results of this work were soon seen in John Arden's *The Happy Haven*, directed by William Gaskill, and Keith Johnstone has used it ever since in his teaching and writing. There has since been a general revival of masks, but often without the purity and discipline of George's method, and so without its strange extra dimension.

The Writers' Group remained strong and lively for about two years. While preparing this article I spoke to Arnold Wesker and asked him what he found most valuable about it. He agreed with me that it was 'the ritual of going and seeing one's friends.' The meetings had all the fun of a party and none of the boredom. But there was more to it than that: we probably reinforced in each other the idea of Direct Theatre – a theatre of action and images rather than words. Perhaps we reassured each other – the support of professional friends meant much to me after the critical disaster of *The Sport of My Mad Mother*. But within two years we had become more successful and so more self-assured. The Writers' Group began to meet less often and then stopped altogether. There were attempts to revive it, but they never took. The need had passed.

Bill Gaskill

Below: Director at work: Bill Gaskill giving notes at a dress rehearsal of N.F. Simpson's *The Hole*, 1958. Avril Elgar and Sheila Ballantine are in the background. (*Photograph: Roger Mayne*)

Below right: Epitaph for George Dillon, 1958. Yvonne Mitchell and Robert Stephens. Written by John Osborne, with Anthony Creighton, before *Look Back in Anger*, this was Gaskill's first production for the Court (after the Sunday-night showing of *A Resounding Tinkle*), and his first production on Broadway. It was also the first play ever to be revived on Broadway in the same season, because of a campaign led by Noël Coward and Tennessee Williams. (*Photograph: David Sim*)

My Apprenticeship

I first came to work at the Court through Tony Richardson. He came from my home town of Shipley in Yorkshire and we had been together at Oxford, where I had deliberately lost my West Riding accent. Tony, with typical shrewdness, kept his, realizing that if we were going to make our mark it was because – rather than in spite – of our provincial background. But this would not have been so if it had not been for the Royal Court.

Tony had met George Devine while working in television, and they almost immediately became very close. George saw Tony as his link with the new generation, and it was due as much to Tony as to

George that *Look Back in Anger* was included in the first season. Tony let me read the play before it was produced, and I was bowled over by its use of language in a contemporary setting. At the time I was working for Granada (who later televized the play), and it was not till the end of 1957 that I actually worked at the Court.

By then the Court had already made its historic impact but it was also extremely successful. *Look Back* had started a year's run on Broadway; Olivier was packing the Palace Theatre in *The Entertainer*; Joan Plowright, the Court's first home-grown star, was the toast of New York in the double bill of Ionesco's *The Lesson* and *The Chairs*; and George Devine was directing Julie Harris in *The Country Wife* on Broadway. All these productions had been launched in Sloane Square, and the new elite spent its time flying back and forth across the Atlantic. George saw himself as the stabilizing influence in the work of the theatre, directing mainly classics and established modern writers. Tony was already reaching out to the film world. It was essential not only to find new writers but also the directors to direct their plays. In 1957 the first series of Sunday night productions was launched; and Tony asked me to direct *A Resounding Tinkle* by N. F. Simpson, one of the prize-winners of a competition organized by the *Observer* for new drama.

The play was fascinating, unlike anything I had directed before, and it was my opportunity to work at the Court. When I started rehearsing with Simpson (known as 'Wally' after the Duchess of Windsor), it was the first time I had worked with a live writer. Wally, though he had no practical experience of theatre and had spent his working life teaching, was very authoritative about his text and how it should be played – particularly with regard to the comic timing. 'Pause longer and they'll laugh,' he would say. I didn't entirely believe him, but something about the gravity of his manner inspired confidence. I was learning at every rehearsal. The performance was on a Sunday night in December 1957 and all Wally's predictions came true. His play was an immediate success, and George arrived back from the States just in time to catch the curtain-up.

The next day he called me into his office beside the circle bar and offered me a job as an assistant to the artistic director, or AAD as it was known. I had met him on several occasions in Tony's flat in George's house by Hammersmith Bridge. He was difficult to get to know, but you could always make contact with his enthusiasms. I remember him describing his visit to East Berlin and his description of Brechtian staging: 'If there has to be a door, you see, it has to be a real door but nothing else.' His craftsmanship and professionalism were rock-like at the base of the Court's work. He had grave doubts about his own talent and a corresponding belief in other directors, particularly young directors. He was the ideal master to be apprenticed to.

Oscar Lewenstein, then general manager, engaged me for £15 a week, half of my television salary, and I started work. I shared an office with the only other AAD – John Dexter. We soon became close friends, in an office which had no windows or ventilation. From there we ran the script department and cast the plays: and the room became a centre for the writers, who were reading plays at five shillings a time. They had no money, and there was no other theatre interested in their work. We would talk about our ideas and write things on the wall. Harold Pinter, whom I had known in rep at Whitby (when he had seduced my ASM), was an understudy and wrote, 'Le théâtre de Bertolt Brecht est un théâtre de Boy Scout – Ionesco.' Keith Johnstone wrote, 'A stage is an area of maximum verbal presence and maximum corporeal presence – Beckett.' And John Arden wrote, 'There's a cock in father's barnyard/ who never trod a hen/ and it seems to me my fair young man/ that you are one of them.' But whether he meant it for me or John Dexter we never found out.

I was already preparing a season of repertoire which was to include a shorter version of *A Resounding Tinkle*; the early play of John Osborne and Tony Creighton – *Epitaph for George Dillon*; and Ann

Jellicoe's *The Sport of My Mad Mother*. Ann's play was way ahead of its time and was predictably slaughtered by the critics. It was withdrawn after fourteen performances, but every night there was an enthusiastic claque of writers and directors shouting at the end. *George Dillon*, which was a moderate success, gave Bob Stephens, who had been with the company since the beginning, his first leading part; and the company, which was a real resident company again, included Yvonne Mitchell, Alison Leggatt, Nigel Davenport, Wendy Craig and Philip Locke.

It was also the time of the first Aldermaston march. Though our degree of political commitment varied, we were swept up in enthusiasm for the movement, and our embarrassment at demonstrating soon disappeared when Jocelyn Herbert started reminiscing about the 30's. Many of us dropped out after the first day, when the rain poured down on the road to Slough. One couple with sparkling eyes, rosy cheeks and knapsacks on their backs were obviously determined to go the whole way, and we soon got to know them. It was Arnold Wesker and his wife Dusty. John Dexter found out that Arnold had submitted a play to the Court, and a relationship was started that led to that wonderful series of productions directed by John and designed by Jocelyn Herbert. The march was being

filled by Lindsay Anderson, who had given Arnold his first encouragement, and very soon afterwards he joined John and me as an AAD. He was rather older than we were, and already distinguished as a documentary film director.

For the next two years or so the three of us, later joined by Anthony Page, worked to establish Arden, Wesker, Simpson, Logue and Jellicoe as the Court writers. We were united by having arrived together and by a belief in what we saw as the Court's real aims – to present new writing in a form of staging centred in the play and without any extraneous decoration from the director or designer. We fought what we saw as reactionary tendencies at the Court – a leaning towards star names, glossy productions of plays set in the Deep South, links with West End managements – though without transfers to the West End it would not have been possible to take the risks we were involved in. George had to keep the balance between us and keep the theatre open. Our last concerted effort as AADs was to insist on the presentation of the Wesker Trilogy. Shortly afterwards Lindsay and I were pushed out of the nest, but John stayed on till 1963, when he and I joined Olivier in starting the National Theatre at the Old Vic.

In 1965, at the critics' lunch when George announced his retirement in a farewell speech, it was greeted politely but with no sense of the importance of the occasion. But Lindsay, whose feeling for the occasion has always been remarkable, leapt to his feet and made an impassioned speech about George. The critics sang *For he's a jolly good fellow*. I was very moved by Lindsay's speech, and although I had turned down the chance of taking over the Court the previous year I realized that the continuity of George's work was more important than working at the National Theatre, and I told George I would do it. Olivier sent a telegram: 'The Lord gave and the Lord has taken away.'

My plan was not only to bring together those writers whose work had been so central to the Court in its early days, but also to return to the idea of a resident company playing in repertoire. George became wildly excited about the prospect of the English Stage Company returning to its original aims and began making budgets and calculating the box office, at which he was brilliant. Soon after, he collapsed during *A Patriot for Me* and never saw any of the productions of my first season, though he recovered sufficiently to be quite caustic about the planning and miscalculations. Almost the last thing he spoke of was the theatre in Sloane Square and how wonderful it was. During the years in which I ran the Court I came to realize how important that stage was in our work.

One Way Pendulum, 1959: Stephen Doncaster's set for Act 2 of N.F. Simpson's 'evening of high drung and slarrit', as he called it. Left to right: Alan Gibson, John Horsley, Robert Levis, Alison Leggatt, Graham Armitage, Graham Crowden. The judge is Douglas Wilmer. (*Photograph: Angus McBean*)

Samuel Beckett

To the Royal Court my deep gratitude and affection. Long may it endure in the spirit of the great inspirer, George Devine.

Samuel Beckett

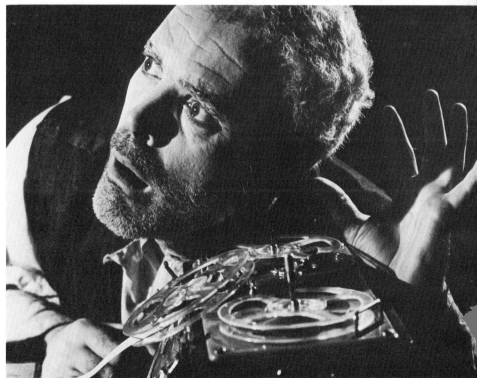

Left: Fin de Partie, 1957. Roger Blin (Hamm) and Jean Martin (Clov) – the original Pozzo and Lucky of *Waiting for Godot* – in the play written for them by Beckett. (*Photograph: David Sim*)

Above: Endgame, 1976. Patrick Magee (Hamm) and Stephen Rea (Clov) in Donald McWhinnie's production – one of three presented at the Royal Court in 1976 to honour Beckett's 70th birthday. (*Photograph: John Haynes*)

Above right: Endgame, 1958. George Devine (Hamm) and Jack MacGowran (Clov). (*Photograph: David Sim*)

Right: Krapp's Last Tape, 1958. Written for Patrick Magee, whom Beckett had met the previous year in the cast of *All That Fall*, when it was broadcast by the BBC. Beckett conceived Krapp for Magee's voice on radio, but turned it, as he wrote, into a companion stage-piece for *Endgame*. This was his first piece of writing in English since the war. (*Photograph: David Sim*)

Two Winnies in *Happy Days. Above left,* Brenda Bruce (1962) (*Photograph: Morris Newcombe). Above,* Billie Whitelaw (1979) (*Photograph: John Haynes*)

Left: Beckett rehearsing Billie Whitelaw. Her voice in *Play,* premiered by Devine in 1964, affected Beckett as Magee's did, and he resolved to write a play for her. According to Beckett's biographer, Deirdre Bair, hers was the inner voice to which he had listened when he wrote *Not I.* (*Photograph: John Haynes*)

Right: Footfalls, 1976. This monologue was written for and played by Billie Whitelaw, spectrally communing with the ghost of her dead mother. 'Will you never have done, revolving it all in your poor mind?' (*Photograph: John Haynes*)

1960–1965

Several major changes began to transform the London theatre scene during this period. In 1960 the Royal Shakespeare Company (RSC), led by Peter Hall, opened a London home at the Aldwych for contemporary as well as classic plays (and, for a time, leased the Arts Theatre as well). In 1963 the National Theatre Company started life under Laurence Olivier's direction, without waiting for an exemplary edifice, at the Old Vic. From now on the English Stage Company had to compete with both organizations – with no hope of matching their resources and (in due course) subsidies – for writers, directors, designers, actors and theatre workers of every kind, as well as audiences.

Both Gaskill and Dexter, urged by Devine, left the Court for the National. Devine remained in control largely single-handed (he had no assistant for a year, and Tony Richardson was often away film-making). He had to tackle increasing administrative responsibilities and acute problems about censorship, box office revenue, reconstructing the building, the relative doldrums of the new drama and, not least, his associates and his own succession. And he did so (though this was not widely realized at the time) with declining health. In the autumn of 1961 he had a nervous breakdown: Richardson deputized during his three-month absence. In the autumn of 1963 he was seriously ill with heart trouble. The Council agreed to appoint a co-director in 1965, but found it hard to recruit anyone willing to shoulder the administrative burden. After Bill Gaskill, Tony Richardson and Michael Elliott had been approached, Lindsay Anderson and Anthony Page agreed – as a temporary solution – to share the direction of the 1964/65 season, following the theatre's reconstruction (see below). They announced that new plays would be presented 'only if they are deemed to be suitable for production and not solely because they happen to be new.' But before the season opened Anderson resigned. Anthony Page – helped, administratively and technically, by Devine – set out with the intention of running a permanent company, as Devine and Richardson had done in 1956, but he was no more successful in establishing it.

After the 1964/65 season had opened with a resounding success – Osborne's *Inadmissible Evidence* – Devine informed the Council that he would resign in the following year. The news was not released until he announced his decision on 25 January 1965 at the annual lunch given by Neville Blond to the critics (at the Savoy Hotel).

Pursuing the search for a wider audience, and for closer links with the theatre outside London, the ESC's artistic committee proposed in 1961 that the Company should link up with three regional repertory companies, interchanging productions. In the autumn the first

66

Above: The Happy Haven, 1960. Frank Finlay and Susan Engel. John Arden wrote it to be played in masks, influenced by George Devine's mask classes. (*Photograph: Roger Mayne*)

Above right: Platonov, 1960. Rex Harrison, Graham Crowden and Peter Bowles. Chekhov's first play, never presented or published in his lifetime, was written while he was a medical student and was discovered in the 1920's, long after his death. This version was translated by Dimitri Makaroff, then revised by John Blatchley, George Devine's assistant, and edited by Devine himself. (*Photograph: John Timbers*)

experiment in implementing this policy was launched with a company based at the Arts Theatre, Cambridge; Norwich dropped out shortly after the Calouste Gulbenkian Trust funded the scheme. Bill Gaskill was in charge. The original plan was to stage ten productions – five new plays, five classics – in Cambridge and two other cities, for three-week runs, over a nine-month season. The advantages to the Court seemed clear: more rehearsal time for new work; 'a regular outlet for unused talent', in directing as well as writing; an 'easing of the burden of production.' The scheme was cut to two months because of costs: three plays were to be mounted by Gaskill in Cambridge, and three Court productions would visit Cambridge and elsewhere. But these arrived before their London run and not (as Cambridge had assumed) *after*; Cambridge felt that it was being used merely as a provincial try-out base. Moreover, as Gaskill pointed out, the Cambridge Arts had no obvious identity; and the experiment had little hope of taking instant root there, or in the

The Changeling, 1961. Mary Ure and Robert Shaw. Tony Richardson's production of this 1622 'half-masterpiece' by Middleton and Rowley was claimed to be the first professional run in London for 250 years. (*Photograph: Sandra Lousada*)

other towns briefly visited. Far more research, planning and experience was required. The venture collapsed after two months, at a cost to the ESC of £2,400. No further attempts were made to establish a regional network or satellite.

Another scheme for expansion in 1961 was the amalgamation of the English Stage Company with the Old Vic, under Devine's overall artistic direction. This was, Devine wrote to Neville Blond, 'our great opportunity to reach a wider public under our own banner, and to keep our dramatists happy, since we can offer a larger stage and a larger scope.' He envisaged a trial period of three years during which a permanent company would play large-scale work at the Vic and smaller pieces at the Court. But in spite of Devine's enthusiasm for the idea – 'the oldest theatre in the country comes to *us* for help and is prepared to swallow its pride,' he wrote to Blond – it came to nothing, because of acute financial difficulties on both sides. Court crises recurred in 1961 and 1963, Neville Blond guaranteed

Above: Claire Bloom and Kenneth Haigh, in Sartre's *Altona*, 1961, described by Kenneth Tynan as 'one of the few indispensable plays of the past decade.' Originally entitled *Les Sequestrés d'Altona*, it was first staged in Paris in 1959, at considerably greater length. The director, John Berry, was the author's choice. (*Photograph: John Timbers*)

Above right: Colin Blakely and Doris Hare in Max Frisch's morality play *The Fire Raisers*, staged at Christmas 1961 in a double bill with the Victorian farce *Box and Cox*, by John Maddison Morton. Originally written as a parable about the rise of the Nazis, it was made to apply to the spread of the Bomb. Blakely, who made his London debut at the Court two years earlier, is among the English Stage Company's major acting discoveries. (*Photograph: Sandra Lousada*)

overdrafts in January and May, and the Arts Council gave an advance on the following year's grant.

Devine's biggest managerial headaches concerned the reconstruction of the Sloane Square building. After the collapse of the Cambridge experiment he set out to find a wider audience and to create what he described as 'an entirely new image for the theatre aesthetically' by remodelling his London base. He planned to eliminate the proscenium arch, replace the hierarchical three-level auditorium with a one-tier showplace, and build an experimental studio behind (or on top of) the Court. These changes were linked with hopes of establishing a new local identity by opening the building through the day for exhibitions, discussions and film shows (like some of the new civic theatres now appearing suddenly on the horizon); of developing training and educational work; of acquiring a second, larger house (perhaps the Chelsea Palace?) and even of setting up a second company, with a permanent base in the West End.

Skyvers, 1963. Barry Reckord's third play was given a Sunday night production in April, and began a successful run in July. David Hemmings (right, with Philip Martin) made his stage debut in *Skyvers* and then disappeared from the theatre into the cinema. (*Photograph: Roger Mayne*)

Right: Exit the King, 1963. Alec Guinness, making his debut at the Royal Court, as Berenger the First. Ionesco's play was the first that George Devine had directed at the Court for more than eighteen months: it proved to be his last production there. (*Photograph: Sandra Lousada*)

During the Court's reconstruction the ESC would run an eight-month season in the West End. Money was promised by the Arts Council, the LCC, Neville Blond and the Gulbenkian Foundation (for training). But the visionary plans collapsed under the weight of a budget at least double the original estimate; the builders' inability to complete the work in anything like the eight months calculated as the maximum time feasible for a West End season; and the refusal (however regretful) of the landlord, Lord Cadogan, to extend the ESC's 28-year lease.

Instead, Devine knuckled under and produced a modest compromise programme at a tenth of the cost (about £22,500). Most of this was paid by a capital grant from the Arts Council. Neville Blond gave £5,000. Devine and some ESC Council members contributed smaller sums when the budget was exceeded. The improvements included a new lighting box at the back of the upper circle; a new stage floor; new counterweights for flying scenery; a bar at the back of the stalls; a rehabilitated Gents; a new stalls floor; a refurbished dress circle. The Court was closed for six months, from March to September 1964. During that interregnum the ESC moved into the West End, in association with H. M. Tennent and Lewenstein-Delfont Productions. It took the recently reopened Queen's Theatre with a projected season of three plays, all directed by Tony Richardson and all planned to feature his wife Vanessa Redgrave. It opened triumphantly with *The Seagull* (Peggy Ashcroft, Peter Finch and Devine were among the prime assets of the cast); but Vanessa Redgrave, who was pregnant, collapsed during rehearsals of Brecht's *St Joan of the Stockyards*. Siobhan McKenna took over the lead, but the play had to be withdrawn after three weeks, at a cost of some £15,000. The third play, *The Way of the World*, was dropped, and the season, which, significantly, had not included one new English work, was abandoned. (Michael Hastings' *The World's Baby* was originally scheduled as the third production.)

There were bonuses for the ESC in this period. At the end of January 1963 Clement Freud's lease on the upstairs room expired, and the space at last became available for the Company's use (though it was not for another six years that it discovered how best to utilize it). More money came from public funds. The LCC made its first grant: £2,500 for 1961/62 (continued at that level for several years). In 1962 the Arts Council, whose grants from the Government were steadily expanding, increased its subsidy from £8,000 to £20,000; and in 1964 it allowed a further increase to £32,500. In that year Chelsea allowed the ESC a 50% reduction in rates, because it is a registered charity: this saved the Court about £1,000 p.a. But the civic subsidy remained at the level of 200 guineas p.a.

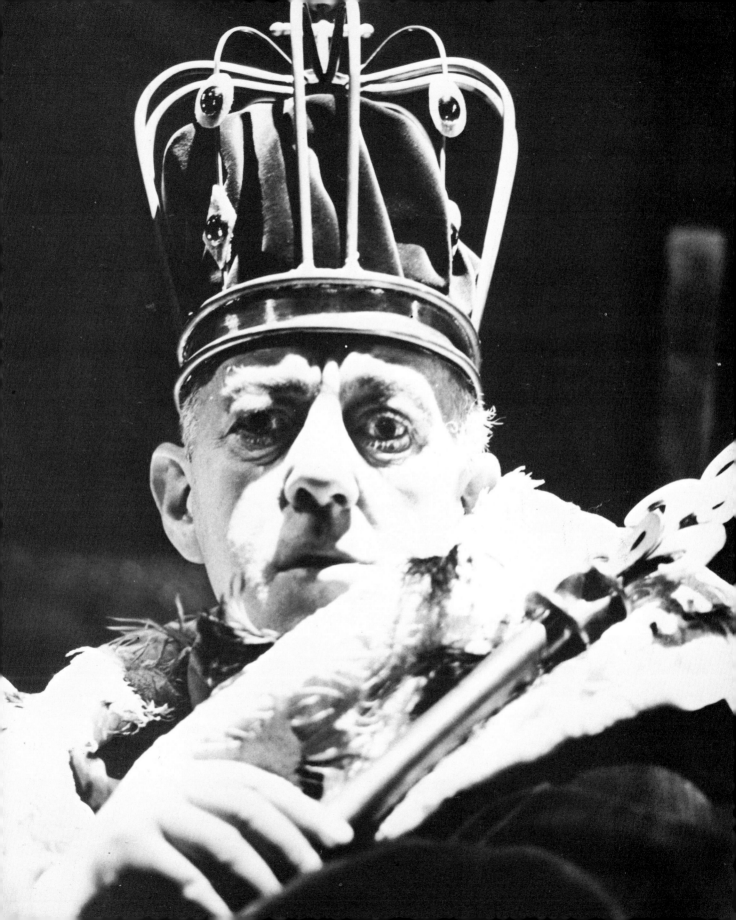

Spring Awakening, 1965. Bernard Adams and Patrick Ellis. Frank Wedekind's much-censored 'children's tragedy', written in 1891 but not staged until 1906, had been kept off the British stage till now by the Lord Chamberlain, principally because it represented masturbation. After the Court gave it a 'club' Sunday night production in 1963, a censored text was licensed for public performance (in a translation by the English Stage Company's literary manager, Tom Osborn). (*Photograph: John Timbers*)

In 1963 one of Devine's dreams materialized when the Royal Court Theatre Studio was opened, under Bill Gaskill's direction. As with many Court ventures, the start was empirical: Jocelyn Herbert discovered that the Jeannetta Cochrane Theatre in Kingsway could be made available free by the Central School of Arts and Crafts. The Studio was (after its first experimental term) granted £2,500 p.a. for three years by the Calouste Gulbenkian Trust; and the National Theatre, with which it was set up, contributed towards the costs. At its inception the aim was outlined as being 'a workshop for actors and at the same time to undertake research into the nature of improvisation and especially public improvisation.' This became the basis of the Studio's work, and it was in the field of improvisation, Gaskill believes, that its most important work was done, with the help of Keith Johnstone. Much of the initial stimulus had come from Devine, who had worked with Michel St Denis at the London Theatre Studio and the Old Vic School on the use of masks and comic improvisation. Devine himself taught at the Studio, demonstrating the basic principles of mask work. Among the public by-products of its work was *Clowning*, a wholly improvised (and almost wholly successful, *vide* the press) show for children staged at the Court on matinees during the Christmas season in 1965/66, under Keith Johnstone's direction; and Johnstone's play, *The Performing Giant*, staged the following spring in the main programme. A direct link with the National proved to be impracticable, but although the Studio survived for no more than three years, it had a significant influence as the only professional acting studio serving the theatre as a whole.

Collaboration over the Studio was linked with the National Theatre's plans for recruiting Devine himself, and for making the Court its 'experimental annexe'. Devine agreed to a 'reciprocal exchange of new plays.' In July 1963 it was announced that the two theatres had concluded an agreement: a joint committee would work out details of how this cooperation could be achieved. But the meetings were postponed; no further plans were announced; the marriage never took place. The Court had, however, a major share in the launching and establishment of the National Theatre Company, not only through the key roles of Bill Gaskill and John Dexter but through a nucleus of such Court actors as Joan Plowright, Colin Blakely, Robert Stephens and Frank Finlay. And the National connection was useful to Devine in recruiting allies whose ears and cheque-books would have remained closed to the Court on its iconoclastic own.

During this period (less fertile, dramatically, than the first five years) Osborne again dominated the Court scene – with *Luther* (1961)

Inadmissible Evidence. When Nicol Williamson was cast as Bill Maitland, the tormented solicitor-protagonist of Osborne's play, in the first 1964 production by Anthony Page (*right: photograph Zoë Dominic*), he had been an actor for only four years. As Maitland he made his debut in the West End and on Broadway. When he returned briefly to the marathon role in the 1978 production, directed by the author, he was a 40-year-old international star in a tax-bracket which apparently excluded the possibility of a West End run. (*below: photograph Donald Cooper*)

A *Patriot for Me*, 1965. George Devine as Baron von Epp, hostess in the historic drag ball scene – whose liquidation was demanded by the Lord Chamberlain. A week before its run was due to end, Devine had a heart attack after his performance. He never worked at the Court again. (*Photograph: Zoë Dominic*)

and *Inadmissible Evidence* (1964), giving prime opportunities to Albert Finney and Nicol Williamson; and the double bill *Plays for England* (1962) and *A Patriot for Me* (1965). The Lord Chamberlain's insistence on banning three scenes in the last of these led to the Council's decision to turn the Court into a club theatre: to see the play you had to pay five shillings for membership of the English Stage Society. *A Patriot for Me* was a critical and box office triumph, but with 25 scenes and a cast of 40 the production lost over £16,500; and censorship prevented any possibility of a West End transfer. (Osborne wrote the part of Baron von Epp for Devine but Anthony Page, the director, offered it to some 30 actors, including Gielgud and Coward; when this failed he actually requested the artistic director of the company to undergo an audition.)

Other outstanding events included Wesker's *The Kitchen* (1961) and *Chips With Everything* (1962), Ann Jellicoe's *The Knack* (1962), and Barry Reckord's *Skyvers* (1963). It was in this period that the first Court plays were staged of Edward Bond (*The Pope's Wedding*, 1962), Peter Gill (*The Sleepers' Den*, 1965) and David Cregan (*Miniatures*, 1965) – all on Sunday nights. Nigel Dennis's third play for the ESC, *August for the People* – written for Rex Harrison – was suddenly withdrawn when the star left a fortnight after its London run opened: the debacle ended Dennis's playwriting career.

Two of the Court's household gods were served – Beckett (*Happy Days*, 1962 and *Waiting for Godot*, 1964) and Brecht (*St Joan of the Stockyards*, 1964, *Brecht on Brecht*, 1962, and *Happy End*, 1965). Two leading Americans were staged: Edward Albee (*The Death of Bessie Smith* and *The American Dream*, 1961) and Tennessee Williams (*Period of Adjustment*, 1962). Alec Guinness took the lead in Ionesco's *Exit the King* (1965), the only play apart from Osborne's to exceed 90% at the box office in this period; but the same author's *Jacques* was part of a three-month 'French season' in 1961 – with Sartre's *Altona* and Genet's *The Blacks* – that cost nearly twice as much as the Arts Council's grant for the year. Among the revivals were Tony Richardson's productions of *The Changeling* (1961) and *A Midsummer Night's Dream* (1962), which was given one of the most severe critical drubbings in the Court's history. More significant was the revival, for a Sunday night performance, of D. H. Lawrence's *A Collier's Friday Night*: Peter Gill's production (his first) led to the revaluation of Lawrence as a dramatist in some of the Court's finest productions.

Among actors who made their London debuts here were Eileen Atkins, Gary Bond, Julian Glover, David Hemmings, Polly James, Ronald Pickup, Lynn Redgrave, Rita Tushingham and David Warner. Jonathan Miller made his debut as a director with *Plays for England*. Guests included Angela Baddeley, Jill Bennett, Claire Bloom,

A Patriot for Me, 1965. John Castle and Frederick Jaeger, with Lew Luton in the background. It was staged, for the first time in the Court's history, under 'club' conditions; but the censor's ban prevented a West End transfer. (*Photograph: Zoë Dominic*)

Bernard Braden, Peter Finch, Rex Harrison, Alec Guinness, Richard Harris, Lotte Lenya, Beatrix Lehmann, Micheál MacLiammóir, Alfred Marks, Siobhan McKenna, Paul Rogers and Robert Shaw.

During the run of *A Patriot for Me* George Devine collapsed with a heart attack. He never returned to work at the theatre to which he had given his life.

Arnold Wesker

Debts to the Court

The first moment of exhilaration must have been on receiving Lindsay Anderson's letter after he'd read *Chicken Soup With Barley*. As a student at the London School of Film Technique, queuing up to see his beautiful documentary *Every Day Except Christmas*, I'd walked up to him one day outside the National Film Theatre and asked him if he would read a story I'd written, *Pools*, which I wanted to make as a film with help from the experimental film fund. He said he would, did, liked it, put it forward. The committee liked it but felt I was too inexperienced to make it.

I next asked Lindsay if he'd read a play I'd written called *The Kitchen*. He said 'Of course.' But when it received no prize or mention in the *Observer* play competition, to which I'd sent it in 1956, I imagined it couldn't have been any good. I would not waste Lindsay's time. Not so with *Chicken Soup*. I knew in my bones I'd written something of power. It was begun in October 1957, finished in six weeks, and here – on 18 December – is what Lindsay Anderson wrote to a young man of 25 who was living at home in an LCC block of flats on the Upper Clapton Road, working part-time in his brother-in-law's basement furniture-making workshop. (I leave out Lindsay's unflattering references to other writers.)

> Dear Arnold, Thank you very much for letting me read the play, which I enjoyed very much, and think is important as well as very *good*. Obviously it needs a reading again; but at first go it held me, convinced me, and presented its problems as well as its people in a complete, *undeniable* way. Can I send it to George Devine to read for the Court? It seems to me exactly the sort of play they should be searching for ... Of course I haven't any idea what their reaction will be: they are rather incalculable people, and of course one can't be sure that the play, being as real as it is, would be a 'success'. But surely they have had enough of that recently to make them ready to put on something as good as this. You really are a playwright, aren't you? I mean there it is, with

Arnold and Dusty Wesker on the Aldermaston March. It was on the March in 1958 that Wesker met John Dexter, who directed the seven Wesker plays staged at the Royal Court from 1958 to 1972. (*Photograph: Lindsay Anderson*)

The Wesker Trilogy dramatized emotional and political changes in an East End, Jewish, socialist family between 1936 and 1956. The three plays were staged together for the first time in 1960. *Above: Chicken Soup With Barley:* Frank Finlay and David Saire. *Above right: Roots:* Joan Plowright, back to camera. Left to right: Charles Kay, Patsy Byrne, Gwen Nelson, Alan Howard (who made his London debut in *Roots* in 1959). *Right: I'm Talking About Jerusalem:* Mark Eden, Terry Palmer. *(Photographs: Sandra Lousada)*

characters as solid as I can imagine, and a whole way of life to them, and the necessary perspective ... I am sure it would act, and stage, most excitingly. The 20 years time-scheme presents its difficulties, of course, but *they* aren't insoluble. Congratulations, as I say, again, and thank you ...

I must have leapt high, to be taken so seriously, to have my permission *asked*: 'Can I send it to George Devine ...?' We had no phone in the flat in those days and I had to conduct my telephone conversations with Lindsay from the call-box on the main road.

The Court, however, did not share his enthusiasm. They asked the Belgrade Theatre in Coventry to mount it and bring it for a week to the Court as part of their celebration of 50 years of English Repertory Theatre. Brian Bailey, the artistic director of the Belgrade, was thrilled with the suggestion but could not offer Lindsay the three weeks' rehearsal he felt were needed, at which Lindsay generously suggested that I consider the offer from a bright young director who had done a couple of Sunday night productions without decor at the Court and who was convinced he could direct the play in two weeks. His name was John Dexter. We met. John walked alongside me on one of the days of the first Aldermaston march, in the pouring rain (he hated both rain and marches), talking, talking, talking about how he understood and knew how to direct the play. His excited, animated wooing was perhaps the second thrilling landmark in those early days.

The third was to arrive at Coventry station and see a poster up with my name on it, then to go into the theatre workshops and see

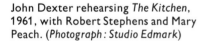

John Dexter rehearsing *The Kitchen*, 1961, with Robert Stephens and Mary Peach. (*Photograph: Studio Edmark*)

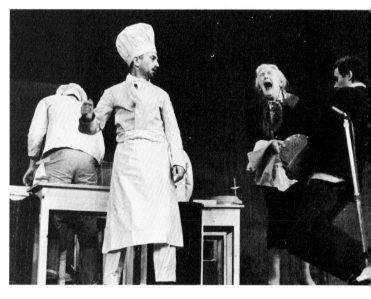

The Kitchen, 1966: at an Old Vic gala performance to raise money for the George Devine Award, Sybil Thorndike, as an elderly waitress, dropped the plates with the line, 'I'm not used to this way of working.' Olivier, Coward and Osborne also appeared. Kenneth Haigh reappeared as Jimmy Porter, Laurence Olivier as Archie Rice, Alec Guinness as Berenger the First, Jack MacGowran as Clov. (*Photograph: Lindsay Anderson*)

Robert Stephens and Wolf Parr in *The Kitchen*, 1961. First staged in 1959 as a Sunday night production without decor, its cast then included Alan Howard, Peter Gill, Patsy Byrne, James Bolam, Gwen Nelson, Nigel Davenport – and Robert Stephens. The 1961 cast, playing an expanded script, included Rita Tushingham, Mary Peach and Harry Landis. When revived in August 1961, newcomers included Steven Berkoff, Glenda Jackson and Windsor Davies. (*Photograph: Studio Edmark*)

carpenters constructing a set for something I'd written at a makeshift desk in a bedroom of a third-storey LCC flat. And the fourth thrill was after the first night of *Chicken Soup* at the Court, when John Dexter and I went upstairs to the restaurant run by Clement Freud – who'd put chicken soup with barley on the menu, ho! ho! – trying to kill time until we could go to the little courtyard in Fleet Street where, at 4 a.m., the papers gathered. John seemed to know about these things. We sat on a kerb, the papers piled on his right side. He read one, greedily, said, 'That's all right,' thrust it to me, grabbed the next one, read quickly, said, 'And that's all right . . . and that's not bad . . . and that's another good one . . . we've done it!' And then I seem to remember we walked over Blackfriars Bridge, or was it Waterloo, and talked about the past and future, no doubt, as the dawn came up. Well, what can I do? Those early days were not only thrilling, they were romantically thrilling. Then came the downs as well as the ups.

George Devine and Tony Richardson were by now interested in

me as a writer of plays. They'd read *The Kitchen*, but thought it was technically impossible to make it work. But was I writing another play? I was, and I outlined *Roots*. They gave me £25 for a first option on it – another thrill; but there's no point in numbering them from here on, since from here on most of my life was thrilling.

Roots was begun in June 1958 and the second typed draft was completed by October. George had put me up for an Arts Council award, news of which I received from him in that phone box on the Upper Clapton Road, and receipt of which enabled me to pay for my wedding in November. We spent the £300 on hiring John Williams' jazz band, Irish dancers, films, and catering for 250 friends and family. Lindsay bought us six steak knives as a wedding present. I know such details are not *about* the Court, but they're certainly *because* of it. Now for the 'down'.

George and Tony didn't like *Roots*. The unseen character of Ronnie, never appearing, worried them. They wanted me to re-write it, to meld the first and second acts together, make the third act into the second, and write a new third act in which Ronnie appeared. What would be his impact on the family – *that's* what the play should be about, they said. I felt they'd missed the point, refused to re-write and withdrew the play. Now for the 'up'.

Belatedly Peggy Ashcroft, a member of the Court's artistic committee, read the play, loved it, thought it ideal for Joan Plowright. She read it, loved it, said she'd do it anywhere. Meanwhile Dexter, who was living with us for the while, read it one day while we were out at work (yes, we still had to), and when I came back leapt into my arms crying that he knew exactly what I was trying to do and knew exactly how to direct it. And then Brian Bailey of the Belgrade read it, and we had a deal.

The first night at the Belgrade was the next landmark. Dexter had drilled the cast to bully the audience into accepting my slow pace and silences. They did. After the first five minutes we turned to each other. It was working. And the reviews agreed. Next morning the Belgrade's restaurant was buzzing with excited actors and staff, and wheeling and dealing was taking place between the Belgrade's and the Court's artistic directors for the play's transfer to Sloane Square.

With the success of *Roots*, Dexter was able to persuade the Court to let him direct *The Kitchen* as one of their Sunday night experimental productions without decor. With such a large cast – 33 – it was felt that two Sunday nights should be given it. The play was mounted with £100 and two weeks' rehearsals, received ecstatic reviews but, strangely, the Court were reluctant to put it into their repertory. About six months later, when another production fell through, they rushed it into their programme for a six-week run.

I dwell upon the Court's retreats and hesitations because it seems to me – and this is what George Devine is to be remembered for – that their real courage, as far as my work is concerned, lay in their continuing to present it even when they seemed not to comprehend its success. The peak, of course, was the presentation of the entire Trilogy in the summer of 1960. But their mistrust of my work continued. They turned down *Chips With Everything* and only agreed to mount it after a commercial impresario, Bob Swash, persuaded them to share the costs.

I don't know how to account for their resistance then, any more than I know how to account for resistance to my new work. Alien, un-English tone of voice? Technical, structural innovations? One step ahead of fashion? Who can tell? Directors did and still do seem to have difficulty in lifting my plays off the page. Nothing has changed.

It is necessary to chart all this so that the next set of impressions make sense. My contribution to this 25th anniversary celebration is to record my debts to the Court. And these, despite their initial resistances, were tremendous.

First, they gave me a physical base. To be able to walk into that building at will, watch rehearsals, meet other theatre people, and feel it was mine gave an invaluable sense of belonging. I've not had it since.

Next, and I'm not sure how fully this is appreciated, they put a spotlight on my plays for the world. The interest in new drama which they stirred up and which was given its first thrust by John Osborne's *Look Back in Anger*, brought the Court to the attention of agents, impresarios and directors from all over the world. We were made 'international writers', almost literally, overnight. This is a launching from which, more than 20 years later, I'm still reaping the benefits.

Third, there were the famous writers' gatherings, which took place mainly in a huge room belonging to Anne and David Piper on Chiswick Mall. We talked, played theatre games, tried out our ideas – not all productive, or intense with discipline, or on a high level, but contributory in subtle ways, technically and human.

And last, perhaps most important of all, the Court gave me a team: John Dexter, director, and Jocelyn Herbert, designer. We made the first five plays together. I can't pretend there weren't frictions, but there is no doubt in my mind that I learned from John how to direct plays, and from Jocelyn the absolute importance of design. The wrong set can utterly destroy the careful rhythms a writer weaves into his work. Jocelyn was and is an inspired designer and modest person upon whom Dexter and I leaned as a human being as well as an artist.

These four elements – the base, international spotlight, writers' group and, especially, the team – all culminated in the fifth element: self-confidence. Of course, many things have conspired to destroy that self-confidence since – careless critics, treacherous actors, unadventurous directors; but nothing, I suppose, can really shake that foundation which I received in those first four years of my association with the Royal Court. They didn't like or understand what I wrote, but they took the risk. I'd like to think they trusted the writer. Perhaps they only trusted the directors – Anderson and Dexter. But whoever and *however*, they gave this writer self-confidence and to them I owe an unreturnable debt – unreturnable, that is, in any way other than through my work.

Jocelyn Herbert

Discoveries in Design

When people ask what it is like designing plays for the Royal Court Theatre they usually do so in a rather commiserating way, as though it must be so very limiting to work in such a small theatre and on such a small stage. I suppose that the answer you give depends on whether you are interested in designing plays or spectacles. It is true that the stage at the Royal Court has its limitations but it has beautiful proportions and a wonderfully intimate relationship with the audience. I would rather design for that stage than for many others.

When George Devine became artistic director in 1956 he was not able to do much about the bad sight-lines at the sides of the auditorium but he did manage to change the whole proportion of the stage by opening the proscenium arch to its fullest height, and he increased the depth of the stage by building out over the orchestra pit and making the stage-level boxes into entrances. This gave the stage an extra nine feet in depth and brought the actors further into contact with the audience.

One of the main limitations of the Court stage is the lack of wing space and a very inadequate scene dock; but over the years it has acquired a very efficient counterweight system, which compensates a bit for the lack of wing space. The stage is also well equipped with traps, including a grave trap and two star traps that actually work. In the early days the switchboard was in a corner at the side of the upper circle and the sound tracks were operated from the stage management room at the side of the stage. Now there is a modern switchboard at the back of the upper circle and a sound desk and recording equipment in a room alongside so that the operators can follow the show from a point where they can see the whole stage, and can take cues visually when the action so demands.

When we started there were no workshops. All the props and small items of scenery were made under the stage – or, when fine, out in the yard. Built elements were made by Stanley Moore, and any cloths were painted in his studio by Royal Court scene-painters. The wardrobe – run by Stephen Doncaster and his wife Wendy – was

83

Serjeant Musgrave's Dance, 1959. Jocelyn Herbert's set for the churchyard at sunset (Act I, Scene 3) in John Arden's 'un-historical parable' about pacifism, set in a snow-bound northern town of 1879. (*Photograph: Snowdon*)

housed in a tiny cottage at the back of the theatre. Within a year or 18 months we had acquired a workshop at World's End – a marvellous, rambling old place where we made and painted our own scenery and props, and where there was room for the costumes to be made as well. It is perhaps ironical, or a comment on the changing values of the times, that during those halcyon days, when financially we were battling for our lives, we still considered that it was essential to have our own workshops. Some years later – after George's death – in spite of the theatre's success and greatly increased Arts Council grant, the workshops were abandoned. The argument was that few new plays were done which demanded much in the way of scenery and costumes, and that they were therefore no longer financially viable.

George Devine wanted to get away from swamping the stage with decorative and naturalistic scenery; to let in light and air; to take the stage away from the director and designer and restore it to the actor and the text. This meant leaving space around the actors, and that meant the minimum of scenery and props, i.e. only those that served the actors and play: nothing that was for decorative purposes only, unless the text, or the style of the play, demanded it. So everything on the stage had to be even more carefully designed and made, as they would be so exposed on a comparatively bare stage, not supported by the trappings of a naturalistic set. This in turn made it imperative for designers to examine the materials they used. No longer would painted scenery (however brilliantly executed) stand such close-up scrutiny and such clear light. Props suddenly became very significant: every book, lamp, chair or table – possibly the only visual elements in a scene. What they looked like, what they were made of, where they were placed on the stage, all these became very important. Perhaps it was the beginning of what I call 'considering the actors as part of the design'; considering where the actors will be on the stage and what they will need as the basis of the design; not creating an elaborate picture and then sticking the actors in it.

We started with a pale, permanent but flexible surround designed by Margaret Harris, within which the plays in the repertory were to be staged. We found that gradually we wanted to use less and less of the surround, and began to use the bare stage and sometimes the bare walls as well. We got rid of borders and exposed the lights: not just by chance, to the first four rows of the stalls, but on purpose to the whole theatre. Out of this grew the luxury of designing a lighting grid to suit each play, i.e. the grid to echo the contours of the set, which made it possible to light an acting area leaving darkness all round, thus creating a surround out of light.

In those early days when George Devine was trying to find authors who would write plays reflecting more closely the times we were living in, as opposed to the drawing-room comedies and revivals of the West End theatres, I remember thinking how little influence contemporary painting and sculpture had so far had on theatre design. The theatre needed a more abstract approach to design. This did not mean that the stage had to look like an abstract painting, or be subject to fashionable gimmicks. It was more an attitude of mind: the belief that photographic naturalism was not the only or the most evocative way of communicating a place or a time. There was also the growing conviction that the bare stage was a very beautiful space and, as with a bare canvas, the moment you put one subject on it – even just a chair – all sorts of things happened. The actor could immediately use the space in so many different ways. It created distance, division of space, movement around, and so on; and the chair, of course, could become so many different things, according to how the actors used it.

Because of this more three-dimensional approach to decor, we looked around and discovered all sorts of new materials that we could use as substitutes for canvas and scene paint: polystyrene, fibre glass, metal, etc. All are superseded now by even more amazing products and techniques but at that time they seemed manna from heaven. Above all we discovered *light*. The enormous development in the quality of lighting equipment has been prompted not only by the increasing demand for control, precision and brilliance, but also by the fact that as naturalistic scenery was less widely used, so lighting became increasingly an integral part of the design. It was this situation which brought about the arrival of the lighting designer, who now plays an essential part in every production team.

Along with this desire to clear away all the clutter went a deep respect for the text, a conviction instilled by George Devine and still uniting directors and designers who worked at the Court while he was artistic director. What we were there to do was to present the play as close as possible to what the author intended. The author was

85

served by all who worked at the Court. He was not likely to have his play turned inside out because of a director's interpretation of what *he* thought it ought to be.

I do not know if it can be said that a design style has characterized most productions at the Court during the last 25 years; but if it has, I think this is largely due to the way that directors working there approach a text and the discipline that this imposes on designers, as well as their having to be inventive and ingenious in coping with the limitations of the stage itself and the often severely limited budgets.

No theatre style, of course, can or should be absolutely rigid. Plays may come along that demand painted cloths, or naturalistic interiors, or some definite indication of period, and these demands have to be satisfied; but they can be interpreted in the terms of 'poetic realism' rather than trying to create the real thing.

I suppose it is inevitable that this piece should have a nostalgic flavour. How could it not? Certainly during those first 10 years of the

Jocelyn Herbert's designs for the Wesker Trilogy. *Left: Chicken Soup With Barley*, Act I. *Right: Roots:* Act I. *Below: I'm Talking About Jerusalem.* (*Photographs: Sandra Lousada*)

ESC's existence at the Royal Court, when George Devine was artistic director, it was a privilege to be working there. We were all incredibly lucky to have been around just at that time. This was not just another theatre putting on plays. We had a sense of purpose and a vision of what part the theatre could and should play in people's lives in the future. The atmosphere was electric, explorative and explosive, the energy amazing. For a brief period our work, and indeed our lives, had a centre.

Albert Finney

Albert Finney makes up for the role of Ted in *The Lily White Boys*, 1960: the other Boys were Monty Landis and Philip Locke. (*Photograph: Lindsay Anderson*)

Recollections of a Lunch

We had been rehearsing *The Lily White Boys* for about two weeks when George Devine suddenly asked me to lunch one day. I had only met him a few times and didn't know him well. Admiration, regard, friendship lay ahead, as did the deep sense of loss when he was gone. To me in January 1960 he was the respected authoritative figure who ran the Royal Court Theatre, and the invitation made me a little nervous. Is this a bollocking I see before me?

'Would you like some red wine?'

'Lovely,' I said, thinking, was that a test, and if so have I failed? Maybe he thinks I drink a lot. Certainly he put me firmly in my place the other day when I imitated Wilfrid Lawson. George thought I was being disrespectful, which I was not, and had talked about the tragedy of Wilfrid's fine talent being beset by demons.

Should I tell him my Barrymore phase is over?

A year earlier, when rehearsing *The Long and the Short and the Tall*, I had been carted off for medical assistance, as I couldn't straighten up. The theatre doctor diagnosed bronchitis and sent me off to bed. Three days later my own doctor came and sent me to hospital for an emergency operation: peritonitis. The Sunday before I'd been at a party and got through a bottle of Pernod, mostly uncontaminated by water. My condition that night and its possible effect on my appendix finally convinced me I would never make a romantic drunken actor. I had done some serious research into alcohol for some months but usually ended up vomiting, and now I knew I hadn't the stomach for it. Now they would never be saying that, but for being so profligate with my genius, I would have been the greatest of them all. No drink and no genius.

I will just have one glass, maybe two, don't want to nod off during afternoon rehearsals anyway.

'How are the rehearsals going?'

'I'm finding the songs tricky, singing is not a thing I'm used to, and I'm not quite sure what 'Brechtian' means. But it's a good part.'

'Yes it is, but being the leading man is not just a question of having

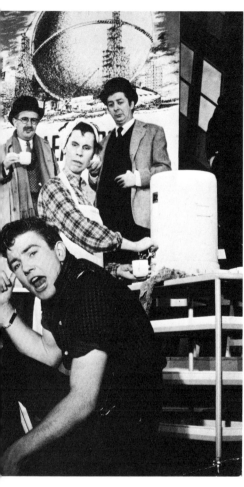

Above: The Lily White Boys, 1960. Behind Finney are Geoffrey Hibbert, Barbara Hicks and Monty Landis. This Brechtian, low-life, satirical musical, with 'play songs' by Christopher Logue, had a score by Tony Kinsey and Bill Le Sage. (*Photograph: John Cowan*)

Above right: Luther, 1961. Albert Finney in the title role. He played it in French and Dutch festivals before the Royal Court opening, and afterwards in Edinburgh and in the West End. Two years later he made his New York debut in Osborne's play. (*Photograph: Sandra Lousada*)

the best part.'

He said 'leading man'!

'It is not just having the most lines or the most laughs, the number one dressing room, or the name in lights over the title.'

With the growing popularity of alphabetical billing perhaps I should change my name to Aaron Aardvark.

'It means you lead and have to be seen to be leading. To commit.'

It is possibly not true to say that I have never been late for rehearsal but I've always believed that you should be ready to start work on time with the eyes open and the mind as alive as possible.

'I don't mean obvious things like knowing your lines and being on time for rehearsals, but showing how much you care for the thing. To encourage your fellow actors to stretch and to dig into the text by demonstrably doing that yourself. Your capacity for work, your enthusiasm, your commitment to bringing it to life. Leading by example.'

Luther, 1961: Jocelyn Herbert's set for the Diet of Worms (Act III, scene 1), when the first Protestant confronted the Holy Roman Emperor and the Church: 'the medieval world dressed up for the Renaissance,' Osborne says in his stage directions. (*Photograph: Sandra Lousada*)

It was all said calmly while he ate, enjoying his lunch. His attention seemed to be on the food yet the point was made and I wanted to get back to rehearsals and justify his faith in me. This is no bollocking, I thought, it is very flattering. He believes in my talent and cares enough to want to nudge it in the right direction.

Was that his greatest talent, seeing some potential, giving it a chance and not being possessive about it, not obtrusive? Unless you thought about it, you might not notice his influence.

Now and again you come across someone who makes you better. George Devine was such a man. I remember feeling great intimacy with him. I do now as I write this, together with that sense of loss. Thanks for lunch, George.

1965-1969

When Bill Gaskill took over as artistic director in July 1965 he set out with the intention of presenting plays in 'true' repertory with a permanent company, returning to the idea pursued by Devine and Richardson at the start of the ESC. His first year featured such pillars of the Royal Court as Ann Jellicoe (*Shelley*), N. F. Simpson (*The Cresta Run*) and Arnold Wesker (*Their Very Own and Golden City*); revivals of *Serjeant Musgrave's Dance* and *The Knack*, together with Thomas Middleton's *A Chaste Maid in Cheapside* and Harley Granville Barker's *The Voysey Inheritance*; new Sunday discoveries like David Cregan, Heathcote Williams and Christopher Hampton; and the first play commissioned from an earlier Sunday author, Edward Bond – the controversial *Saved*.

It was (and is) an impressive programme of names; but Gaskill's luck was out, the chemistry failed to work, the critics were generally hostile and the audiences stayed away. Box office takings averaged only 32% and the ESC faced a consequential loss of some £45,000 within six months. Gaskill and his Council were persuaded – not least by the Arts Council – to revert to short runs and ad hoc casting. Thereafter, for three years, there was no deficit. In the following two years the box office average rose to 50%, and in 1968/69 to more than 57%, although most of the new plays fell below that figure: *Saved*, for instance, played to less than 40% despite all the publicity. Mixing old plays with new, Gaskill achieved an overall box office success.

During Gaskill's regime by far the most successful event at the box office (though the most reviled by the reviewers) was his production of *Macbeth* (1967) with Alec Guinness and Simone Signoret (in bright light throughout, on a sandpaper set with no hint of scenery) which played to over 98%. Next most successful, financially, were Osborne's *The Hotel in Amsterdam* (96.2%), *Roots*, revived for school matinees (82.7%), the D. H. Lawrence season (76.3%), Osborne's *Time Present* (75.5%), Gaskill's revival of *Three Sisters* (75.2%) and the revival of *Look Back in Anger* (66.0%). Fortunately for the basic success, maintaining the right to fail, the Arts Council subsidy went up dramatically – from £32,500 in 1964/65 to £88,650 in 1966/67 and £100,000 in 1967/68, a level not exceeded for another five years.

Gaskill's regime was marked, even more bruisingly and perilously than Devine's, by struggles with censorship. So many cuts were demanded by the Lord Chamberlain in *Saved* that it was resolved (with the agreement of the Arts Council and the Court's lessee, Alfred Esdaile) to stage it only for members of the English Stage Society. But after a police visit to the theatre the Lord Chamberlain, in a spasm of unprecedented activism, issued summonses against Gaskill, Esdaile and Greville Poke (secretary of the ESC) on the grounds that *Saved* was not a bona fide club production: a member of

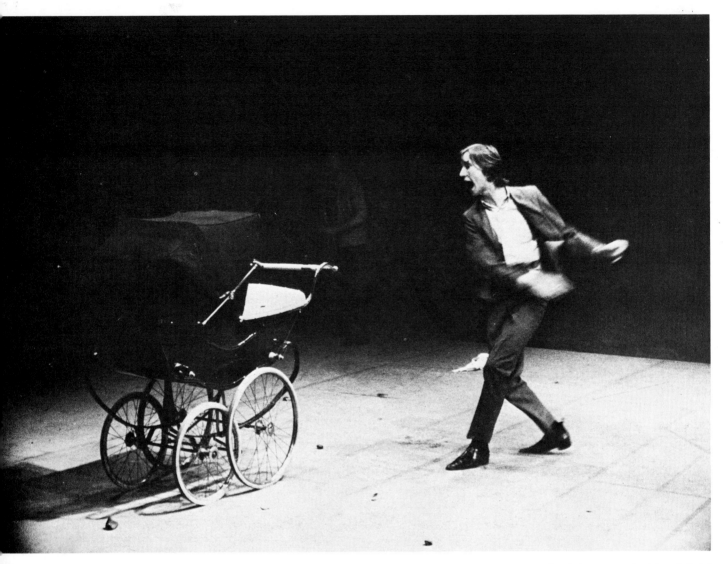

Saved, 1965. Dennis Waterman in the scene that the Lord Chamberlain didn't like. The play, commissioned from Edward Bond, had to be staged under club conditions. Its production led to a court case – and a moral victory for the English Stage Company in its fight against theatrical censorship. (*Photograph: Snowdon*)

his staff visiting the play had not been asked for proof of his 'club' membership.

Although the magistrate found against the Court, the ESC was fined only £50 in costs, and Gaskill, Esdaile and Poke were conditionally discharged. From now on it was clear that it was illegal to stage plays anywhere without a licence from the Lord Chamberlain, whether or not they were presented under club conditions – a result that defeated his apparent object in bringing the prosecution. This moral· victory, which accelerated the end of the Lord Chamberlain's powers over the theatre, was followed two years later by another battle over a Bond play – *Early Morning*. When this was banned in toto by the Lord Chamberlain (although now at his last gasp) because of its irreverent treatment of Queen Victoria, Gaskill proposed to stage it under club conditions. On this occasion, however, the Arts Council refused to acquiesce (fearing, apparently, that this might hold up the abolition of censorship which seemed

Front page of the London *Evening
Standard*, 14 February 1966.

imminent) and threatened to withhold its grant for the period of the
run if Gaskill persisted. It was decided, accordingly, to give *Early
Morning* two consecutive Sunday night performances. On the first,
police visited the theatre, interviewed Gaskill and made their
presence felt. No action followed, but the second performance was
cancelled on Esdaile's insistence. Instead a matinee – described as a
'critics' dress rehearsal' – was given for invited guests, who were not
charged for their seats. *Early Morning* was the last play banned by the
Lord Chamberlain, whose long reign over the drama was terminated
by the Theatres Act of 1968 on 28 September. Gaskill and the ESC
celebrated, early in 1969, with a season of Bond plays, performed
publicly and uncensored for the first time. Later that year the author
was given the stamp of official recognition as a cultural asset fit for
export: *Saved* and *Narrow Road to the Deep North* were toured by the
ESC through Europe under British Council auspices.

It was towards the end of this period that the 'fringe' or
'underground' theatre began to take root in Britain. The People
Show and CAST (Cartoon Archetypical Slogan Theatre) started in
1965. The Oval House in Kennington was opened as a fringe venue in
1966. But it was not until a year or so later that a sector of the British
theatre was suddenly radicalized, politically and theatrically, by the
visits of such American companies as the Open Theatre and La Mama;
by the establishment of Jim Haynes's Arts Lab in Drury Lane, the
impact of Ed Berman's Inter-Action and Charles Marowitz's Open
Space (all three enterprises run by Americans); and the pressure of
world events – in France (the *événements* of May '68), Czechoslovakia
(the Prague spring and the Russian invasion), Vietnam (the escalation
of the war) and Northern Ireland. New companies were founded: the
Portable, Freehold, Red Ladder, Pip Simmons. An Arts Council
committee was appointed to investigate 'New Activities'. A new
press outlet was opened – *Time Out*. With the abolition of the Lord
Chamberlain's censorship, a new freedom of speech was available.
And, prompted by the example of the Edinburgh Festival that same
year, a new circuit of makeshift showplaces in halls, clubs and
adaptable rooms began to take shape and kept spasmodically alive.

The English Stage Company met the challenge in its own way,
thanks to Bill Gaskill. One major event of his 1965–69 regime was the
opening of the Theatre Upstairs, in the club-rehearsal room at the
top of the Royal Court. In March 1968 club performances of 'an
experimental nature' were started to test its possibilities as a studio
theatre, long dreamed of by Devine and his associates. Fourteen
productions – short plays, acting solos, mimes – were staged, free, by
unpaid actors, authors and directors (they included Sam Shepard's
Red Cross and John Arden's *Squire Jonathan*). As club revenues

Their Very Own and Golden City, 1966. Sebastian Shaw as Wesker's veteran trade union organizer and Ian McKellen, standing on his hands, as the crusading architect whose dreams of Utopia crumble. (*Photograph: Zoë Dominic*)

averaged some £2,000 p.a. some members of the Council opposed any change of use. Alfred Esdaile championed its transformation by two entrepreneurs into 'a club for young accountants'. But Gaskill's plans were supported. Helped by an interest-free loan from the English Stage Society and an adjustment of the Arts Council subsidy (£5,000 added to the grant and £5,000 less in guarantees) the room at the top was converted into a public auditorium measuring about 30 by 40 feet, and seating up to 120 (on occasions as few as 35). It opened on 24 February 1969 with David Cregan's *A Comedy of the Changing Years*.

The first year was, in the words of its director Nicholas Wright, a 'critical disaster', partly because it exposed many London reviewers, for the first time, to some of the mixed theatricalisms of the 'fringe'. With so tiny a box office capacity it could scarcely be expected to make a profit (even with transfers downstairs or to the West End) or even necessarily cover production costs; but these were so much smaller than those of the main theatre that the right to fail, and the

The Voysey Inheritance, 1966. Avril Elgar and John Castle in Harley Granville Barker's play, first staged at the Royal Court in 1905 during the Vedrenne-Barker regime. (*Photograph: Lewis Morley*)

chance to try again, were given an extended lease. Helped by the English Stage Society and by ad hoc private sponsors, the Council kept the Theatre Upstairs going, and in spite of occasional closures in the past 12 years it has staged, up to date, over 180 productions.

Relations between the Court and the critics were frequently sourer than was usual in the London theatre of the 60's, partly because the Court was a theatre of so unusual a kind: a kind which, Court people felt, was neither liked nor understood by many reviewers, while some journalists believed that the ESC expected a special immunity from criticism. There seemed to be a perennially explosive incompatibility between the Court's idea of a critic's responsibility to the work and the theatre (and of the qualifications needed to be a critic) and the reviewers' sense of responsibility to their readers and their editors (especially in the popular press). Court scepticism about reviewers' wisdom was reinforced by the contrast between dismissive reactions to the first nights of many plays and the later acceptance of these plays as pillars of the contemporary drama.

When his production of *Macbeth* was bombarded with derisive notices in 1967, Gaskill threatened to exclude the critics of several national papers from future Court productions because of the triviality and shallowness of first night reviewing which failed to take account of the theatre's record and the seriousness of its intentions. After a turbulent public row the threat was withdrawn; the reviewers continued to come to Sloane Square; but mutual understanding did not perceptibly improve. Two years later in another *cause célèbre*, where Lindsay Anderson took the initiative, the Court announced that it would no longer send free tickets to Hilary Spurling, theatre critic of the *Spectator*, because it did not find her 'attitude to our work illuminating, and we do not believe that it furthers our relationship with the public.' Three critics responded by refusing to review Court productions. Six months later, after prolonged debate, public and private, the Arts Council applied financial pressure: it threatened to withdraw its grant if the Court did not resume relations with Mrs Spurling. The Court conceded, still brandishing its principles – 'that theatre critics who accept invitations to review seats have responsibilities and duties and that the theatre should have the right to withhold free seats. . . .'

Bill Gaskill seemed ready to challenge theatrical or social *idées reçues*, for the Court's sake, when the need appeared obvious. And he defied theatrical convention, once again, in February 1969, after *Life Price* – Jeremy Seabrook and Michael O'Neill's play about a child-murder – played for the first 10 days to virtually empty houses, in spite of respectful notices. During the last two weeks of the run all

Below: Controversial design: Christopher Morley's bright, bare and empty box for *Macbeth*, 1966, with only one door and no darkness. The set later became the model for design work in the RSC. (*Photograph: Snowdon*)

Below right: Garland made this comment in *The Daily Telegraph* (1 November 1966) after Bill Gaskill's threat to stop inviting critics after their press reception of *Macbeth*. (*Reproduced by kind permission of* The Daily Telegraph)

Right: Controversial casting: Alec Guinness and Simone Signoret in *Macbeth. (Photograph: Snowdon)*

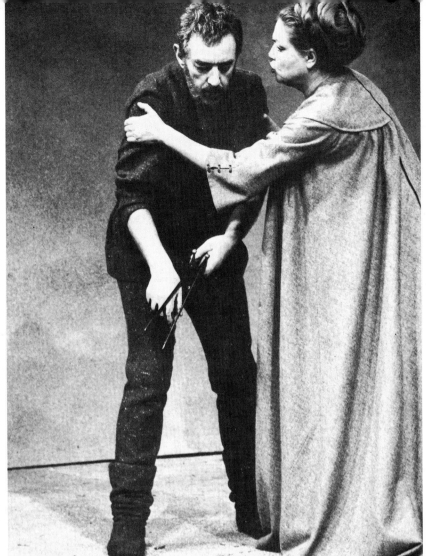

"WE'RE WITH YOU MR GASKILL".

Ubu Roi. The Polish Royal Family.

Marianne Faithfull, Avril Elgar and
Glenda Jackson in Edward Bond's
version of Chekhov's *Three Sisters*, 1967.
(*Photograph: Douglas H. Jeffery*)

Ubu Roi, 1966. *Above left*, *Ubu Thinking*
and, *left*, *The Polish Royal Family*: two
designs by David Hockney for this
version of Alfred Jarry's 1896 shocker,
adapted by Iain Cuthbertson.
(*Photographs courtesy Petersburg Press*)

seats were offered free, and *Life Price* played to capacity. Gaskill
declared, 'We want to be a public theatre, with free seats, not a
private theatre for a minority.' Proposals were made for staging one
or two free-seat productions a year, or offering some free-seat
performances in all productions. But the insuperable problems of
cost, yet again, blocked any hope of further experiment along these
lines.

George Devine died on 20 January 1966. He was 55. John Osborne
wrote of him, in the *Observer*:

> In 10 years as artistic director of the Royal Court Theatre,
> George Devine was almost solely responsible for its unique
> atmosphere, which anyone who knew him knew to be a
> reflection of his unique temperament. . . . Hundreds of writers
> and actors owe their present fortunes and favour to him. I am in
> the greatest debt of all. It seems extraordinary to have been so
> fortunate.

The George Devine Fund was set up after his death to finance an
annual award to a promising artist, whether playwright, director,
actor or scene designer. Not long after the death of his adversary,
Ronald Duncan finally resigned from the Council of the English Stage
Company.

After the first Gaskill year few of the Court writers from the
previous decade appeared in the programme. Sunday night authors
included Joe Orton (*The Ruffian on the Stair*, 1967), Peter Gill (*A
Provincial Life*, 1966), whose *Over Gardens Out* was staged Upstairs in
1969; Heathcote Williams, who made his Court debut in 1966 with
The Local Stigmatic; John Antrobus (*Captain Oates' Left Sock*, 1968);
Michael Rosen, whose *Backbone* (1968) was promoted to a run. David
Cregan's second Sunday-nighter, *Transcending* (1966), achieved the
same promotion, and was followed that year by *Three Men for
Colverton*, *The Houses by the Green* (1968) and *A Comedy of the Changing*

99

Years (1969). Other Court debuts included those of John Hopkins (*This Story of Yours*, 1966); Michael O'Neill and Jeremy Seabrook (*Life Price*, 1969); and Mike Stott (*Erogenous Zones*, 1969, Upstairs). Two plays by Charles Wood were staged: *Fill the Stage With Happy Hours* (1967) and *Dingo* (1968), which the National Theatre would not present because so many radical changes were demanded by the Lord Chamberlain. This was staged under club conditions. The main debuts of the period were those of Christopher Hampton, who became the Court's first resident dramatist shortly after the Sunday night performances of *When Did You Last See My Mother?* (1966) and went on to write *Total Eclipse* (1968); and David Storey, with *The Restoration of Arnold Middleton* (1967), directed by Robert Kidd, followed by *In Celebration* (1969), which inaugurated a justly celebrated stage partnership with Lindsay Anderson. Another outstanding event in Gaskill's regime was the establishment of Edward Bond as a major playwright with *Saved* (1965) and *Early Morning* (1968) – both commissioned by the English Stage Company – and *Narrow Road to the Deep North* (1969).

Among other significant productions was that of *Marya* by Isaac Babel, one of Stalin's most distinguished victims. Adapted by Christopher Hampton, it was chosen to mark the 50th anniversary of

Above left: Time Present, 1968. Jill Bennett (left) – with Katherine Blake – as John Osborne's first stage heroine, Pamela Orme. (*Photograph: John Timbers*)

Above right: Dingo, 1968. Michael Francis, Barry Stanton and Henry Woolf in Charles Wood's play about the 'aftermyth' of desert warfare, staged under club conditions because the author and the English Stage Company refused to accept the Lord Chamberlain's veto on many passages. (*Photograph: Douglas H. Jeffery*)

Left: The Hotel in Amsterdam, 1968. Joss Ackland, Judy Parfitt, Ralph Watson, Paul Scofield as four of the conversation-piece characters in the shadow of the offstage megalomaniac film director, KL. (*Photograph: Zoë Dominic*)

Right: Three Men for Colverton, 1966. Sylvia Coleridge and Richard Simpson in the fourth of six David Cregan plays to be staged at the Court between 1965 and 1969. (*Photograph: John Haynes*)

100

the Russian Revolution. The play had been banned while being rehearsed in 1934 and had never been staged: Babel was arrested in 1939, and died, officially, two years later. In 1967 Bill Gaskill's production of *Three Sisters*, translated by Edward Bond, aroused controversy because Marianne Faithfull was in the cast; and his choice of Simone Signoret as Lady Macbeth provoked (as we have seen) even more violent argument. His less provocative revivals were *A Chaste Maid in Cheapside* (1966) and *The Double Dealer* (1969). Alfred Jarry's surrealist classic, *Ubu Roi*, was revived in 1966 with the veteran vaudevillian, Max Wall, in the lead, a prime example of the cross-casting – transcending traditional 'legitimate' borders – that has fitfully distinguished Court policy. Otway's *The Soldier's Fortune* (1967) marked Peter Gill's debut as a director of period plays.

The major venture in revivalism during the Gaskill regime was the rehabilitation as a dramatist of D. H. Lawrence, whose plays were ignored in his lifetime. Peter Gill's Sunday night production in 1965 of Lawrence's first, written in 1909, had led the way; in 1967 Gill's production of *The Daughter-in-Law*, staged for the first time since Lawrence wrote it in 1911, was so well received that in 1968 it was presented again, with *A Collier's Friday Night* and *The Widowing of Mrs Holroyd*. Few events at the Court have been accorded such unanimous critical rapture as this special Lawrence season.

The English Stage Company played host to three influential American companies during this period: the Open Theatre (1967), the Paperbag Players (1967) and the Bread and Puppet Theatre (1969). The Open Theatre's production of Jean-Claude van Itallie's *America Hurrah* was banned by the Lord Chamberlain, largely because of 'unflattering references to a friendly head of state' (President Johnson), and was therefore staged for members of the English Stage Society only. Although a transfer to the Vaudeville Theatre was arranged, the lessee withdrew from the deal at the last moment, fearing action by the Lord Chamberlain or the LCC, even if 'club' conditions were observed. (Charles Wood's *Fill the Stage With Happy Hours* was presented instead, as an emergency substitute.)

In Gaskill's first year he was helped by two associate directors, Iain Cuthbertson and Keith Johnstone. They were followed, briefly, by Desmond O'Donovan. Throughout this period a key figure backstage was Jane Howell who, in addition to directing a wide range of plays – *Twelfth Night*, *Roots*, *The Voysey Inheritance*, *Serjeant Musgrave's Dance*, *Narrow Road to the Deep North* and others – ran the Schools Scheme and aided Gaskill and the Court in many different ways. Two Scottish newcomers made their debuts as directors on the London stage here in this period: Robert Kidd (*When Did You Last See My Mother?*) and Bill Bryden (*Journey of the Fifth Horse*).

The D.H. Lawrence season, 1968. As Christopher Hampton says, 'Its influence on a whole line of work in the theatre and on television was far-reaching.' *Left: The Daughter-in-Law.* Victor Henry and Anne Dyson. *Below: A Collier's Friday Night.* Christine Hargreaves and John Barrett. *Right: The Widowing of Mrs Holroyd.* Judy Parfitt and Michael Coles. (*Photographs: Douglas H. Jeffery*)

In the field of design Gaskill started by employing John Gunter as resident designer, the first since 1956, followed briefly by Christopher Morley. One conspicuous innovation was the employment of two leading painters as theatre designers – David Hockney for *Ubu Roi*, and Patrick Procktor for *Total Eclipse*. Deirdre Clancy made her London debut as costume designer with *The Daughter-in-Law*.

Another key figure of Court history to emerge in this period was Andy Phillips, the chief electrician, who became one of the country's leading lighting designers. In the first ESC decade Devine always looked after the lighting himself; none of his associates and pupils could match his enthusiasm and expertise (except, perhaps, for Richardson). Phillips not only showed the directors how it could be done, but he refined the skill and widened the scope of his craft, preparing the way for his successors – notably Jack Raby – in a theatre where lighting has been, from the start, a cardinal element in the design and composition of productions.

In addition to Jane Howell, another woman played an important part in the counsels of the Court at this time: Helen Montagu, who was general manager from 1965–72. We may take this opportunity to record the debt owed by the English Stage Company to her, to her predecessor, Doreen Dixon, and to her successor, Anne Jenkins, still valiantly coping with the Court (her job has been a virtual feminine monopoly from the start, with the notable exception of Pieter Rogers); and to the women who have, most of the time, done the work of casting director – Pauline Melville, Corinne Rodriguez, Patsy Pollock, Simone Reynolds, Lindy Jones and especially Miriam Brickman and Gillian Diamond; to Harriet Cruickshank, whose jobs in the past decade have included those of Upstairs manager, press officer and Council member; to Lady Melchett and Mrs Gestetner of the ESC Council; to Lois Sieff, for some 20 years the English Stage Society's indispensable dynamo and to Elsie Fowler, the Court's legendary housekeeper for 17 years.

Jack Shepherd

'Don't Talk About It – Do It'

I auditioned for the Royal Court repertory company in the summer of 1965. I gave them a speech of Edmund's from *King Lear*, which involved, for reasons that aren't clear any more, walking around with my arm outstretched and suddenly looking up into different corners of the room, and a scenario of my own all about a meths drinker being thrown out of a police station. I failed. They thought I was interesting, but crazy.

Undeterred, I wrote them a letter about wanting to be at the centre of the action, which was then, in my opinion, the Royal Court, and wanting to be in new plays, about our society, and so on. It was an honest letter, written in desperation, and it worked. I was let in to the company, at the lowest level. I was to be an understudy in *Saved*. I remember reading the play for the first time. My reaction was very precise: I felt as if I'd been punched on the nose.

I once worked out how many productions I had been in at the Court. I counted 36. I added them all up again last week. No matter how hard I tried, I couldn't get the figure any higher than 31. These productions included plays in the main theatre, the Theatre Upstairs, and those performed on a Sunday night, once only, with hardly any money at all, and for hardly any money at all. One of the hardest things for an actor is to go on stage not knowing the lines properly. This often happened on a Sunday night. Afterwards the playwrights used to say that they were 'very pleased', and sometimes, more grimly, that they had 'learned something'. If the latter, they would be seen drinking alone in the circle bar. No one wants a drink with a playwright who has just learned something.

More fun were Keith Johnstone's improvised 'clowning' sessions. These would take place on a Sunday night too. We, the actors, would sit on chairs at the front of the stage, and after being primed by Keith and, sometimes, suggestions from the audience, we would set off on a series of strange improvised journeys. Keith would then retreat into the wings to watch, though he was often given to bounding on stage unexpectedly (like a Demon King in woolly pullover and glasses) to

Ubu Roi, 1966. *Above:* Jack Shepherd as Mother Ubu with Max Wall, the music-hall master who at the age of 58 made his debut as Ubu in the straight theatre – one of the most successful examples of Royal Court casting across conventional theatrical frontiers. (*Photograph: Zoë Dominic*). *Above right:* David Hockney's design: *Mère and Père Ubu.* (*Photograph courtesy of Petersburg Press*)

alter the scene, or give us fresh instructions.

Since one of the rules of these 'clowning' sessions was not to know what you were going to do until you did it, and not to think about what you were saying until you said it, the results were often surrealistic. I remember once being a crow hovering above the Crucifixion on Good Friday. Somehow Roddy Maude-Roxby had spread himself, as it were, beneath me, as Christ on the cross. I was then joined by another crow, played by Anthony Trent with flapping arms. A mysterious conversation ensued. I can't remember what we talked about. This was in 1967, in the days of flower power and widespread acid-tripping. Afterwards Roddy had a lot of trouble with some Americans who thought he really was Christ, and that the second coming was at hand.

'Lead us,' one of them said, a girl, with inward-looking eyes and straggly blond hair.

'No,' said Roddy, and hurried out of the building.

106

The Royal Court Actors' Studio was still operating at this time. Junior members of the company, such as myself, were encouraged to attend. There were classes in basic skills, movement, method acting, clowning, comic masks, full masks, and so on. Bill Gaskill used to take improvisation classes in which he would set out to explore the world of the epic narrative. These sessions were often very baffling.

'An old woman comes down to the river,' he said once. 'I want someone to act the narrative contained in that sentence.'

Everyone cringed. After a long silence an actor was picked out. A man.

'You want me to act out the sentence, "An old woman comes down to the river",' the actor repeated.

'Yes,' said Bill after another long silence.

The actor then tied a pullover round his head, hunched his shoulders, and started walking, as he hoped, towards the river.

'Start again,' said Bill, almost immediately. 'What you are showing me is ... "*The* old woman comes down to the river." I want *an* old woman. Can you show me *an* old woman? Without using a headscarf, and without hunching your shoulders?'

The actor looked scared. 'I don't know,' he said.

'Try it again,' said Bill.

And so it went on.

I don't remember Victor Henry attending any of Bill's classes. He had theories of his own at this time. I remember him telling me that if you played a scene with your head on one side you could make middle-aged women cry. It had never occurred to me to want to do that but I showed interest, arguing that it seemed unlikely.

'Just watch me,' he replied. So I watched him one night, as Sparky in *Serjeant Musgrave's Dance*, playing a love scene with his right ear resting absurdly on his shoulder. I looked around the auditorium and, sure enough, middle-aged women were crying all over the place.

Nearly all Victor's best work was done at the Royal Court in the late 1960's. He was the epitome of a dangerous actor. When he walked on stage he always reminded me of a gunfighter looking for someone to shoot or, failing that, to bite. He could also be a dangerous person. Everyone who knew him (before his terrible accident in 1972) has their own repertoire of extraordinary and contradictory stories. He was the only truly ungovernable person I have ever known.

For a brief period in 1968 the space upstairs became a late-night drinking club. It even had its own fruit machine until, it was rumoured, some enterprising thug called in at the office and suggested to the management that they might want 'protection'. The story may well be apocryphal but the fact remains that the machine disappeared a few days after the rumour started circulating. It was a very free and anarchic time. People started putting shows on in the club. I produced one about a man trying to cross the world in a straight line. Victor Henry organized one called *Booze* – a series of recitations and songs about the delights of drinking. From these inauspicious beginnings the Theatre Upstairs was born.

One of the first productions Upstairs was more of an event than a performance. It was an intended satire on Enoch Powell and his inflammatory speeches on race, called *The Enoch Show*. Unfortunately for the cast (myself included) the National Front had infiltrated the audience. They threw chairs and stink-bombs, and chanted: 'Get them out!' I think *everyone* was frightened. Especially the instigators. When the police arrived the chanters ran out of the building and joined up with others who were already marching around Sloane Square holding flaming torches and chanting slogans. When the show started up again it seemed wildly inappropriate.

Teeth 'n' Smiles, 1975. Jack Shepherd – with Cherie Lunghi – as Arthur, the Cambridge dropout turned songwriter who is the central figure in David Hare's play. (*Photograph: John Haynes*)

I remember life at the Court as being very intense at this time (1969). The Edward Bond season had proved a formidable challenge for everyone involved. In *Narrow Road to the Deep North* it was not always clear to me what the lines meant. So, whenever I got the chance, I would seek out Edward Bond and ask him.

'What is Shogo trying to achieve at this point?' I would ask.

'He's lying,' Bond would reply. Or something equally inscrutable.

In the end he got fed up with my questions, and emptied an ash-tray full of sand and cigar-butts on my head.

'Why ask me?' he said.

Two years before, when I'd played in *The Restoration of Arnold Middleton*, David Storey had been similarly uncommunicative. Later, I heard him talking on a television programme about acting. He was asked what he said to actors when they asked him about the meaning of his text.

'I don't think you should tell them anything,' he said, gently. 'Let them discover it for themselves, so that when they finally get there, the realization will seem so much more *momentous*.'

The problem is getting there.

During the period when I worked intensively at the Court a defined way of rehearsing the actors (of getting there) was in the process of being evolved. The actors were encouraged to regard themselves as servants of the play. The text had to be spoken in such a way that the audience would be drawn to the narrative of the play – not the charismatic (or otherwise) nature of the performance. A good actor was someone who could draw attention to the thing that was said, as opposed to the way it was being spoken. Naturalness, not naturalism. Altruism, not egotism. And above all, in rehearsal, there was no substitute for *doing*. As Bill Gaskill repeatedly said: 'Don't talk about it – do it.' And much more.

What made it difficult was that a lot of the theory tended to run right across the grain of an actor's instinct. It was very hard to find a synthesis.

It still is.

David Storey

Working With Lindsay

We were driving along a back street in Huddersfield, looking for locations for the projected film of *This Sporting Life*, and lamenting the fact that there was nowhere to eat, when Lindsay Anderson enquired if, apart from the screen adaptation of the novel, I'd ever written a play. We stopped at a corner pie-shop and it was only a little later, the pangs of hunger satisfied, that I remembered there was a play: it had been written two years earlier, in 1958, when, despairing of ever getting a novel published, I'd come home one half-term from the school where I was teaching (at the back of King's Cross Station) and, over a period of three days, written a play about a schoolteacher who was cracking up.

'What's it like?' he said.

'I can't remember,' I said. 'I haven't even typed it out.'

The progression of events after that I don't clearly recall, but at some point I am walking across the road from the Royal Court Hotel to the Royal Court Theatre and Lindsay, who is walking beside me, calls out to a grey-haired figure ahead who, carrying a sheaf of papers and smoking a pipe, turns and says, 'I've read your play. It *may* be worth doing,' and I am introduced to the legendary figure of George Devine.

A plan had been convened to do the play with Richard Harris, as a warm-up to the film: the date was postponed, then finally cancelled. Two subsequent proposals to do the play hung fire for several months, then petered out; the play was enquired about by television, and turned down on four occasions; it was examined by a number of repertory companies – and unanimously rejected; finally, it was asked for by the Royal Shakespeare Company, from whom, subsequently, I never heard. Six years after its submission to the Royal Court it was taken up by the Traverse Theatre, on the initiative of Gordon McDougall, a former Court assistant director, and produced in Edinburgh in November 1966. The following summer, seven years after its arrival at Sloane Square, it appeared on the stage of the Royal Court, directed by Robert Kidd, its title changed

Preparing for *The Changing Room*, 1971. David Storey, Edward Judd, Lindsay Anderson, Barry Keegan and a sporting-life professional in conference on a rugby field. (*Photograph: John Haynes*)

through a period of fluctuating hopes and disappointments from the initial *To Die With the Philistines* to *The Restoration of Arnold Middleton*. In those days, the time of 'The Second Wave', it was considered a success and prompted me to write, in quick succession, a number of plays, the best of which were performed at the Royal Court over the following three years.

I hadn't attended the rehearsals of *The Restoration of Arnold Middleton* and my knowledge of the theatre previous to that was restricted, since childhood, to not more than a dozen visits. Not having been invited to the rehearsals of *In Celebration* I was surprised, therefore, in the middle of the first morning, to receive a telephone call asking if I might be coming. Over the next few days I watched the events in the rehearsal room with an increasing sense of boredom. Nothing appeared to happen except the endless arrangement of cups and saucers, the laying down and taking up of coats and bags, the movement from point A to point B by way of point C, to be

In Celebration, 1969. Alan Bates, James Bolam, and Brian Cox as three sons returning to a Yorkshire mining town for their parents' 40th wedding anniversary. Five years after the play's first production the original cast made a film version, under Lindsay Anderson's direction, for the American Film Theatre. As Anderson says, it is 'probably the most complete and authentic record of Royal Court playing and direction' preserved on film. (*Photograph: Zoë Dominic*)

reconstituted as a move to point C by way of point B. The expected discussion of interpretation, significance and effect, of emotion, temperament and motivation – when I could really get going on what the play was all 'about' – never occurred: not only did it not occur but, whenever it showed the least inclination to do so it was quickly and unmistakably discouraged. 'None of That in Here' was very much the motto. I watched in some confusion in much the same way as a spectator might watch a football match, the rules of which had never been divulged.

It was only at one of the previews that the significance of what I was watching became apparent: the lights came up at the end of the performance and I turned to find a figure standing behind me with tears in its eyes – the artistic director of the theatre, Bill Gaskill, on whose initiative Lindsay had been invited to direct the production, glanced down at me and smiled.

The 'mechanics' I'd been watching over the previous four weeks were nothing less than the visual equivalent of those same 'mechanics' which had absorbed me in the writing of the play: I had no more then thought of motivation and interpretation, of significance and effect, than had the director in putting the text together on the stage; rather, my time had been taken up with getting the words out economically and making sure that if someone

112

did have a cup of tea there was sufficient time for the kettle to boil, for the tea to mash, and for the tea, once poured, to be handed to the appropriate character. Watching Alan Bates, Jimmy Bolam, Brian Cox, Bill Owen and Constance Chapman, Fulton Mackay and Gabrielle Daye through – as it were – the illumination offered by Bill Gaskill's tears, the 'mechanics' of the rehearsals were suddenly revealed to be the medium through which experience, not in an abstract sense, but in all its particularities, could be discovered. The 'revelation' of *In Celebration* expanded into what might be described as a method of working when, for technical reasons, I was obliged to take a more active part in the next production, *The Contractor*.

If the technicalities of arranging coats, cups, saucers, trays, books, shoes, slippers, cushions, cigarettes and matches had appeared confusing in the previous play, the problems of erecting a marquee on a proscenium stage, the laying down of a dance floor, the raising of coloured awnings, the dressing of the tent in a manner suitable for a wedding – and the dismantling, the packing and the removal of the same – appeared insuperable. A great deal of the credit in showing that it could be done must go to the designer, John Gunter – and, in *believing* it could be done, to Lindsay, the play's director. Not only would the tent not go up by the end of the third week of rehearsal, but by the end of the fourth week when it did go up it wouldn't stay there: at some crucial point the poles would creak, the ropes quiver, and a slow subsidence of the canvas would indicate that the 'mechanics' of the play were still not right. Only on the first public preview did the roof of the tent, assembled in three large pieces, stay aloft, and the running time of the play, as a consequence, was brought down from the three hours and twenty minutes of a run-through to a more approachable two hours plus.

It was the image at the end of *The Contractor* which had prompted, in the writing, the beginning of the next play, *Home*: a white, metalwork table around which the Contractor toasts and is toasted by his workmen, and which in *Home* comprises, together with four metalwork chairs, the sole 'furniture' of a play which, halfway through the writing, I discovered was taking place in a lunatic asylum.

I gave Lindsay the text in a passageway at the Royal Court and, after holding it for a while, he handed it back and said, 'You'd better give it to me in more auspicious circumstances,' asking for it back when someone came into one of the offices, and saying, 'Look, this is the next new play: do you think, on looking back, people will say this was a significant moment?' and, later, having read it, adding, 'Well, we'd better start at the top,' a remark which led, a short while later, to our sitting in the artistic director's office at the Royal Court and gazing across its narrow width at the smiling and distinctly apprehensive

face of John Gielgud, a meeting characterized by his saying, 'I was *sure* you didn't like me, Lindsay,' and Lindsay's query, 'Which part do you want?' Ralph Richardson, at this stage, had also been approached and a meeting was arranged in a house overlooking Regent's Park where the door was opened by a figure barking like a dog and who, on turning away from us, kicked out its legs and neighed like a horse. . . .

The beginning of rehearsals for *Home* was like watching two horses galloping along while, perched on a delicately fashioned carriage behind, a driver called out, 'Whoa! Stop!' finally turning to his fellow passenger and saying, wryly, 'Well, we'd better let them have a run . . .' If *The Contractor* had seen the empirical method of directing at its most demanding, *Home* saw it at its most discreet:

'It isn't possible for an actor to sit on a stage without moving, Lindsay, for 25 minutes.'

'Is it 25 minutes?'

'It feels like 25.'

'Move, in that case, if you feel like it, John.'

Until a point had been reached:

'It's strange, but once sitting here, I don't feel I want to move again.'

'Don't, in that case.'

'I shan't.'

One critic observed:

'So perfect is the spell cast, indeed, that on the second night during one of the deeper silences, a mouse strolled on the stage, looked calmly round, and having satisfied its curiosity wandered off again ... it would not surprise me that [he] too had been exhaustively rehearsed, his entrance and exit timed within the flick of a tail.'

It was watching *The Contractor* one evening, when it was revived at the Fortune Theatre, that prompted the idea of setting a play in a football changing room: as each character in *The Contractor* came on

The Contractor, 1969. As a teenager David Storey had worked during his school holidays for the Wakefield firm of tent-makers who designed the marquee used in this play. In the first act it was erected, in the second it was lined and decorated, and in the third it was dismantled. *Far left*: Philip Stone, T.P. McKenna. *Left*: Bill Owen, as the contractor, is on the right. *Right*: Billy Russell, Adele Strong, Christopher Coll, Judy Liebert. (*Photographs: Tom Murray*)

and introduced itself, I imagined a not dissimilar occasion at a rugby league club where, before a match, the players assembled, all 'ordinary' men but transformed by the occasion into something else; the changing room was a room where people 'changed', and, in turn, a place which was 'changed' by the people in it.

In this sense, the physical momentum of *The Contractor* and the emotional momentum of *Home* were combined in *The Changing Room* production; in the first act 23 characters are introduced to the audience, establish themselves and identify their roles: the human structure of the rugby team and its helpers is fused to the dynamic of the match.

Perhaps because the human resources were so formidable, *The Changing Room* represented the fruition of the empirical method of writing (starting with a blank page and seeing what would happen) and the empirical method of directing (letting the actors come on and seeing what they presented before the shape of each performance was gradually determined); the plays that came afterwards were variations on this method – *The Farm*, its atmosphere likened to the familiarity of feeling evoked in *In Celebration*, and *Life Class*, where the fixed locale was animated, and structured, by the people who came into it.

These plays, together with *Cromwell* and, latterly, *Mother's Day*, occurred during the height of what might be described as the Royal Court's 'Second Period'. Its third, all being well, is just beginning. Let us hope that it too, like the one preceding it, is animated by a spirit which is as much a consequence of that theatre's history as it is of any feeling peculiar to our time – where the desire to please has not superseded – in fact, is synonymous with – the desire to discover, explore and illuminate new ground.

Christopher Hampton

Sloane Square Lessons

When the Royal Court agreed to give my first play a Sunday night production in the summer of 1966 no one at the theatre mentioned to me that it was to be directed by someone who had never before been responsible for a professional production; but then, on the other hand, I kept to myself the fact that I had never seen a play at the Court. And one way and another there was nothing in those preliminary meetings to suggest that over the next four years the theatre would play an increasingly central role in my life or that I had found, in Robert Kidd, a director whose collaboration was to mean a great deal to me.

At that time I was still an undergraduate and it was therefore not until two years later that I found myself made a member of the theatre's staff in what now seems to be a characteristically impulsive and haphazard way. A few weeks before my finals I travelled down from Oxford to see John Osborne's *Time Present* and afterwards went upstairs to what was then a club to watch some improvisation exercises, in which Bill Gaskill was taking part. When these were over, Bill, who seemed in a very buoyant mood, asked me what I planned to do after my finals. I replied truthfully that I hadn't the least idea. 'Well, then,' he said, 'I suppose you'd better come here.' In this way I became the first resident dramatist in London. It was, however, explained to me that I should not be misled by the pomposity of the title, which had enabled the theatre to get an Arts Council grant for me. The Royal Court would make my salary up to £24 a week (at that time a sum on which it was easy to live quite adequately) and in return I would be expected to supervise the script department.

So I passed into a world which was the antithesis of the amiable civilities of Oxford. I attended the weekly meetings, where plays were passionately defended or scornfully attacked; I crept into the upper circle to watch rehearsals; I joined marauding bands to visit theatres, subsidized or unsubsidized, in the West End and, though often bewildered, grew used to the command: 'Well, I don't think we can stay here' – which brought us out on to the street at the interval

116

Christopher Hampton (right),
photographed in 1976 with Robert
Kidd, who had directed all his plays
since the Sunday night showing in 1966
of *When Did You Last See My Mother?*
(*Photograph: John Haynes*)

or even before; I sat alone in Exeter or Crewe watching new plays; I met playwrights in the office I had finally managed to secure (the size of which can perhaps best be conveyed by saying that all meetings had to be conducted standing up) and tried to succeed in the almost impossible task of encouraging them while at the same time explaining that the Royal Court was not going to do their plays; I defended the writers I believed in as best I could ('I suppose you're responsible for this,' Lindsay Anderson said to me in a thunderous aside audible to the actors who were giving a rehearsal reading of *Lay-By* and to the authors, who slightly outnumbered the cast – and this was long after I had left); above all, I sat in my dingy Earl's Court basement reading scripts. In short, as resident dramatist, there was only one function I could find no time to perform: writing.

Bill Gaskill was sympathetic enough to this difficulty to say that if I could find an assistant myself I could have one, and a minuscule amount of money was set aside for this purpose. Within a couple of weeks I had recruited David Hare and by the end of my year's stint (after which I was due to take a job at Bristol University) I had all but completed my play *The Philanthropist*. The arrangement, however, seemed to be working so well that I was asked to stay on. The Arts Council would not renew the grant but no doubt something could be hammered out. By this time I felt so at home there that I made my apologies to Bristol, negotiated, in quintessentially Royal Court fashion, a 20% drop in salary and settled down for another year.

After a year there I felt I had absorbed, by osmosis, the Royal Court ethos, a dubious entity that I see I can no longer avoid discussing. I had been startled when i'd arrived by the violence of people's opinions. Temperamentally disposed to like rather than dislike the work I was called on to consider, I was shocked by the savagery and contempt with which the work of certain established writers, theatres and actors was attacked. This, I supposed, was the source of the Court's reputation for arrogance and clannishness. Only gradually did the positive aspect of this daunting stance become clear to me: it meant

117

Julian Holloway and Victor Henry in *When Did You Last See My Mother?*, 1966. When it moved to the Comedy Theatre, Christopher Hampton became (at 20) the youngest playwright in living memory to have a play presented in the West End. (*Photograph: Morris Newcombe*)

that on the rare occasions when someone, anyone, felt very strongly in favour of a play or a project, their enthusiasm was taken seriously. Thus, for example, a play (like my first) sitting in the out-tray, together with a reader's report which concluded, 'I see no reason why we should do this play,' could be picked up by a stage manager and steam-rollered into production.

Then again, those of us who were just beginning had no grasp of the bitterness of the struggles of the first ten years of the Court's existence. The Lord Chamberlain disappeared during the run of my play *Total Eclipse*, so that in the last week of the run the play was a couple of minutes longer than it had been when it opened. For me this was an amusing detail, but for those to whom censorship had meant summonses, fines, threats and persistent hostility or at best indifference from the press, it was a real victory. For years people had been running at closed doors, using their heads as battering rams; now the doors were open and all my generation had to do was saunter through them. No wonder we were sometimes bemused by the extreme positions and emphatic prejudices of the concussed veterans.

More important than all this was the fact that the place still was a writers' theatre; and scrupulous attention to the text and its demands overrode any other considerations. Thus, the plays might contain any amount of rhetoric, but the productions were un-rhetorical, simple, lucid and concerned to draw attention to the play rather than to themselves. The acting was intense and confiding but free of artificiality and bravura effects. The design was evocative, austere and economical. The lighting was meticulous but discreet. In other words, everything was made to depend (sometimes fatally) on the truthfulness of the writing.

Finally, there was the Court's attitude towards success: deep-seated suspicion. No writer previously successful elsewhere in London could ever hope to be welcomed to Sloane Square wholeheartedly. Assistant directors responsible for productions

118

John Grillo (as Verlaine) and Michele Dotrice in *Total Eclipse*, 1968, which Hampton wrote before he graduated from Oxford. From 1968 to 1970 he was resident dramatist at the Royal Court. (*Photograph: Douglas H. Jeffery*)

which were successful with critics and public would find themselves instantly dismissed. Once again, though, these reflex responses did have their positive side. More than any other theatre, before or since, the Court was able to nurse along difficult and challenging writers towards a final grudging acceptance. The celebrated 'right to fail' is without doubt a staple ingredient of any progressive theatrical enterprise, and if it sometimes seemed more like an encouragement to fail, this was surely an error in the right direction.

The two plays of mine to receive productions while I was working at the Court provide a neat illustration of these principles. The first, *Total Eclipse*, was not immediately accepted, but one day Bill Gaskill and Robert Kidd appeared unexpectedly in my room at Oxford and asked me to read it to them. Reassured in some way by this, they scheduled the play, which proceeded smoothly through rehearsals amid many expressions of confidence and even restrained enthusiasm, and opened to generally indifferent reviews. It ran for three weeks to 60% audiences. *The Philanthropist*, on the other hand, although it was accepted at once, had a far bumpier ride. Firstly, it took almost a year of agonizing postponements and setbacks before we had the play cast. Then, the rehearsals were cocooned in an atmosphere of profound and, to me, inexplicable gloom. I rewrote furiously, to no avail. Cuts were made. The title of the play was

Alec McCowen as the philologist hero of *The Philanthropist*, 1970. 'My trouble is that I'm a man of no conviction – at least I *think* I am.' (*Photograph: John Haynes*)

endlessly discussed and condemned. A ghastly and interminable meeting in Bill Gaskill's office wrung from him a final, irrevocable verdict: 'Well: it's the play.' At the first preview it was soon apparent that his judgement was as unerring as ever, and even at this distance, such is the influence of the place on me, I can't find fault with it. The play was disgracefully successful, so much so that I've always felt I left under something of a cloud. Because, the week after *The Philanthropist* opened, I was finally cast out into the world.

Since that time, in the latter half of the 1970's, it's generally held that the Court has faltered and lost its way, and various arguments have been advanced to account for this, none of which I find convincing. It has always been run by instinct rather than by programme, so that its progress is bound to be erratic. Most important, it is no longer, as it was in 1966, virtually the only outlet for serious new work, and if the offspring are as healthy or even occasionally healthier than the parent, that is not necessarily to the Court's discredit. At any rate, I shall always be grateful to Bill Gaskill for taking me on, doubly so as I don't know if he ever entirely approved of my writing. At Oxford I had learned how to enjoy myself – but it was the Royal Court that gave me an education.

Edward Bond

Edward Bond rehearsing the non-professional cast of his latest play, *The Worlds*, in 1979. They are members of the Activists Youth Theatre Club, established in 1976 as part of the Court's Young People's Theatre Scheme. (*Photograph: Chris Davies*)

The Theatre I Want

The ESC was founded when the UK was a theatrical backwater. It was so partly because of censorship and partly because the theatre was almost exclusively middle class. The novel still had cultural status and George Devine hoped to attract novelists to the theatre. He got a surprise. He attracted a social group that had largely been unheard in the theatre – working-class writers and others who shared their point of view. The ESC wasn't ready for this. It had no philosophy. It merely wished to do new plays and pay its way. However, you cannot create art without a philosophy nor can you sustain an artistic movement without one.

New writing needs new acting, new directing and new audiences. You will get the audiences only when you have the other things. And to get the other things there has to be a new creative discipline. To interpret man and society in a new way, to recreate the relationship between the individual and society so that, in a changed world, society may be just and the individual given both freedom and moral responsibility – to do the artistic side of that, to create the images which help men to live in understanding of their lives, is difficult. It requires energy, concentration, constant reassessment and struggle. You cannot compromise. Human history has reached a critical and probably decisive point. If we survive the next 150 years we will survive the next 10,000.

Our time may be compared to those others – such as the Greek civilization and the Renaissance – when men started to live in new ways, to think new thoughts, to accept new moral responsibilities and to forsake old gods. If they'd failed to do this, the new economic relationships of those times, the new ways of sustaining life, would not have worked. We are passing through another such time, and it requires (as it did in the past) a reinterpretation of what it means to be human. I've tried to work out the implications of this in what I call 'the rational theatre'. I have had to do this in order to find out how I could write. But it isn't a private philosophy; it deals with the public relations within society. This doesn't mean that I expect

121

everyone to write like me! I, like most writers, gladly learn from other writers. But we do have to agree on certain things if we are to share a common purpose. It seems to me that you cannot any longer create art without socialism and that therefore it is not only nonsense to ask an actor to act in Beckett one night and in Brenton the next – it is also nonsense to expect the audience to enjoy one and then the other. If they did, we have to say that they don't understand either. Now this is a hard thing to say because it sounds (to say the least) unfair and it seems to invade matters of taste. Well, that is what history does: it brings its quota of necessities, and in interpreting these we create freedom and art.

For many reasons the ESC has never had a philosophy (socialist or otherwise) in the sense I have described. That is why it has often wandered. It might have had a philosophy different from the one I propose: I believe that in the analytical intensity necessary to art that philosophy would have created works of decadence and reaction, but at least audiences would have known what world the ESC said we were in, and the actors and directors would have been able to learn how to portray that world. But I am convinced that trying to do Beckett one week and Brenton the next would be just as absurd and culturally pernicious. It would encourage an Edwardian attitude to

The Bond season, 1969. *Below: Saved.* Left to right: Richard Butler, Kenneth Cranham, Patricia Franklin, Queenie Watts. *(Photograph: Donald Cooper).* *Below right:* Jack Shepherd and skeleton in *Early Morning. Right: Narrow Road to the Deep North.* Gillian Martell and Kenneth Cranham. *(Photographs: Douglas H. Jeffrey)*

the playing-fields and battlefields of art, as if it were to be chosen as a new shirt is chosen, on grounds of taste, comfort and variety – and as if changing your life or creating justice were as easy.

There are many practical difficulties in the way of establishing the theatre I want. Probably a permanent company would be necessary; perhaps this could be combined with a touring company. I think of Joint Stock as in some ways being the Royal Court in exile; and I don't know, but perhaps creating it was an attempt to solve some of the practical problems of running the Court in the way I would wish it to be run. Certainly I will be told that my suggestions for the Court are impractical, that money creates its own problems and you cannot live by the idea. A warning: that is also what people have always said when they sold their soul to the devil.

Would the state allow such a theatre to exist? Yes, if its work had international authority. And this would be possible. I am sure, from meeting the younger generations of writers who have developed

123

The Worlds, 1979, in the Theatre Upstairs. Written for young people – 'we have to teach them how to change society' – it dramatized the kidnapping of an industrial boss by young terrorists during a strike. British critics were not invited. (*Photograph: Chris Davies*)

since the ESC was founded, that the writers are there. And the Court is still uniquely qualified to be their home. The Royal Shakespeare Company's Warehouse Theatre is (however reluctantly) subordinated to the needs of the Great Bourgeois – William Shakespeare. The National Theatre, probably because it *is* a national theatre, feels obliged to be the home of all the talents. And unfortunately I think that this (in spite of all the National's good-will) makes it difficult for it to be the home of a New Theatre. After all, the nation is old, and that part of its culture which is now senile ought to be rejected.

I think many would say with regret that the Court has ambled on and off for years, usually dragging in an audience only when it put on a play that appealed to the Edwardian taste that passes for culture in the London press; or when it appealed directly to a rigidly defined social subsection, who would not support it when it changed its appeal to some other such subsection. It does not – cannot – have a regular new audience because it has not dedicated itself to creating a radical new culture, one that will create a moral and practical consciousness appropriate to life in the last years of this century. After all, in this largely theatre-less society most people have to be taught what theatre is.

When he started, Devine did not fully know what he was doing, and ever since then the Court has not accepted the responsibilities that go with being the sort of place it claims it wants to be – even though these responsibilities are now clearer. We have all made mistakes, and we can learn from them. What now happens to the Court depends entirely on what decisions it makes in this matter. If it became what it should be, then, yes, the state might try to shut it down – and it might then find new friends. If it tries to avoid its true responsibilities . . . well then, yes, it might amble on. But it will not be the home of the New Theatre. It is still trying to share the old audience when it must create a new one; too often it tries to refurbish the old culture when it must create a new one.

1969–1972

In August 1969 Lindsay Anderson and Anthony Page agreed to return to the Royal Court and share the artistic direction with Bill Gaskill. Peter Gill later joined them as an associate director. During the period of their triple control (no more than two members of the triumvirate were in office at the same time) a great deal of new work was staged, both Upstairs and Downstairs. Stars abounded: so did experiments.

The major events in the main theatre included the production of three plays by David Storey – *The Contractor* (1969), *Home* (1970) and *The Changing Room* (1971). All were directed by Lindsay Anderson and all transferred to the West End. There was Christopher Hampton's *The Philanthropist* (1970), another commercial success of a different kind; Edward Bond's massive, undervalued *Lear* (1971); and Osborne's *West of Suez* (1971), with Sir Ralph Richardson in the lead. *Live Like Pigs* and *The Sport of My Mad Mother* were both revived in 1972, but there were no new plays from John Arden or Ann Jellicoe. N. F. Simpson contributed *Was He Anyone?* (1972, Upstairs). A notable writing debut was that of E. A. Whitehead, whose *The Foursome* (1970) was the first Upstairs production to transfer to the West End; *Alpha Beta* followed in the main theatre in 1972.

One of the Court's most remarkable (and least characteristic) products, Heathcote Williams's *AC/DC*, was premiered Upstairs in 1970 and later staged below – the first Upstairs transfer Downstairs, and the first Upstairs play to be toured. Other new Downstairs plays included Frank Norman's *Insideout* (1969); Michael Weller's *Cancer* (1970); *Slag* (1971) by the recently departed resident dramatist, David Hare (with which Max Stafford-Clark made his debut here as a

The Theatre Upstairs, as set for *The Enoch Show*, 1969. This is among the most conventional shapes into which this flexible play-space has been moulded. The room measures 30 ft by 40 ft, and can hold up to 120 seats. When it opened, all seats were 7s 6d (37½ p). (*Photograph courtesy of TABS, published by Rank Strand Electric*)

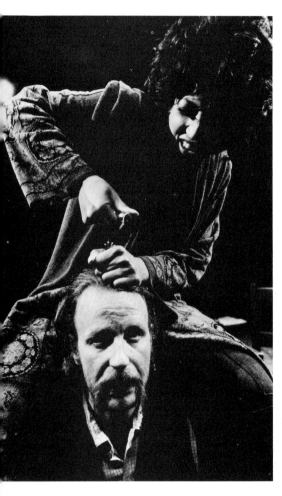

Above: Victor Henry and Sheila Scott-Wilkinson in *AC/DC*, Upstairs, 1969. Heathcote Williams's 'counter-cultural classic' – which Ronald Bryden described as 'an extraordinary explosion of verbal and imaginative energy' – was staged Downstairs later in 1969. (*Photograph: John Haynes*)

Above right: *The Sleepers' Den*, Upstairs, 1969. Eileen Atkins and Madoline Thomas in Peter Gill's first play, originally staged as a Sunday night production in 1965. (*Photograph: Douglas H. Jeffery*)

director); Denis Cannan's *One at Night* (1971); John Antrobus's *Crete and Sergeant Pepper* (1972); Charles Wood's *Veterans* (1972), starring Sir John Gielgud and John Mills; and Donald Howarth's *Three Months Gone* (1970), another West End transfer, starring Diana Dors.

New writers staged at the Theatre Upstairs (directed by Nicholas Wright until March 1971, and then by Roger Croucher until August 1972) were Howard Barker (*Cheek*, 1970), Howard Brenton (*Revenge*, 1969), Stanley Eveling (*Dear Janet Rosenberg, Dear Mr Kooning*, 1969), Wilson John Haire (*Within Two Shadows*, 1972), Athol Fugard (*Boesman and Lena*, 1971), Barry Hines (*Billy's Last Stand*, 1970) and Mustapha Matura (*As Time Goes By*, 1971). Peter Gill's *The Sleepers' Den*, given a Sunday night performance four years earlier, was staged for an Upstairs run, following the premiere there of *Over Gardens Out*. In spite of the Theatre Upstairs, Sunday night productions were still occasionally staged: they included Stephen Poliakoff's professional debut in London, *Pretty Boy* (1972); and, in 1970, Keith Dewhurst's *Pirates*, with a cast of 29 and music by Steeleye Span. The same author's *Corunna!*, with the same folk group but no more than five in the cast, was staged Upstairs in 1971. Both musicals, which had a somewhat longer life outside the Court, were directed by Bill Bryden.

Increasingly the Theatre Upstairs began to act as a venue for fringe

Christie in Love, Upstairs, 1969. Brian Croucher and William Hoyland. Howard Brenton wrote this play, his first success, for Portable Theatre, founded the previous year by David Hare and Tony Bicat. (*Photograph: John Haynes*)

companies – Portable Theatre, Traverse Theatre Workshop, the Pip Simmons group, Freehold, Incubus, for example. And in 1970 the Court as a whole celebrated the new theatrical phenomena, in all their wild variety, with *Come Together*, the festival of fringe theatre and extra-theatrical groups, when Bill Gaskill had the stalls of the main auditorium removed to make a promenade, and the stage was built out over the first four rows, with tiered seating on it. For three weeks in October, throughout most days and late at night, the underground theatre erupted through the Court's two showplaces and into Sloane Square. Multi-media, neo-Dada, environmental and agitprop work was mixed up with high jinks, dirty jokes and straight plays. Under the aegis of Bill Bryden (later a pillar of the National Theatre), the People Show, Brighton Combination, CAST and the Pip Simmons Theatre Group took their place in the bill beside Marianne Faithfull and the Gentle Fire, demonstrations of vomiting from a scaffold by the performance artist Stuart Brisley, a Stockhausen

127

premiere, and the surrealist pub theatre of Ken Campbell's Road Show. Plays by Samuel Beckett, Howard Brenton, Peter Terson and Heathcote Williams were staged. Green hamburgers and purple steak pies were served by Peter Kuttner, rock and jazz were played, argument was provoked, barriers were exploded. You could see several unprecedented events in a day for only five shillings. It seemed that the Court would never be the same again. That fiesta of cross-fertilization has not been repeated. Nor has the experiment in pricing – or architectural metamorphosis.

The new politicization of the fringe was scarcely reflected in the

Jill Bennett and Diana Dors in *Three Months Gone*, 1970, the third play in Donald Howarth's Anna Bowers trilogy but the first to be staged at the Court. *All Good Children*, the first in the trilogy, had been commissioned by George Devine but was never produced in Sloane Square. (*Photograph: John Haynes*)

English Stage Company's own work except, perhaps, in the productions by Pam Brighton under the Young People's Theatre Scheme (see page 191). Edward Bond's *Passion*, commissioned by the Campaign for Nuclear Disarmament, was performed on Easter Sunday 1971 by Royal Court actors under Bill Bryden's direction – not at the Court but on the steps of the grandstand at Alexandra Park Racecourse.

Relatively little work from abroad was staged during the 1969–72 period. Foreign plays included Marguerite Duras' *L'amante anglaise*, performed in French in 1969 by the Madeleine Renaud-Barrault company, and in English as *The Lovers of Viorne* (1971), for which Peggy Ashcroft returned to the Court; and Harald Mueller's startling play about post-war German youth, *Big Wolf* (1971). Beckett's *Happy Days* was staged in French by the Madeleine Renaud-Barrault company in 1970, and three Beckett plays were staged Upstairs. Brecht's *Man is Man* (1971), directed by Bill Gaskill, was a major Downstairs event,

Uncle Vanya, 1970. Paul Scofield and Ralph Michael in a new version by Christopher Hampton. When Scofield began the role he was the same age as Vanya: 47. This was only his third Chekhov performance in 30 years: he had twice appeared as Konstantin in *The Seagull*. (*Photograph: Keystone Press Agency*)

Paul Scofield and Anthony Page, who directed him in *Uncle Vanya* in 1970. Unusually, but aptly, Chekhov's subtitle – *Scenes from Country Life* – was retained. (*Photograph: Zoë Dominic*)

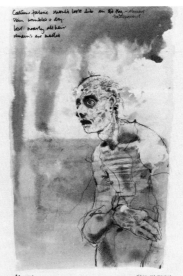

West of Suez, 1971. Ralph Richardson as Wyatt Gilman, the literary celebrity at the heart of Osborne's play, set in a post-colonial island society. ('I still cling to the old bardic belief that words alone are certain good.') (*Photograph: John Haynes*)

The Lovers of Viorne, 1971. Peggy Ashcroft as the murderess, a role played at the Royal Court in 1969 by Madeleine Renaud in the original French text, *L'amante anglaise*. This was Dame Peggy's first appearance at the Court since 1959 – and a decade of work with the Royal Shakespeare Company. (*Photograph: John Haynes*)

Lear, 1971. Deirdre Clancy's design for the ghost of the gravedigger's son, who becomes a kind of Edgar-Fool to Edward Bond's Lear. The author later described his play as 'an attack on Stalinism, as seen as a danger to Western revolution and on bourgeois culture as expressed in Shakespeare's Lear.'

Right: Lear, 1971. Harry Andrews (making his debut at the Court) in the title role. The Bond play has 18 scenes and 70 speaking parts. (*Photograph: John Haynes*)

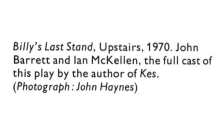

Billy's Last Stand, Upstairs, 1970. John Barrett and Ian McKellen, the full cast of this play by the author of *Kes*. (*Photograph: John Haynes*)

accompanied Upstairs by *The Baby Elephant*. There were few other revivals but these included Christopher Hampton's version of *Uncle Vanya* (1970), with Paul Scofield; Peter Gill's production of *The Duchess of Malfi* (1970); Frank Wedekind's *Lulu*, adapted by Peter Barnes (1970); and *Hedda Gabler*, adapted by John Osborne (1972), with Jill Bennett.

From 1968 onwards an increasing number of new plays originated elsewhere; and many of the writers seen for the first time at the Court had already made their debuts in theatres on the fringe. In 1971/2, according to John Elsom in his book *Post-War British Theatre*

Cheek, Upstairs, 1970. Left to right: Tom Chadbon, Kenneth Cranham, Liz Edmiston and Cheryl Hall. This was Howard Barker's first play: the next three were staged Downstairs. (*Photograph: John Haynes*)

(1976), there were 480 premieres of new plays in Britain, and 238 of these were staged by London fringe theatres.

During this period the quest for a second, larger theatre continued. Unsuccessful talks about expanding into Hammersmith were followed by negotiations with governors of the Old Vic for use of the historic theatre in the Waterloo Road after the National Theatre's departure. Collaboration with independent West End managers became more intimate: Michael Codron (who joined the Council) was asked to become a partner in staging several plays at the Court, which would have stretched the Company's resources and its financial credit with the Arts Council. This kind of co-partnership – as in *The Philanthropist* and *The Changing Room* – increased, with frequent benefits (when all went well) for the bank balances of both the ESC and the management concerned, and for the vigour and variety of the West End scene.

The English Stage Company – and, indeed the British theatre – suffered a sad loss at this time. The tragic death of Neville Blond on 4 August 1970 removed not only an indispensably tough chairman and business-like ally, but also a devoted, generous and fighting friend of the ESC. Without him it would probably not have survived its first decade. The Court's debt to him, publicly acknowledged by Devine at his resignation, became clearer as the years went by. Several crises in the next decade might perhaps have been avoided had he remained in the chair. The Neville Blond Fund was set up in his memory, to subsidize new talent in the future.

The Council asked Greville Poke to take over as chairman, but as he had strongly opposed the Company's stand over the Hilary

Below: The Foursome, Upstairs, 1971. Left to right: Paul Angelis, Sharon Duce, Philip Donaghy, Clare Sutcliffe, stretched out on John Napier's set – six tons of sand. E.A. Whitehead's first play was also the first Upstairs play to be transferred to a West End theatre. (*Photograph: John Haynes*)

Below right: Within Two Shadows, Upstairs, 1972. Left to right: Frances Tomelty, Brenda Fricker, Peggy Marshall, Eve Belton, Garfield Morgan. This was the first play about the Ulster troubles to reach the London stage. Its author, Wilson John Haire, was a Belfast carpenter brought up as a Catholic in the Protestant Shankill Road. (*Photograph: John Haynes*)

Spurling affair he felt unable to accept the offer, though he continued as honorary secretary. Neville Blond was therefore succeeded, jointly, by Oscar Lewenstein and Robin Fox, both of whom had known the Company from the inside since the early days. Fox's sudden death six months later, on 21 January 1971, was another blow to the ESC – not only because of his managerial expertise in matters of transfers and contracts but also because of his considerable personal influence, charm and popularity at the Court. When he died, Oscar Lewenstein assumed sole responsibility as chairman.

Come Together, 1970. *Above:* Stuart Brisley, having taunted the audience while he ate brown bread and drank water and his group built a scaffold, climbed to the top of it and vomited. *Above right:* Laura Gilbert of The People Show, the first, most prolific and most persistently influential of the performance art groups. (*Photographs: John Haynes*)

Below left: Alpha Beta, 1972. Albert Finney and Rachel Roberts in E.A. Whitehead's second play. Their performances are preserved in a film version made for television and directed by Anthony Page. (*Photograph: John Haynes*)

Big Wolf, 1972. Leon Vitali, Mike Kitchen, Mike Brady, Nigel Terry. Harald Mueller's play about German dead-end, urban war-orphans was first staged as a Saturday morning show in 1971, with a cast drawn from local schools. (*Photograph: John Haynes*)

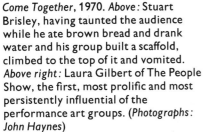

John Gielgud

A Vote of Thanks

The Royal Court has always had a certain magic for me. As a schoolboy during the First War I travelled by tube to Westminster from Gloucester Road every morning in my rubbed top-hat and stiff collar, and I would bend down to look out of the window at the enticing posters of J.B. Fagan's productions of Shakespeare. Fagan was to give me one of my earliest repertory engagements in the early 1920's at Oxford, but I had managed to see a number of his Court productions: *Twelfth Night*, with Arthur Whitby's inimitable Sir Toby; *The Merchant of Venice*, with Maurice Moscovitch; *Henry IV Part 2* and *Othello*, with Godfrey Tearle, Basil Rathbone and Madge Titheradge. Also I was taken to the first night in 1921 of *Heartbreak House*, in which the audience became very drowsy in the last act until they were woken up by the bomb explosion at the end of the play.

I do not remember seeing many plays at the Court in the next decade, when I was acting myself in other theatres most of the time, but I once appeared as Rosencrantz – or was it Guildenstern? – in a few matinees of Barry Jackson's 'Hamlet in plus fours' (Colin Keith-Johnston) during the General Strike. In one of Jackson's expensive Court experiments, Tennyson's *Harold*, I hoped to be asked to play the hero but I was turned down in favour of the young Laurence Olivier.

When *Look Back in Anger* was produced Olivier was immediately converted to the kitchen-sink school, as it was then christened, and was to be one of the first so-called West End stars to undertake a quite new kind of work in his superb performance in *The Entertainer*. There was some talk of my appearing with him at the Court in Anouilh's *The Rehearsal* but I was not able to take it on at the time when he suggested it. Much as I admired *Look Back in Anger* myself (rather to my surprise) I did not imagine that the new writers would want me in any of their plays, and I gave some rather ill-advised interviews saying that I was out of sympathy with Brecht and Beckett. I also lost touch with George Devine, as I now greatly regret, since we had worked together a great deal through his early career. When I

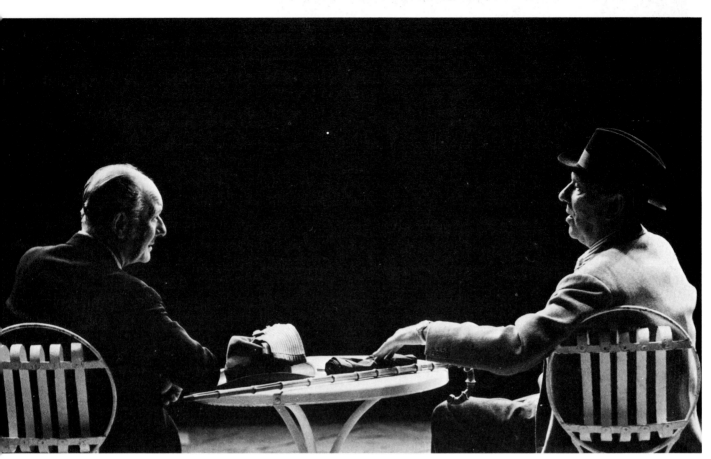

Veterans, 1972. Bob Hoskins and John Gielgud in Charles Wood's comedy about the making of *The Charge of the Light Brigade*, the film – directed by Tony Richardson – for which Wood wrote the script. (*Photograph: John Haynes*)

Above left: Home, 1970. John Gielgud and Ralph Richardson, making their debuts at the Royal Court under the English Stage Company. Their performances are preserved in a video version made for a New York television channel. (*Photograph: John Haynes*)

Left: Knight at ease: John Gielgud at a rehearsal of *Veterans*. As late as 1972 Gielgud and other stars were paid no more than £50 a week at the Royal Court. (*Photograph: John Haynes*)

was asked by William Gaskill, Lindsay Anderson and David Storey to appear in *Home*, Devine was already dead.

The text of *Home* naturally intrigued but also somewhat mystified me. Construction, situation, dialogue – all was quite unlike anything I had ever been asked to tackle; there was no clue to background or detailed directions but, as I had greatly enjoyed Storey's earlier play, *The Contractor*, I thought I would like to take a chance. I had not liked Lindsay Anderson when I had met him on two previous occasions – once in England and once in New York – and I had the impression that he did not like me either, but David Storey approached us both with much confidence and charm. And once I began to work, the atmosphere of the rehearsals began to become enormously sympathetic and exciting, especially as my old friend Ralph Richardson was in the play, as well as two brilliant actresses, Mona Washbourne and Dandy Nichols.

Lindsay's quiet and subtle method of handling the production

Bingo, 1974. Gielgud as Shakespeare, with Arthur Lowe as Ben Jonson, in Edward Bond's play, sub-titled *Scenes of Love and Death*. It was originally produced at the Northcott Theatre, Exeter, the previous November, with a different cast. (*Photograph: Douglas H. Jeffery*)

appealed to me tremendously, though we were all dismayed by the difficulty of learning the text correctly and convincing ourselves and one another of the essential task of communicating the play's implications. Jocelyn Herbert contributed with inimitable charm and purpose. And the theatre seemed to welcome us as friends and colleagues and did not, as we feared, find us stuck-up West End Establishment figures, hidebound by tradition and a superior attitude towards experiment and innovation.

I am intensely grateful for the experience of *Home*. It gave me the greatest pleasure and encouragement to persevere in a new field so late in my career, and I shall always remember the play and all connected with it with the greatest affection and satisfaction.

David Hare

Time of Unease

I first went to work at the Court in the terrible wet November fogs of 1968. I had started a small travelling group called Portable Theatre and was living off my tiny one-tenth share of the gate. Christopher Hampton, fearing I would not survive the winter (he had visited my flat and invoked Gorky to describe how I lived), suggested that I start to read scripts, and within two months I took over from him as literary manager, there being no particular competition for the job because the wage was £7.10s a week.

I shared the same misconceptions many people had, that the Royal Court would be a political theatre, which it wasn't, and a writers' theatre, which it only rarely was. And it took me a long time to understand what its virtues were, partly because I found the people who worked there so strange. It's hard to remember now, but George Devine's famous remark that you had to choose your theatre as you would your religion did mean something then, and the body of people who worked at the Court were fiercely partisan about it, though quite what the exact tenets of the religion were, was, for an outsider, often fairly hard to grasp. I could see what everyone was against, because I was usually against it too – the hysterical torture of Shakespeare's texts at the RSC, or the absurd degrading comedies we had to endure in the West End – but when it came to defining what we were *for*, well, it was harder. It was almost a faith.

The faith had been tempered in adversity, a fact which, again, people can now barely recall. Nobody's work in the English theatre since 1945 had been so misrepresented as William Gaskill's at the Court. A small group of loyalists had ridden out the storm, and in all the important things had been proved right: the austere bare-stage style of the productions would all too soon be the dominant staging cliché of the day, and Bond in particular was coming to be valued, not as the sadistic maniac of the critics' imagination, but as one of the original writers of his time. But the psychological cost of surviving the constant critical abuse had been very great: the staff were arrogant, touchy, entrenched. And a boy from university, as I was,

Teeth 'n' Smiles, 1975. Hugh Fraser with Helen Mirren as the lead singer of a disintegrating rock group at a Cambridge May Ball in David Hare's autobiographical play. Tony Bicat (co-founder, with Hare, of Portable Theatre) wrote the lyrics, and his brother Nick Bicat wrote the music. (*Photograph: John Haynes*)

David Hare rehearsing at the Court, 1975, with Dave King (hidden) in *Teeth 'n' Smiles*. After working at the Court as, successively, literary manager and resident dramatist from 1967 to 1971, he played the same roles at the Nottingham Playhouse in 1973. In 1974 he was co-founder of the Joint Stock Theatre Group. (*Photograph: John Haynes*)

floating in, scarred from no battles, having seen nothing of the fight, found their prickliness incomprehensible. In a way I was destined never to get on.

I do remember those years as a time of almost perpetual unease, as I had one fight after another in the place. Every project had to be lobbied for by a medieval series of trials, which became more complex and severe in 1969 when a triumvirate of directors – Lindsay Anderson, William Gaskill and Anthony Page – took over the theatre, and developed an attitude to new work which made the championship of new scripts so arduous and humiliating that it's a wonder people stuck their necks out at all. No, they did not want plays from Howard Brenton (one artistic director said he should be taken out and buried in a hole in a field); yes, they *had* promised unconditionally and irrevocably that as an act of faith in the seven writers involved (Howard Brenton, Brian Clark, Trevor Griffiths, myself, Stephen Poliakoff, Hugh Stoddart, Snoo Wilson) *Lay-By* could be scheduled for a Sunday night performance, but now they had decided to *read* it and it was no longer a good idea; yes, I was now resident dramatist, but not for a moment should I take that to mean they had any intention of doing my plays. (All resident dramatists in this period had their plays rejected: it became a feature of the job.)

I resigned a couple of times and was once farcically sacked for leaving in the interval of a particularly dreadful production, because, they said, it was letting the side down (there were more appeals to public school sentiment at the Court than in any institution I have known). But when I went to collect my wages nobody had remembered to stop them, so I simply went on appearing and nobody mentioned the matter again. I was absurdly out of step with their taste, and yet out of an odd mixture of resentment and respect, I never stopped wanting to prove the value of the writers I liked.

What then did we have in common, and why did I last even two and a half years in the job? I think what struck and cheered me there from the first day was finding a group of people who assumed, without a moment's self-doubt, that the dominant culture of the day was garbage, because the values of the society were rotten; that, in particular, literary affairs in this country are largely in the hands of a sold-out right-wing middle class who can't write; and that therefore in artistic matters you must, at whatever cost, trust your own experience and believe nothing you read in newspapers. I found this attitude wholly sympathetic, and nothing that has happened to me since has disabused me. Indeed the most heartening aspect of the London theatre in the last few years has been the growth of a constituent audience for new work who seem to come in deliberate defiance of critical taste. I believe it is partly the good work of the

Slag, 1971. Lynn Redgrave and Anna Massey in Hare's second play, commissioned by Michael Codron, about three women teachers living without men: Barbara Ferris completed the cast. The play was staged in New York three months before the Royal Court premiere. (*Photograph: Alex Agor*)

141

Lay By, 1971. James Warrior and Catherine Kessler in a Portable Theatre production staged on a Sunday under club conditions for members of the English Stage Society. This play was sparked off at a Royal Court meeting of writers and directors as an experiment in collective authorship, cued by a newspaper cutting about a violent rape in a lay-by. David Hare's six co-authors were Howard Brenton, Brian Clark, Trevor Griffiths, Stephen Poliakoff, Hugh Stoddart and Snoo Wilson. (*Photograph: Snoo Wilson*)

Court which has encouraged this audience, and its existence is increasingly reassuring.

The other thing the Court taught me was to value aesthetic excellence. At the time my sole interest was in the content of a play. I thought the political and social crisis in England in 1969 so grave that I had no patience for the question of how well written a play was. I was only concerned with how urgent its subject matter was, how it related to the world outside. As I came to realize that no common beliefs held the Royal Court together, I also slowly appreciated that there was therefore only one reason why writers chose, as they then did in great numbers, to give their work to the Court first, and that was the likelihood that it would be better acted, better designed, better lit, better directed, in short better *presented* than anywhere else, that here the text would be respected, the rehearsals would be serious, the commitment to the project in hand would be real, however bizarre the running of the theatre outside the rehearsal room. And that by encouraging the writer with their great care for the values of presentation, the directors were actually enabling writers to say richer and more complex things than they would have been able to if, like me, they were bundling an exhausted travelling company out of a van and on to an open floor.

I believe that the Court in the early seventies was primarily an aesthetic theatre, not a political one. And the reason why it then lost the loyalty of so many writers in the following years was because it finally refused to move into the field of English politics, although it was presenting excellent political work about the Third World. A direct confrontation finally occurred between those who wanted the Court to be a socialist theatre and those who wanted it to be a humanist theatre and, no question, the humanists won. It is for that reason that many of the best plays of the seventies were not performed at the Court, because there was, in an older generation, a squeamishness about moving into a directly political field. I believe this was a tragedy for the Court, and it is taking time to recover.

Lindsay Anderson

Lindsay Anderson on the set of *Home*, 1970, his thirteenth production at the Royal Court, and his first in New York. (*Photograph: John Haynes*)

The Court Style

I remember very well the English Stage Company's first production at the Royal Court in 1956. Or rather I remember very well the impression it made on me, for strangely enough the impression is much stronger than my memory of the play, which was *The Mulberry Bush* by Angus Wilson. At that time I had no professional connection with the English Stage Company. I was not even a professional of the theatre: I had been a documentary film-maker for some years, and I had been a film critic (not a reviewer) in various specialized magazines. I was a friend of Tony Richardson, who had followed me at Wadham College, Oxford (by chance, George Devine, Tony Richardson and I were all ex-Wadham men) and through Tony I was around when preparations were being made for the opening of the ESC's first season at the Royal Court. It was a confident, hopeful time.

Thus I went to *The Mulberry Bush* as a friend, wholly in sympathy with what I took to be the aims of the Royal Court enterprise. These went far beyond the simple encouragement of new work or of new writers that seems now to be the accepted lore. Indeed, no account of why the theatre started – at least as far as George Devine and Tony Richardson were concerned – can be complete without some appreciation of the historical context, and of the state of the London theatre and of British cultural morale generally in the mid-1950's. We were still in the post-war doldrums. Nothing that was done in the theatre related in any stimulating or significant way to what was happening in Britain or in the rest of the world. Non-commercial drama was generally 'poetic' drama, represented most successfully and most reputably by T.S. Eliot and Christopher Fry. The Royal Court impulse was a 'realist' impulse, and its ambitions extended to the representation on the London stage of 20th-century European classics, and even classical revivals. Style, it was understood, was just as important a part of the theatrical experience as theme or content. George was no sentimentalist, and nor was Tony. They had no favourable predisposition towards writing just because it was 'new'.

The impact on me of *The Mulberry Bush* was above all stylistic, though not in a formal or decorative way. The play itself had dignity and even a certain pathos because it was, above all, serious. It was a play of ideas, not very profound and not perhaps particularly original: in its development, it was even a little silly. But it was seriously written and seriously presented. There was a blessed absence of that 'desire to divert' (and particularly, of course, the desire to divert an English middle-class audience, out for an amusing evening) which had always maddened me in West End theatre. The playing was natural, civilized, unforced. And the presentation was similarly lucid and economic. The settings were realistic, but not fussily or extravagantly naturalistic: they stood out with elegant clarity against a pure, white surround. There was no bowing and scraping to us, the audience; and there was no bullying either. In English culture, where 'serious' is most often used as a mocking epithet, this made the experience a refreshing and even a touching one.

Such were to be the characteristics of what I would call the Royal Court 'style'. It was this style which for so many years made the theatre unique – an achievement much more elusive to definition than the achievement in terms of writers discovered and new plays performed. I think it is also the quality whose loss is most keenly to be regretted.

I had never directed in the professional theatre before I did my first production at the Royal Court in 1957. One day, out of the blue, the Court received a play from Kathleen Sully, an author whom Tony Richardson knew I much admired. He sent me the play, which I read and much liked, and suggested that I should direct it for a Sunday night production without decor. So I did, and it went well enough for me to be invited the next year to direct a play by Willis Hall called *The Disciplines of War*. Always drawn by the emotive power of popular songs, I suggested we retitle the play *The Long and the Short and the Tall*. Again the play went well, and I was invited to become one of the assistants to the artistic directors, together with Bill Gaskill and John Dexter. So my theatrical career began.

Being completely inexperienced in the professional theatre, I did not at first realize what a unique place the Royal Court was. Its freedom from theatrical 'camp' was total. Perhaps this was the strong university influence; certainly it was a reflection of the personality of George Devine. The atmosphere at Sloane Square was never particularly 'intellectual' but it was pretty intelligent and most of us, I am afraid, displayed a rather arrogant intolerance of approaches and standards other than our own. The theatre, it was taken for granted, was always 'about something'. Because our values were anti-establishment, it was generally assumed that the Court could be

Home, 1970. Mona Washbourne and Dandy Nichols. (*Photograph: John Haynes*)

described as a Socialist theatre. This was largely nonsense. It was not even a very intellectual theatre. The tone was far more humanist than intellectual. Liberal, if you like, in its strong rather than its soppy sense. And this commitment inspired all the choices, and was the basis of the style.

Royal Court acting, therefore, tended to be unmannered (not unmannerly), emotionally open, and realistic in class terms. I believe that our production of Alun Owen's first play, *Progress to the Park*, which I directed for a Sunday night in 1960, was the first time that Liverpool accents had been used freely, authentically and un-selfconsciously on the London stage. When we auditioned young actors and actresses in those days we usually had to ask them where they came from, and then to repeat their audition pieces, not in the 'acceptable' accents into which they had been drilled at drama school but in the natural accents of their youth. The results were almost always revelatory. (Today, of course, all this will seem simplistic, obvious in the extreme. For some years now the joke has been that middle- and upper-class actors are at a disadvantage in the theatre, and must ape a working-class accent if they are to have any hope of employment, which is nonsense, even if in certain quarters there has developed an inverted snobbery, just as odious as the establishment snobbery of the past. But let it not be forgotten that when Albert Finney graduated from RADA, the old *News Chronicle* ran a competition for its readers to select a new name for this brilliant young actor, since 'Albert Finney' was obviously too plebeian to be acceptable in West End lights. And when Tom Courtney played Konstantin in an Old Vic production of *The Seagull* in 1960,

immediately after leaving drama school, more than one critic commented scornfully on the impossibility of an actor in a play by Chekhov speaking with what was plainly a Northern accent.)

In spite of his university education, then, George Devine was not an academic: he was an actor as well as a director, as stimulated by practice as by theory, hierarchic, not afraid of instinct, and anxious to learn. This made him unique in my experience as director of a theatre. He knew about almost everything; he was good at everything, though naturally better at some things than at others; he loved and respected talent, and he was not jealous. He was devoted above all to the service of the theatre – the theatrical experience; not the theatre as a 'vehicle' for ideas, which is in itself a form of philistinism, though rarely recognized as such; and not the theatre as a laboratory for aesthetic experiments. There were quite a lot of plays and writers to whom George simply did not respond, generally on humanist, less often on artistic grounds. But if he did not respond

146

The Changing Room, 1971. David Storey
returned to the Rugby League world of
his first novel, This Sporting Life, in what
one critic, Michael Billington, described
as a 'seamless blend of acting, writing
and direction'. Left: John Barrett,
Warren Clarke, Brian Glover.
(Photograph: John Haynes). Above: left to
right, John Price, Alun Armstrong,
Geoffrey Hinsliff, Mark McManus,
Michael Elphick, Frank Mills, Matthew
Guinness, Edward Judd, Paul Dawkins,
Edward Peel, Warren Clarke, David
Hill. (Photograph: Lindsay Anderson)

to a writer, he was never afraid to say so – and their work would not
be performed at the Royal Court.

This idea of the theatre as a total experience may sound rather
obvious. But it is a more subtle idea than it may seem, and examples of
it are not so easy to find. The Royal Court was a theatre with a strong
tradition of direction: yet it was never a directors' theatre. The text
always came first, and writers were to be cherished and encouraged.
But they were not to be mollycoddled. There was never any
suggestion that a director should use a text in order to show off his
own prowess or personality; at the same time, particularly in the
early days, he was expected to work with his author, guiding him
where necessary and where possible, through revisions and rewrites.
As the years have passed, of course, this equilibrium has been lost.

As with direction, so with design. A design aesthetic, of expressive
simplicity and refined realism, was part of the Royal Court policy
from the start. That surround of white net did more than provide
continuity to the succession of Royal Court productions. It was also
an artistic, even a moral, statement in itself. It did not long survive,
alas, as directors of varying principles and personalities succeeded
each other: but the principle remained embedded in the consciousness of all. The designer's responsibility was to express and interpret
the text. Perhaps even to enhance it. But certainly never to use it, or

Life Class, 1974. Frank Grimes, Rosemary Martin, Alan Bates. As in some other Storey plays, the author wrote from personal experience of its background – a provincial art school. He went to one in Wakefield before going on to the Slade in London. (*Photograph: John Haynes*)

overpower it. In all, the Royal Court aesthetic had a good deal in common with the Periclean ideal:

φιλοκαλοῦμεν μετ᾽εὐτελίας καὶ φιλοσοφοῦμεν ἄνευ μαλακίας

We pursue beauty without extravagance and knowledge without effeminacy.

I hope I have not made the Royal Court seem high-falutin' or artistically self-righteous. We were all too cocky and too disrespectful for that. The real lesson we learned, never to be forgotten, was that seriousness is not the same thing as smugness; and that there is nothing more wearisome than 'camp'. We learned that a theatre dedicated to the service of the playwright is not the same thing as a 'literary' theatre. And we learned that a theatre in which the director was encouraged and expected to provide as personal an interpretation of a text as he is capable of is not the same thing as a 'directors' theatre', in which the director *uses* a text to display his talent and draw attention to himself. The best 'notice' that a director can get is praise for his playwright and praise for his players.

One of the most extraordinary things about the Court style is that it lasted so long – over twenty years. George Devine, to my personal sorrow, never saw a play by David Storey. (I am speaking, of course, only of my own productions at the Royal Court in later years.) But if he had, I'd like to think that he would have responded to their poetry, their realism uncluttered by naturalism, their elegance 'without extravagance'. Their seriousness and their laughter, their vision of society untouched by the crudity of propaganda. And all their splendid actors – surely the most consistent glory of our stage.

These are some of the things I mean by the Royal Court 'style'.

1972–1975

In 1972, faced with the imminence of Bill Gaskill's resignation, after years of hard labour at the Court, the Council of the ESC consulted Lindsay Anderson, Anthony Page and Peter Gill about how much responsibility each was willing and available to take in the future artistic direction of the Royal Court. In the event the Council's chairman, Oscar Lewenstein, agreed to assume artistic control of the company, at the cost of abandoning his work as a commercial impresario. Lindsay Anderson and Anthony Page continued as associate artistic directors, and Albert Finney joined them, at Lewenstein's invitation. Greville Poke, who had been secretary of the ESC from the start, succeeded Lewenstein as chairman.

'Looking back,' Lewenstein wrote later, 'I do not think that an artistic director with three very much part-time associates is a good structure.' Personality problems aside, the right to fail was becoming increasingly, perilously expensive. The chances of commercial success were diminishing because of economic pressures on the West End, and the widening gap between the theatre of comfort and the theatre of commitment. Dozens of groups with less cumbersome superstructures of command, no bricks-and-mortar burdens and, perhaps, less internecine strife – or creative tension – at the top were staging new work before the ESC got to it or had made up its mind to do it. But this was a conspicuously fertile period at the Court, nevertheless: 80 productions were staged, 60 of them world premieres, of which nine transferred to the West End. And although the 38 Downstairs events cost some £400,000 to produce, the 42 Upstairs ones cost only about £75,000.

In November 1972 the ESC was given another opportunity to

Savages, 1973. *Below*: Frank Singuineau as the Indian chief in Christopher Hampton's play, which was inspired by an exposé of the genocide of Indians in Brazil published by the *Sunday Times Magazine. Below right*: Paul Scofield, as a British diplomat in Brazil, and Tom Conti, as one of the urban guerrillas who holds him as a hostage. (*Photograph: John Haynes*)

The Sea, 1973. *Right:* Deirdre Clancy's drawing for Mrs Rafi, the character played by Coral Browne in Edward Bond's comedy. *Below:* Left to right: Gillian Martell, Margaret Lawley, Adrienne Byrne, Coral Browne, Alan Webb, Susan Williamson. (*Photograph: John Haynes*)

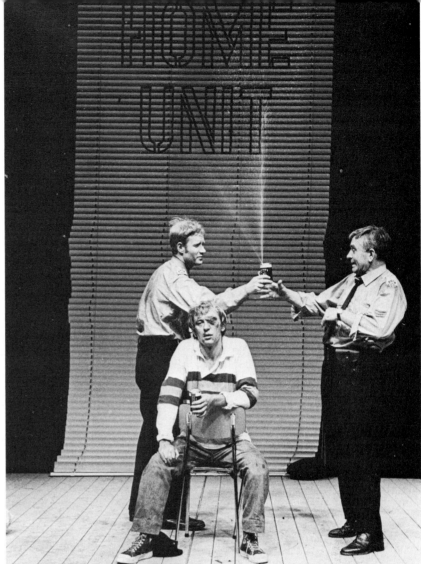

Struan Rodger, Mark McManus and Ed Devereaux in *The Removalists*, 1973, which was given the first George Devine Award made outside the British Isles. Its Australian author, David Williamson, worked with two compatriots as director and designer, Jim Sharman and Brian Thomson. (*Photograph: John Haynes*)

Magnificence, 1973. Geoffrey Chater, as a Tory Minister about to be blown up, and Kenneth Cranham as the terrorist who tries to do it. Howard Brenton's play was commissioned by the Court (from the Neville Blond Fund). (*Photograph: John Haynes*)

expand outside the Royal Court when the Old Vic governors – 10 years after their approach to Devine – invited it to take over the Waterloo Road lease on the departure of the National Theatre Company. The Council agreed, subject to the availability of the necessary financial aid from the grant-giving bodies. In the following summer a policy statement prepared by Oscar Lewenstein was approved by the Council, the Old Vic governors and the Arts Council drama panel. But Anthony Page and Lindsay Anderson (on his return from film-making) were sceptical, and in December the artistic committee of the ESC voted against it. As the National Theatre's departure from the Old Vic was delayed, the prospective budget for the merger between the Court and the Vic grew – and so did doubts about the feasibility of the project. The Arts Council delayed its approval; and in 1974 it was vetoed by the ESC Council, to the bitter disappointment of Oscar Lewenstein and Greville Poke.

Among the main events of the period – and, indeed, of the British

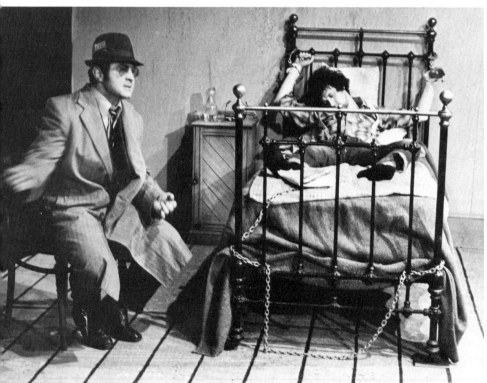

Above left: Sam Shepard. His first play to be publicly produced at the Royal Court was *La Turista*, given its European premiere in the Theatre Upstairs (as its third production) in 1969. Since then the Court has staged six plays by this Pulitzer Prize-winning American visionary playwright and musician.
Above: The Unseen Hand, Upstairs, 1973. Richard O'Brien and Warren Clarke.
Left: Geography of a Horse Dreamer, Upstairs, 1974. Bob Hoskins and Stephen Rea. (*Photograph: John Haynes*). *Right:* Tooth of Crime, 1974. Mike Pratt and Diane Langton. (*Photograph: Mick Rock*)

theatre of the past 30 years – was the production in 1974 of three plays from South Africa: Athol Fugard's *Statements After an Arrest Under the Immorality Act* and (with John Kani and Winston Ntshona) *The Island* and *Sizwe Bansi is Dead*. (The latter was first produced Upstairs in September 1973.) These works (and their performance) were received by reviewers with unprecedented enthusiasm, not only for their theatrical impact but also for their moral force. It is worth recalling that they would probably have never been staged had the Lord Chamberlain's censorship survived because, apart from the fact that their political content might have been deemed offensive to a 'friendly power', they were largely improvised and unscripted before production.

Three plays by another South African writer, David Lan, were also staged Upstairs – *Bird Child* (1974), *Paradise* (1975) and *Homage to Bean Soup* (1975). Michael Abbensetts, a writer from Guyana who made up his mind to be a playwright when he saw *Look Back in Anger* in

Montreal, made his debut in 1973 with *Sweet Talk* and later became resident dramatist at the Court. Mustapha Matura scored a critical and commercial success with *Play Mas* (1974), which transferred to the West End.

The major Court playwrights were all productive during this period: Osborne (*A Sense of Detachment*, 1972); Wesker (*The Old Ones*, 1972); Bond (*The Sea*, 1973 and *Bingo*, 1974); Storey (*Cromwell*, *The Farm*, 1973 and *Life Class*, 1974); Hampton (*Savages*, 1973); and Beckett (*Not I*, 1973, performed astonishingly by Billie Whitelaw, and sharing a bill with *Krapp's Last Tape*). Howard Brenton was represented by *Magnificence* (1973), which Gaskill had commissioned. From Barry Reckord came *Give the Gaffers Time to Love You* (1973); from John Antrobus *Captain Oates' Left Sock* (1973) and *Mrs Grabowski's Academy* (1975); from Heathcote Williams *Remember the Truth Dentist* (1975); from Wilson John Haire *Echoes from a Concrete Canyon* (1975); from Ken Campbell *The Great Caper* (1974), the record-breaking loss-maker of the period – but, Oscar Lewenstein said, 'It is difficult to see how the English Stage Company could refuse to do a play of such interest and originality without abandoning its purpose.'

Other writing debuts included those of three novelists – Edna O'Brien (*A Pagan Place*, 1972); David Caute (*The Fourth World*, 1973); and Paul Bailey (*A Worthy Guest*, 1974) – but none followed with further plays. More significant was the stage debut of Caryl Churchill, after writing several short plays for radio: *Owners* (1972, Upstairs) was followed by *Objections to Sex and Violence* (Downstairs) three years later, and by other plays for the Court and elsewhere. *The Pleasure Principle* (1973), the first solo play at the Court by Snoo Wilson, followed his participation in two collective works to which the ESC played a reluctant host: *Lay By* (1971) and *England's Ireland* (1972). His collaborators in the latter work, staged as a Sunday-nighter, included Howard Brenton, Brian Clark, David Edgar and David Hare. Brenton and Edgar worked together on another example of politically aggressive cartoon theatre, *A Fart for Europe*, staged Upstairs in January 1973. The new theatre brutalism influenced *The Rocky Horror Show*, the brilliantly original musical by the Australian team of Richard O'Brien and Jim Sharman, which proved to be one of the Court's most profitable by-products. It transferred to two converted cinemas in the King's Road, and later to Broadway and the West End, where it ran for seven years after its Upstairs opening – a show-business institution whose Royal Court origins had long been forgotten.

For once, there was no Brecht at the Court. The only revivals – apart from Peter Gill's exhumation of D.H. Lawrence's *The Merry*

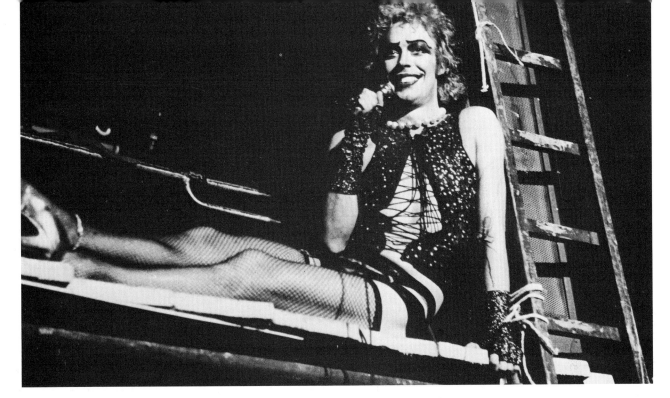

The Rocky Horror Show, Upstairs, 1973. Tim Curry as Frank N. Furter in the Court's greatest box office export success. This rock 'n' roll fantasy musical, based on a Frankenstein theme and the archaeology of old-movie addicts, transferred successively to two Chelsea cinemas and the Comedy Theatre in the West End, where it ended its London life seven years after its Upstairs opening. *(Photograph: John Haynes)*

go Round in 1973 – were those of Joe Orton's three full-length plays – *Entertaining Mr Sloane*, *Loot* and *What the Butler Saw* – by three different directors, Roger Croucher, Albert Finney and Lindsay Anderson respectively. The Orton season, a final flourish of Oscar Lewenstein's regime, achieved considerable success at the box office: as high, for *Entertaining Mr Sloane*, as 91%. Next to that came, encouragingly, Hampton's *Savages* and Bond's *Bingo* (both 89%); Storey's *Life Class* (88%), Beckett's *Not I* and *Krapp's Last Tape* (87%), Storey's *Cromwell* (83%), and the South African season (82%). Only three plays fell below the 30% mark. The new writers were finding an audience – and some were making a profit for the Court. But not enough. In 1973/74 there was a deficit of £10,000. In the second half of 1974 the Court lost £50,000. The Arts Council paid £20,000 of this with a supplementary grant, but a deficit of £40,000 was carried forward into 1975.

Among other innovations of this period were the appointments of the first woman resident dramatist, Caryl Churchill; and the first woman literary manager, Ann Jellicoe. The first competition for young playwrights was organized. And in 1972 the Council agreed to introduce staff meetings, 'at reasonable intervals' – a belated measure of industrial democracy. Special Sunday night fund-raising events in 1974/75, under the auspices of the English Stage Society, included concerts by Bettina Jonic, George Melly (a Saturday night), Nicol Williamson, Dave Allen, Cleo Laine and John Dankworth, and Alan Price.

Athol Fugard*

The Gift of Freedom

When I was 26 I came to England from South Africa for the first time, and the first play I saw in London was *Rosmersholm* at the Royal Court, with Peggy Ashcroft. The second Court production I saw was *Rhinoceros*, with Olivier. I wanted very much to work in that theatre and I tried to get a job there in stage management, but I didn't succeed.

I went back to South Africa and I went on acting, writing plays and directing; I worked with my group in Port Elizabeth, the Serpent Players, but it wasn't until 1966 that I worked in a London theatre – and then it wasn't the Royal Court, but the Hampstead Theatre Club, where I directed and acted in my play *The Blood Knot*.

My relationship with the Royal Court started with *Boesman and Lena*. Yvonne Bryceland and I had done it in Cape Town, then Johannesburg, and Nicholas Wright asked us to bring it to London. I didn't have my passport then – the South African Government took it away for four years, after my 1966 trip to England – but when they

Athol Fugard as Boesman, in a South African production of *Boesman and Lena*, with his Port Elizabeth company, the Serpent Players.

*In conversation with Richard Findlater

finally gave it back, Yvonne and I came over to London. I received nothing but encouragement from Bill Gaskill, Lindsay Anderson and Anthony Page, and I knew then that the Court really was a writers' theatre, in a way I had never imagined to be possible.

Coming out of Nicholas Wright's initiative I can remember very clearly the moment after a performance in the Theatre Upstairs when I met a little gnome whose name turned out to be Oscar Lewenstein. Oscar was responsible without any question for my play moving from the Theatre Upstairs for a further limited run to the Young Vic. And that was the start of a very important relationship for me. I just trusted that man, and he trusted me to a degree that is always bewildering.

When Oscar heard there was another play of mine being performed in South Africa he telephoned me in Port Elizabeth and asked if he could read the script. I said, 'There's no script.' He said, 'I've got this date in the Theatre Downstairs.' I said, 'I don't want the Theatre Downstairs. I want the Theatre *Upstairs*.' That was the one I knew. He hadn't read or seen the play, and yet he offered me the theatre for *Sizwe Bansi is Dead*. It was a gross demand on my side, and total faith on his. I found it difficult to believe that a story as South African as this could have any significance outside my country, and I was plain scared. I wanted to stay in a small space with an audience of 70 people or so. Later he came along to the Irish Club where I was rehearsing it with the actors and on the way back to the Court he said, 'You've chosen to open Upstairs. But I think this play has got a life Downstairs. We'll do it there afterwards. I believe you've got another play you haven't told me about called *The Island*. Can I read

Boesman and Lena, 1971. Yvonne Bryceland. Athol Fugard directed this production, and those of his other plays staged at the Court, but he has not acted in them. (*Photograph: John Haynes*)

the script?' Once again I had to say to Oscar, 'There's no script to read.' 'What have you got that you could give me?' he asked. I had some rather indifferent recordings of a performance in South Africa, and I played those to Oscar and Albert Finney. And they accepted it. They *responded* to it. They took chances in a way that I think is almost disappearing from the theatre. Then came an even more difficult problem. They said, 'We've heard there's a *third* play,' and that was the play Yvonne and I wrote in South Africa – we couldn't produce it there – *Statements After an Arrest Under the Immorality Act*. That is how the South African season came to the Royal Court.

Sizwe Bansi is Dead, Upstairs 1973 and Downstairs, 1974. Winston Ntshona (*left*) and John Kani (*below*), the cast and co-authors, who originated the play in South Africa with Athol Fugard and the Serpent Players. (*Photographs: John Haynes*)

John Kani and Winston Ntshona in *The Island*, 1974: 'a play that raises respect for the human race,' said Irving Wardle in *The Times*. (*Photograph: John Haynes*)

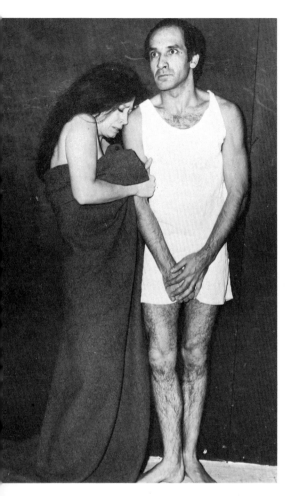

Yvonne Bryceland and Ben Kingsley in *Statements After an Arrest Under the Immorality Act*, 1974, staged with *The Island* and *Sizwe Bansi is Dead*. 'The season will shine gloriously in the history of the English Stage Company,' said the *Stage*. 'It helps to restore dignity to the theatre and also to man himself.' (*Photograph: John Haynes*)

I felt that there was an area of trust in that place that was very special, a space that allowed me to make mistakes. I don't think I've ever encountered that anywhere else. They just let me get on with it. The Royal Court gave me the most incredible freedom I've ever experienced in a professional theatre. It was a family, starting with the ushers, the men behind the bar, the man in the ticket office, all the way to the top with Oscar. He was like a godfather to me, and the Court was just home, a little embattled enclave, strong and supportive. I haven't a single bad memory of the Royal Court. Not one. I'm not saying that because of this book; it just happens to be the truth. I don't know what it is that has given the Court its very special identity as a playwrights' theatre. It's just that, for me, the ambiance, the environment, were there, and I found it so easy to slot myself in, coming from God alone knows where, 4,500 miles away. I felt totally comfortable, in spite of my usual gross insecurities as a writer and director. It afforded a kind of protection that no other theatre had offered. It still commands attention and gives protection – not like the fringe.

I don't want to disentangle here the complex motives which go into making a piece of hopefully significant theatre in South Africa. It's very hard to separate the degree to which you are working as an 'artist' and the degree to which you are using theatre as a survival mechanism. We had control of a craft which is called theatre and could make something a lot of people couldn't, but we *had* to make it because if we didn't there was no point in staying alive. My debt of gratitude to the Royal Court includes the fact that there was never any attempt to iron out the wrinkles in the complexity of what we were doing. I can remember how very delighted Oscar was if the problem was very complicated, very ambiguous, and very paradoxical, when he said that they would really bloody well have to work hard to get the point. There was such trust, such encouragement for me. It was absolutely unique and totally sustaining. For a time I found there a reconciliation between warring elements in my nature – my sense of wanting to be a writer and to define the nature of the stage experience, knowing that the actors are not just interpreters but have potentially an incredible contribution to make.

I will be grateful to the Court till my dying day. I have just one regret: that I never acted there, though Oscar wanted me to.

Mustapha Matura*

A Certain Quality

Mustapha Matura. Formerly a stockroom assistant, this Trinidad-born author saw his first work (*Black Pieces*) staged by Roland Rees at the Institute of Contemporary Arts in 1970. *As Time Goes By*, his first play at the Royal Court, was commissioned by the West End impresario Michael White.

I was never caught up in the romanticism and idealism about the philosophy of the Royal Court and the tradition of George Devine. I didn't know much about that. I knew little about the theatrical world when I came to London in the late 1960's. I saw the Court as a place with a special reputation and when I worked in Sloane Square I responded to what was actually *there*, not to the *idea* of it all. For some other writers the English Stage Company didn't come up to their expectations, when they first worked with it, but I didn't have any expectations. I was neither disappointed nor surprised. But I was very grateful – and I still am.

It was Roland Rees who gave me my first real encouragement and my first professional production in 1970. He staged three short pieces – which I'd written without ever hoping to get them performed – at the Institute of Contemporary Arts (*Black Pieces*). And it was Michael White, the West End impresario, who commissioned my first full-length play – *As Time Goes By* – after seeing those pieces at the ICA. We offered *As Time Goes By* to the Royal Court, naturally, but they could only offer us a Sunday night production then, so we offered it to the Traverse in Edinburgh, who were delighted to do it. That production came to the Court, Upstairs, in September 1971, and was the beginning of my association with the theatre.

What struck me at the time was the remarkable attention that the Court people paid to detail, in all aspects of the production, the *care* that went into everything. It was something of a revelation to me to see theatrical work at that level. But it wasn't until a couple of years later that a play of mine was started there, thanks to Oscar Lewenstein. And it was thanks to him that I really got into the skin of the Court, and felt at home there as a writer.

I remember that I was walking up the stairs at the Court one evening, and Oscar called to me from behind. He asked me what I was doing. I said, 'I've just written a play.' He said, 'I'd like to read it. Please send it to me.' It was an immediate and encouraging response. And then, after I'd sent it in, he said he liked it and asked me to come

*In conversation with Richard Findlater

Matura at the Court. *Left: As Time Goes By*, 1971. Robert Coleby and Stefan Kalipha. *Right: Rum an' Coca-Cola*, 1976. Norman Beaton and Trevor Thomas. (*Photographs: John Haynes*) *Far right: Play Mas*, 1974. Lucita Lijertwood. (*Photograph: Tom Busby*)

in and talk about it. We talked, he suggested some changes, they were acceptable to me, and when I'd made them we started to discuss how it should be staged and who should do it. It sounds simple but it wasn't. Making it seem so, for a writer, was one of Oscar's gifts. It was a big decision for him to make at that time, because we knew that *Play Mas* was going to be expensive, and the Court was going through one of its economic crises. But he went ahead and the success of the production had a lot to do with Oscar's personality. I think he was a wonderful influence at the Court.

Play Mas was my first experience of being intensely involved in a production, all the way through, instead of just turning up at rehearsals once a week, maybe. That was marvellous for me. I had a function. I felt needed – and I was. I had the inside knowledge which they wanted for reference. But it wasn't only that – and it wasn't only me. I know that from talking to other writers. In those days you felt a commitment, to the Royal Court, but you also felt a commitment, *from the Royal Court to you*. It was one of those intangibles that make all the difference to your work. One tangible example of what I mean is what happened when Ann Jellicoe became literary manager at the Court. She immediately phoned a lot of writers like myself who had worked there in the past and asked us to come round and talk about what we were doing and what ideas we had about the Court's future. It was that kind of direct interest and encouragement and communication that really distinguished the Court from other theatres.

Another of the good things about working there was the way in which Jocelyn Herbert, say, or Albert Finney would come in, watch rehearsals and maybe give their advice on one point or another. You had all this experience to draw on, and it seemed a *natural* happening. You didn't have to ask them: they came on their own initiative, giving up their time. And they did it because, you felt – very strongly – they wanted the play to succeed. There used to be a great deal of pride involved among everyone working at the Court. Not just the director and the author, but the fireman and the cleaner. You felt

162

special working there. You knew that whatever the Court staged it would have a certain *quality*. You might not like the production, you might not agree with what they were doing, but you could be sure of that quality of work in the staging. It takes a lot to build that kind of certainty, that kind of trust. They understood the problems of the author, and they served the play well.

But the real importance of the Royal Court, I think, is not so much in the building itself and the plays that are staged there. It's the approach to the theatre that has been fostered there, the kind of thinking about theatre work that has been encouraged, the writers and artists who have been started, and helped, and developed by the English Stage Company. It has created a school. And going back there is, for many of us, a bit like going back to school: we have a kind of love/hate relationship with the Royal Court, whatever we think of the place now as compared with our own times there. It gets attacked all the time, of course. Thinking about what I've just been saying myself I'm surprised at quite how complimentary I've been. I haven't always felt like that. But the passionate response that the Court stirs up in so many of us says a lot for the place. You may think its great days are over. You may disapprove of its programme. But you can't be indifferent to it. Nobody who has any concern for the theatre can be indifferent to the Royal Court.

163

Oscar Lewenstein

Oscar Lewenstein. Five years after starting his theatrical career as general manager of the Glasgow Unity, he became general manager of the Royal Court, until 1954. In 1955 he began his career as a commercial impresario. A founder-member of the English Stage Company, to which he and his own company brought 19 plays, he was its chairman from 1970–72 and its artistic director from 1972–75. (*Photograph: Eileen Lewenstein*)

Jubilee Memories

In the 26 years since the English Stage Company was formed, during most of which I have been linked with it either as a member of the Council, as a co-producer of many of its productions, as chairman, or for three years as artistic director, there were, as in all theatrical ventures, many disappointments, disillusionments and even disasters. However, as this is a celebration of the English Stage Company's 25th birthday, the editor has rightly suggested that we should concentrate on the positive achievements, and I am glad to contribute below some happier memories of those years.

1 Watching the first night of *Look Back in Anger* at the Royal Court with Kenneth Haigh. For me Ken will always be the very embodiment of Jimmy Porter. If ever an actor was born to play a part, he was born to play Jimmy. Hearing those lines come winging from the stage, lines the like of which one had never thought would be heard on the English stage, which half the audience were shocked to hear, whilst the other half were delighted. I was with my then partner, Wolf Mankowitz, in the front row of the dress circle, and John Osborne was in the same row. I remember it still, as the curtain fell, half the audience applauding, the other half silent.

2 Sitting in the dress circle at the dress rehearsal of Ionesco's *The Chairs*. The Court was almost empty. Suddenly George Devine as the old man and Joan Plowright as the old woman seemed to take over the theatre. There they were in that circular room full of chairs and their invisible guests. The performance cast a spell over the few of us who were there. I turned to Jocelyn Herbert, whose first set for the Court this was, and said, 'This is what it's all about, isn't it?' She agreed; she had felt the spell too. Thinking about George Devine's performance in this play reminds me of many other outstanding performances he gave. He was not a star actor but on many occasions his was the performance you remembered. I think particularly of his Mr Shu Fu the barber in Brecht's *The Good Woman of Setzuan* and as Dorn in *The Seagull*. When Dorn said, 'I don't know, maybe I don't understand anything, maybe I've gone off my head, but I did like that

164

play. There is something in it. When that child was holding forth about loneliness, and later when the devil's red eyes appeared, I was so moved that my hands were shaking. It was fresh, unaffected . . . Ah, I think he's coming along now. I feel like telling him a lot of nice things about it,' this was not just a play but our own lives upon the stage. All that scene had the same wonderful connection with George's life in the theatre.

3 Looking at *The Blacks*, and particularly the women in it. The director, Roger Blin, did not speak English and he chose the cast mainly for their appearance. The result was that it looked magnificent in the decor of André Acquart, but at times the actors' thick accents made the difficult text impossible to understand. 'They say you are difficult to understand,' said Genet. 'Be still more incomprehensible.' It was not a success, but still I see clearly in my mind Rashidi Onikoyi dangerous as Mr Archibald Absalom Wellington; Bloke Modisane obsequious as Diouf; and most clearly of all I remember Felicia Okoli

165

as Miss Stephanie Virtue Secret-Rose. I can still hear this beautiful Nigerian woman speaking 'softly as in a state of somnambulism,' as the stage direction says, 'I am the lily-white Queen of the West. Only centuries of breeding could achieve such a miracle!' Ah, Felicia, where are you now?

4 Enjoying the audience of the Theatre Royal, Brighton, being shocked. It was and is easy to shock them – are they still the same audience that was there before the war? Memories of *The Making of Moo*, the play that, as Ken Tynan wrote, 'introduced the full gaiety of blasphemy to the English theatre' and Charles Wood's *Veterans*, where every time Bill Hoskins said the word 'fuck' a seat went up announcing the departure of a member of the audience, and he said that word quite a number of times in one memorable speech. There was shock at the Court too. 'Oh, Lady Redgrave, how *could* you!' cried a member of the audience, throwing a shoe at Rachel Kempson in the course of John Osborne's *A Sense of Detachment*. My wife was moved to tears by

166

this play, which expressed all Osborne's heartfelt concern for England. The Brighton audience is particularly roused by a titled actor. The protests at *Veterans* were in large measure directed at John Gielgud for appearing in such a play. The same protests were heard when Ralph Richardson appeared in the first production of Orton's *What the Butler Saw*.

5 Waking up the morning after the first night of Ionesco's *Rhinoceros*, reading the critics and realizing that we had a hit. The first night had taken place under great technical difficulties, with Orson Welles directing the backstage staff on a walky-talky set from the front of the theatre, and I had feared the play had not come across. But all was well and it enjoyed a capacity run at the Court, followed by a transfer to the Strand Theatre. I saw this play first in Barrault's production in Paris with my dear friend Cecil Tennant, who helped me with his usual enthusiasm to set it up. He was a good friend to the English Stage Company. Everything seemed to go well in the planning stages of this production. Laurence Olivier accepted the part of Berenger, Orson agreed to direct, and Zero Mostel agreed to play Jean: a splendid trio. Then Zero was knocked down by a bus in New York and had to withdraw. He played the part with great success in New York some time later. He was the only actor I knew who could turn into a rhinoceros without the aid of make-up.

6 Working with Lindsay Anderson on *The Lily White Boys*. I read a notice by Ken Tynan about this play when it was originally presented without songs, by an amateur company. After I read the script I thought it should be turned into a play *with* songs. Lindsay agreed and we recruited Christopher Logue to write the lyrics, and Tony Kinsey and Bill Le Sage to do the music. The final result, presented at the Court with a fine cast including Albert Finney, Georgia Brown, Shirley Ann Field and Ann Lynn, was, I think, the nearest thing to a Brechtian satire produced in England. Working with Lindsay was exciting and enjoyable in those days.

7 Watching *St Joan of the Stockyards* in 1964. When Vanessa Redgrave had to withdraw, Siobhan McKenna, who had played Joan in an earlier production I had arranged in Dublin, gallantly stepped in and took the part. The critics hated it but for me the production by Tony Richardson, with Jocelyn Herbert's fine decor, was one of the most enjoyable I have ever had a hand in. The most openly Marxist of all Brecht's plays, to have it playing in the Queen's Theatre in the very heart of the West End was a joy I shall not forget. What an heroic piece it is. Poetic and heroic – it only lacked a working-class audience to enjoy it.

8 Taking over St Martin's Lane for John Osborne. Jointly with the ESC, my company presented his two plays *Time Present* at the Duke of

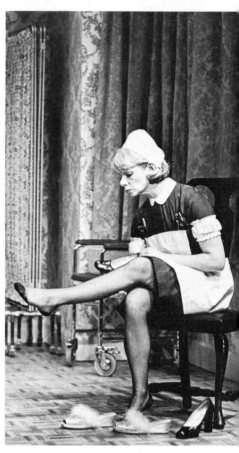

The Orton season 1975. *Above: Entertaining Mr Sloane.* Beryl Reid and Malcolm McDowell. *Right: Loot.* Jill Bennett. *(Photographs: John Haynes). Far right: What the Butler Saw.* Betty Marsden and Kevin Lloyd. *(Photograph: David Montgomery).* These plays were directed by Roger Croucher, Albert Finney and Lindsay Anderson respectively. Orton's other plays – *The Ruffian on the Stair* and *The Erpingham Camp* – had been staged at the Court in 1967 as a Sunday-nighter, a few weeks before the author was murdered.

York's and *The Hotel in Amsterdam* at the Albery (then the New Theatre). Later these were joined for a short time by *Look Back in Anger*, revived at the Court and transferred to the Criterion. All three were directed by Anthony Page. It was a great pleasure to come out of my office in Goodwin's Court and see the whole of one side of lower St Martin's Lane occupied by John's plays. And to watch Paul Scofield as Laurie in *The Hotel in Amsterdam*, particularly in the great love scene in Act 2 where he says to Annie: 'Because . . . to me . . . you have always been the most dashing . . . romantic . . . friendly . . . playful . . . loving . . . impetuous . . . larky . . . fearful . . . detached . . . constant . . . woman I have ever met . . . and I love you . . . I don't know how else one says it . . . one shouldn't . . . and I've always thought you felt . . . perhaps . . . the same about me.' Paul picked out these words and phrases and held each of them for a moment before going on to the next.

9 The season of South African plays directed and co-written by Athol Fugard was, I think, the high point of my time as artistic director. And the opportunity to present a season of Joe Orton's three full-length plays was a happy way for me to end my term of office. I originally hoped that the three associate artistic directors would each direct one of them. Lindsay and Albert did but unfortunately Tony Page was not able to commit himself – though in the end it turned out that he

could have been free. So Roger Croucher, then director of the Theatre Upstairs, took on the direction of *Entertaining Mr Sloane*. This season was a great success and, I think, established Joe's position in the British theatre. It was good to see *What the Butler Saw* given the recognition it deserved.

So, despite fights and disappointments, we finished the three years during which I had been artistic director with a show of unity. There was pleasure and satisfaction in that.

1975–1980

When Oscar Lewenstein told the Council that he had decided to leave at the end of his three-year contract he also told them it seemed to him that, in spite of their past differences, Lindsay Anderson was the obvious choice as his successor, if the Council wished to continue with the current policy. The Council, wishing it, expressed a unanimous hope that Anderson would accept. He declined, however, because he felt he was not the right man for the job at that time. It required considerable administrative ability which was not, he thought, his strong point. The artistic directorship was therefore put out to competition: 49 applications were received, eight applicants were interviewed, and the two most favoured were appointed jointly, at their own suggestion. Both Robert Kidd and Nicholas Wright, who took over the Court in the autumn of 1975, were experienced in the ways of that theatre (though few others). Kidd, born in Edinburgh, had worked as a stage manager; he made his directing debut with the Sunday night debut of Christopher Hampton's *When Did You Last See My Mother?* and was appointed an assistant director in 1967. Wright, born in South Africa, had been casting director before becoming an assistant director in 1968 and the first director of the Theatre Upstairs in 1969.

The programme for their first year in the main theatre looked impressive. There were new plays by David Hare (*Teeth 'n' Smiles*), Howard Barker (*Stripwell*), Edward Bond (*The Fool*), Christopher Hampton (*Treats*), Peter Gill (*Small Change*), David Storey (*Mother's Day*) and Mustapha Matura (*Rum an' Coca-Cola*). There were productions of *Waiting for Godot*, *Endgame* and a triple bill – *Play, That Time* and *Footfalls* – to celebrate Beckett's 70th birthday. There was a

Peter Gill rehearsing Tom Courtenay and Bridget Turner in Edward Bond's *The Fool*. Courtenay played the Northamptonshire 'peasant-poet', John Clare. (*Photograph: John Haynes*)

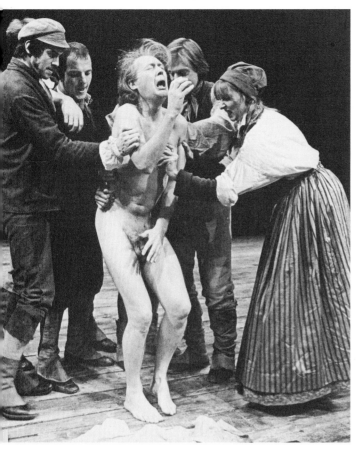

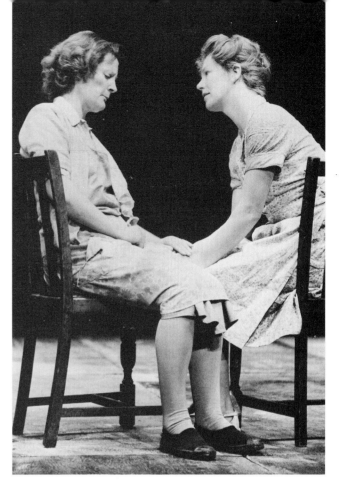

The Fool, 1975. Nigel Terry, Brian Hall, John Normington and Sheila Kelly. (*Photograph: John Haynes*)

June Watson and Marjorie Yates in Peter Gill's *Small Change*, 1976, an intimate portrait of childhood and adolescence in working-class Cardiff, expressed in a quartet of mothers and sons. (*Photograph: Zoë Dominic*)

Treats, 1976. Stephen Moore and Jane Asher in Christopher Hampton's fifth play, which transferred to the Mayfair Theatre. 'I write from some compulsive image or situation . . . It's about two subjects I seem to keep coming back to, cruelty and apathy.' (*Photograph: John Haynes*)

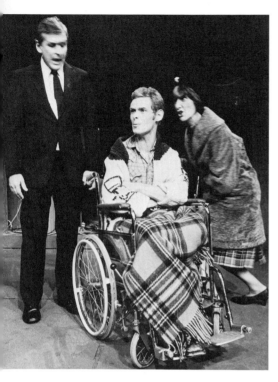

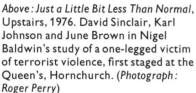

Above: Just a Little Bit Less Than Normal, Upstairs, 1976. David Sinclair, Karl Johnson and June Brown in Nigel Baldwin's study of a one-legged victim of terrorist violence, first staged at the Queen's, Hornchurch. (*Photograph: Roger Perry*)

Above right: For the West, Upstairs, 1977. Rudolph Walker as Idi Amin in the first Royal Court play to be transferred to the National Theatre. This was staged 21 years after Michael Hastings' first play was produced at the Court (directed by John Dexter) when he was a 17-year-old tailor's apprentice. (*Photograph: John Haynes*)

successor to *The Rocky Horror Show*, by Richard O'Brien and Richard Hartley: *T-Zee.*

As a response to the current economic crisis that dominated the start of their regime, they closed the Theatre Upstairs, from October 1975 to May 1976. But it reopened with a remarkable Joint Stock documentary about Angolan mercenaries, *Yesterday's News*, directed by Bill Gaskill and Max Stafford-Clark. It went on to stage the Joint Stock productions of Caryl Churchill's latest play, *Light Shining in Buckinghamshire*; and it introduced two new authors to the London stage – Michael McGrath (*Amy and the Price of Cotton*) and Nigel Baldwin (*Just a Little Bit Less than Normal*), an early example of what might be described as the theatre of the disabled.

The main theatre's revival of *Sizwe Bansi is Dead*, early in January 1977 was perhaps the most profitable, to date, of the regime's productions. By the time it had opened its run, however, the Kidd-Wright partnership was over. The young artistic directors had run into trouble from the reviewers, at the box office, with the Arts Council and inside the Court world itself. Although the Hare and Hampton plays transferred, they made scarcely any profit for the Court. Moreover, neither cash nor immediate kudos was gained by the new Howard Barker, David Storey and Edward Bond plays: with a cast of 22 and 70 costumes, *The Fool* cost, in spite of ingenious

The Winter Dancers, Upstairs, 1977. Jack Shepherd and fellow-Indians in David Lan's fifth play. A graduate in social anthropology, the author was moved to write *The Winter Dancers* after reading a study of the Kwakiutls of Vancouver Island. (*Photograph: John Haynes*)

economies by the designer, the record sum of over £18,650, far in excess of the budget. A new Nigerian work, *Parcel Post*, played to under 20% of the box office and added sharply to the losses. And *T-Zee*, from which great lifesaving rewards had been hoped in the wake of *The Rocky Horror Show*'s smash hit, was a flop. During the last nine months of 1976 the average takings were only about 35% (compared with the norm of 55%). This may be seen in perspective as a reasonable figure for such a programme, considering the risk factor and the widening gap between likely revenue and possible subsidy. Ten years earlier, when production costs were far lower, Bill Gaskill had estimated precisely this figure of 35% as the practical box office capacity for an all-year programme of new work. But by 1 April 1976 the accumulated deficit was nearly £28,500. In the following nine months it amounted to more than £27,000. There was a bank overdraft of nearly £6,000. Thanks to Michael White, Lois Sieff and Bernard Delfont (who underwrote the costs) a special performance of *A Chorus Line* wiped nearly £16,800 off the deficit. Yet in the prevailing circumstances of 1976 the Court seemed, to many friends as well as enemies, to be in grave danger.

This could not be blamed exclusively on the relative inexperience of Kidd and Wright (though the effort was made) nor on their run of signally bad luck. Economic realities were catching up with the

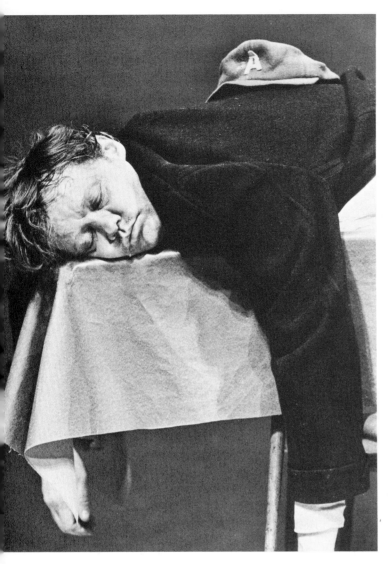

Above: Curse of the Starving Class, 1977. Dudley Sutton in the first Sam Shepard play to be world-premiered in the downstairs theatre. (*Photograph: John Haynes*)

Above right: Fair Slaughter, 1977. John Thaw and Max Wall, as a veteran British revolutionary (failed) holding his political talisman, the severed hand of Trotsky's train-driver, whom he had met in Russia in 1920. (*Photograph: John Haynes*)

Court. West End managers were less ready to risk new work, and no revivals were staged by Kidd and Wright. Without lucrative transfers the Court's only salvation seemed to be a much bigger Arts Council subsidy which recognized the theatre's national role as well as the heavy costs of the building and the prime responsibility to stage new work. That did not appear, as yet, to be a political or economic possibility. Another possibility began to be investigated in the late autumn of 1976 by the alarmed Council of the ESC, which set up a sub-committee to examine the situation and recommend a change of artistic direction. Since September average takings had dropped to 29%, and a huge deficit was looming up. The instalment of the Arts Council subsidy due at Christmas had already been largely anticipated. The Council therefore asked the Arts Council if it could make a further cash advance on the subsidy for the year beginning in April 1977, even though the Government had not yet informed the Arts Council itself what the total grant for that year would be.

Stuart Burge, artistic director at the Royal Court from 1977–79. After working for twelve years as an actor he began his career as a director in 1948, winning an international reputation as a versatile freelance. While he ran the Nottingham Playhouse (from 1969–73) one of his productions, *Lulu*, visited the Royal Court. (*Photograph: Tony McGrath/The Observer*)

The Arts Council agreed, but it did so with what later appeared – to many Court staff, directors, actors and authors – to be an ultimatum, although it had given somewhat similar warnings in previous financial crises to earlier artistic directors here and at other subsidized theatres. The ESC was told that it must operate within its existing cash resources, that it should reduce its accumulated deficit 'substantially', and that it could expect no more than £242,000 for 1977/78 (an increase of 10%). 'It is hoped that you can evolve a programme that is at once artistically exciting and financially successful,' wrote the Arts Council's finance director. When the ESC Council agreed to these proposals in December Robert Kidd at once told the chairman (to whom he had already, in November, signified this intention) that he would resign. This automatically cancelled Nicholas Wright's appointment. A month later, on 13 January 1977, Kidd released his letter of resignation to the press, accusing the ESC Council of selling the Court down the river, and the Arts Council of threatening the theatre's closure. Major newspapers, including those whose critics had been far from unanimous in their approval of the Court for years past, spoke out in its support. The *Sunday Times* said its closure would be a 'major disaster'. The *Guardian* observed, 'No other post-war theatre in Britain has such a remarkable record.' The *Daily Telegraph*, which stood at the opposite pole, politically and artistically, to much of the work created at the Court, declared, 'If there is a single British theatre which has changed the face of post-war Britain, it is the Royal Court. For twenty years we have looked to it for new writers, new directors, new ideas.'

A crisis of confidence exploded at the Court among its artists and workers, who attacked the ESC Council for its handling of events, and demanded a radical change in the structure of the Company's management, and the composition of the Council. Meetings of actors, writers, directors and other theatre workers were called, in a remarkable demonstration of loyalty inspired by the Court and of the widespread concern among those who had worked there about its future. Requests were made that representatives of those who worked at the Court should be elected to the Council. Edward Bond went further, proposing that the ESC should be run by its workers, past and present. This was strongly supported by, among others, Oscar Lewenstein. Meanwhile the ESC Council had appointed a new artistic director, Stuart Burge (who was released by Peter Hall from his engagement to run the Cottesloe Theatre), and had asked Sir Hugh Willatt to set up a small independent sub-committee to recommend changes in the ESC management structure. The Willatt report was accepted, months later, by the Council, who then offered their resignations, but agreed to continue until a new Council could

175

be formed – with two staff representatives (later increased to three). By then, as the Company recovered its financial balance (helped by a special grant of £20,000 from the Arts Council towards reducing the deficit), there was a decline in the urgency of demands for reform, for workers' control and for a new home. The obituaries of the English Stage Company proved to be premature, once again. But the underlying problems remained – intensified by the growing pressures of the time – beyond the scope of the Willatt committee. And they still persist.

Stuart Burge, who took over as artistic director in April 1977 at the age of 59 (four years older than Devine at his death), had not worked for the Court before, except as a visiting director: he was the first outsider in 21 years. During the first year of his regime the rise in running costs and overheads was slowed down, in spite of inflation; production costs were cut; the number of cost-saving visiting productions increased; a new form of try-out was introduced – the Rehearsed Reading (with a Gulbenkian subsidy); and one new play, Mary O'Malley's *Once a Catholic*, followed its Court success with a West End transfer. Within two years the deficit had been wiped out.

The biggest success of Burge's regime at the Court was the 1978

Above: Once a Catholic, 1977. June Page, Anna Keaveney and Jane Carr in Mary O'Malley's first full-length play – set in a London convent school in 1965 – which went on to a long West End run. (*Photograph: John Haynes*)

Right: Mary Barnes, 1979. Patti Love (in the title-role) and Simon Callow. David Edgar's play (from Birmingham) was based on the true story of what happened to a diagnosed schizophrenic who was treated by the radical therapy of a community centre instead of being sent to a mental hospital. (*Photograph: John Haynes*)

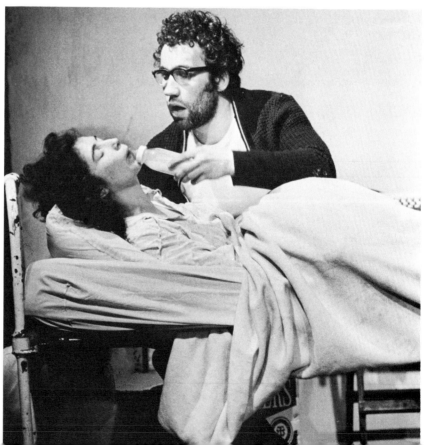

Flying Blind, 1978. Peter Postlethwaite. This black farce by Ulster writer Bill Morrison was set among the troubles in Northern Ireland; it was first staged at the Liverpool Everyman. (*Photograph: John Haynes*)

revival of Osborne's *Inadmissible Evidence*, with Nicol Williamson incomparably in the lead again. This was one of the major theatrical events of the decade, in a class of its own, but the play was not seen in the West End because of the star's tax-status – a prime example of conspicuous waste. It was closely followed, in box office popularity, by David Edgar's *Mary Barnes* (from the Birmingham Rep Studio) and Martin Sherman's *Bent* (a co-production, 1979) which transferred to the West End. Two notable new plays to do good business were Nigel Williams's *Class Enemy* (1978), which moved from Upstairs to Downstairs within a month, and Caryl Churchill's *Cloud Nine* (from Joint Stock, 1979). And there were two successful revivals – *The Good Woman of Setzuan*, with Janet Suzman in the lead, staged in conjunction with an outside management; and Edward Ravenscroft's *The London Cuckolds*, an unjustly neglected Restoration comedy, directed by Burge. The Beckett connection was maintained with *Happy Days*, supervised by the author, with Billie Whitelaw.

New authors in this period included Ron Hutchinson (*Says I, Says He*, from the Sheffield Crucible, and *Anchorman*), Bill Morrison (*Flying Blind*), Leigh Jackson (*Eclipse* and *Reggae Britannia*), John Byrne (*The Slab Boys*, from the Traverse), David Leland (*Psy-Warriors*), Alan Drury (*An Empty Desk*) and Alan Brown (*Skooldays*, followed by *Wheelchair Willie*). New plays came, too, from Barrie Keeffe, Howard Barker, Nigel Baldwin, Heathcote Williams, John McGrath, Peter Barnes, Snoo Wilson, Mustapha Matura and David Lan. Michael Hastings, first staged at the Court in 1957, returned with *For the West* (transferred to the National Theatre), *Full Frontal* and *Carnival War a Go Hot*. *Curse of the Starving Class* (1977) continued the long Sam Shepard connection with the Court. Another American author, Thomas Babe, saw his *Prayer for My Daughter* promoted in 1978 from the Theatre Upstairs to the downstairs auditorium.

Stuart Burge demonstrated that the Court could still welcome and develop new talent, of several different kinds and in ways that no other theatre could equal, although it could no longer afford to develop so much of it on its own – especially now that the long era of subsidy by authors was ending. Pressure from the Writers' Guild and the Theatre Writers' Union on the Royal Court, together with the National and the RSC, resulted in 1979 in an increase in commissioning fees for the main theatre to £2,000, and to £1,500 for the Theatre Upstairs. (Writers were also promised attendance fees of £75 a week.) Subsidy by actors and other theatre workers continued and still continues today: it was not until 1975 that the top salary of the stars was increased from £50 to £75. (And as late as 1980 Jonathan Pryce was paid £85 a week for Hamlet, which was then the Equity minimum, though far below the national minimum wage.) Burge was

177

helped to survive in his balancing act, despite inflation, by increases in the Arts Council grants and guarantees. For 1978/79 the subsidy was £305,000. In 1979/80 it rose to £385,000.

By then there was a new artistic director at the Royal Court and in 1978 Howard Newby, novelist, radio producer and former top-ranking BBC executive, had become chairman of the Council in place of Greville Poke, who had given more than 20 years of devoted, unstinting service since its formation.

The meteoric career of Robert Kidd ended tragically early, after long and recurrent illness, in 1980. He was 37.

Bent, 1979. Tom Bell and Ian McKellen in Martin Sherman's box office hit about homosexual love among the horrors of Hitler's concentration camps. (*Photograph: John Haynes*)

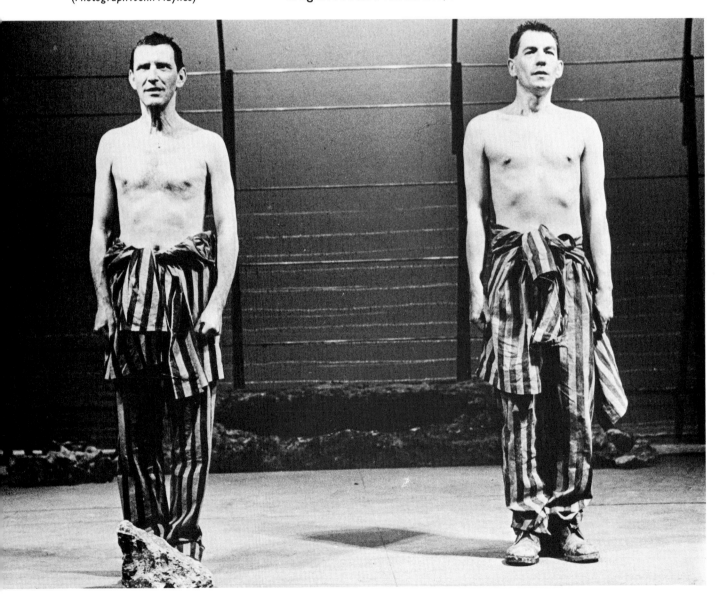

Hamlet, 1980. Jonathan Pryce in Richard Eyre's landmark production, one of the triumphant classical revivals which have given new opportunities to leading actors – and helped the Royal Court in times of trouble. (*Photograph: John Haynes*)

In the autumn of 1979 Stuart Burge was given leave by the ESC for up to six months in order to direct *Sons and Lovers* for a major television serial, and Max Stafford-Clark was invited to deputize for him. When it became clear in December that Burge could not return by the spring, Stafford-Clark agreed to continue until the end of 1980; he was later invited to be Burge's official successor as artistic director, until April 1983. Stafford-Clark had worked at the Edinburgh Traverse as artistic director, became director of the Traverse Workshop Company and founded Joint Stock with Bill Gaskill. At the Court he had directed 14 productions (when the ESC opened there he was a schoolboy) and had been an associate director since 1977. When taking over in 1980 he promised a 'totally traditional' programme of 'idealism tempered by compromise.'

During his first year new plays were presented by Barrie Keeffe (*Sus*), Howard Barker (*Love of a Good Man*) and Peter Sheridan (*The Liberty Suit*), all produced by visiting companies. Two visiting revivals were D. H. Lawrence's *Touch and Go* and John McGrath's *Trees in the Wind*. But the main theatre staged two major home-grown premieres: Nicholas Wright's *The Gorky Brigade* and David Lan's *Sergeant Ola and His Followers*. The Theatre Upstairs presented new plays by Caryl Churchill (*Three More Sleepless Nights* – with the Soho Poly) and Sam Shepard (*Seduced*). *The Key Tag* by Michael McGrath (a George Devine Award winner) was given a rehearsed reading in October and staged Upstairs in February. David Mowat's *The Guise*, given a rehearsed reading in August 1978, returned to the Court in a Foco Novo production in October 1979. Edward Bond's latest play, *The Worlds*, was, remarkably, staged Upstairs by the Activists of the Young People's Theatre, under the author's direction. Andrea Dunbar's first play, *The Arbor*, directed by Stafford-Clark in the Young Writers' Festival in March 1980, Upstairs, was staged downstairs in an expanded version in June. This was a notable example of the Court's continuing discovery of new contemporary voices, and of the scrupulous response of the director and his actors to the simplicity and truthfulness of the text.

From mid-November 1979 the main auditorium was closed for two months for redecorating and reseating at a cost of £40,000, met entirely by private donations after a sustained fund-raising campaign. A significantly high proportion of the funds was raised from inside the theatrical profession – another mark of the loyalty still felt towards the old theatre in Sloane Square.

By the autumn of 1980 the main event of Stafford-Clark's regime so far was not, however, a new play, but the revival of an old one: Richard Eyre's production of *Hamlet*, with Jonathan Pryce as the prince. This was a smash hit at the box office and was hailed by some observers as the first definitive re-interpretation since 1965 (when David Warner was the RSC hero). It was also taken as a sign that the alternative theatre, of which Stafford-Clark has been a leading activist, was changing its attitudes towards the classical tradition on which it had, effectively, turned its back for the past decade. Finding, serving and staging new plays remained, and will remain, the main purpose of the Royal Court but economic pressures have obliged Stafford-Clark to consider extending runs where possible beyond the traditional Court limits, as well as increasing the number of co-productions with other companies in order to spread production costs, and reaffirming the need for a mixed economy, aesthetically and financially, of old and new plays.

Nicholas Wright

A Shared Aesthetic

The first play I saw at the Royal Court was *Major Barbara*. The English Stage Company had been started a couple of years before, and I'd read everything I could about it. It sounded left-wing and unstuffy: I was very attracted to it and wanted to work there.

It was a first night. The foyer, which was narrow and very dark, was packed with people in evening dress, fanning themselves with programmes, which in those days had a commemorative first-night gold star pasted on the cover. If this seems at odds with the theatre's radical reputation, I can't say it seemed so at the time. The performance was preceded by God Save the Queen played on what sounded like an ostentatiously wheezy gramophone. Most of the audience stood up, some remained seated, and quite a lot of people hovered between the two, or stood up late and sat down early. Having come from abroad, I was delighted: the gesture had exactly the ambiguity that foreigners admire in the English.

But what struck me most was the persuasiveness of Alan Webb as

Nicholas Wright rehearsing Warren Mitchell in *The Great Caper*, 1976. Born in Cape Town, Wright joined the English Stage Company as casting director in 1967; in the following year he directed a Sunday night production of his own play, *Changing Lines*. He was joint artistic director at the Royal Court (with Robert Kidd) from 1975–77. (*Photograph: Mick Rock*)

Undershaft, the munitions magnate. (More ambiguity: the Royal Court was famously linked with the CND movement, then at its height.) It was an ironic, humorous performance: graceful and very simple, so that you felt you could see the actor's own temperament through it. Joan Plowright played Barbara. She had become a leading actress purely through her work for the Court, and I'd expected her performance to be somehow in opposition to that of an actor who seemed to me very elderly, steeped in a traditional school. But when she and Webb played together their styles didn't jar at all: they inhabited the same world.

It was to be another eight years before I got a job at the Royal Court. I'd made friends at drama school with George Devine's daughter Harriet, and used to turn up regularly at her home on Sunday afternoons. Her mother Sophie never seemed to mind how many people were there and was equally nice to everyone. We used to sit around talking about the theatre and playing games while she made tea and a big cake and did the washing-up, or sat at the kitchen table with her box of paints, doing costume designs for the next day. And in this way I'd got to know a few of the directors who worked at the Court. None of them ever gave me a part in a play there, and secretly I knew my acting was too bad to deserve one. And when I stopped trying to act, and decided to learn to direct plays, I didn't think it would be any use asking any of them for a job. I was pretty in a stupid-looking way, and had made matters worse by getting nervous and chattering idiotically to all the people I most wanted to impress. It seemed to me that I'd made such a bad impression that the only way to get into the Royal Court would be in disguise.

A surprising number of first plays are written for pragmatic reasons: to give the author a whacking part to play, or a play to direct. My first play was written to prove to the Royal Court that I was intelligent enough to work there. I started by getting a job on a movie. The work was mainly herding sheep around Dorset, but I was getting paid about ten times as much as an ordinary shepherd, which meant that when shooting was finished I would be able to take time off to write. And I began to feel already that I was getting nearer the Court, since the movie was being cast by Miriam Brickman, who had been a pioneering casting director there. Her successor, Pauline Melville, was now an actress and in the cast. Stage two was buying a typewriter and going to Greece. I can't say I thought much about the actual play until I'd sorted out these technical questions and found the right island, where I found the play took much longer to write than I had expected – nearly a month. Back in London I sent it to the Court under a *nom de plume*: E. Jefferson, after Eddie Jefferson, a jazz singer I admired.

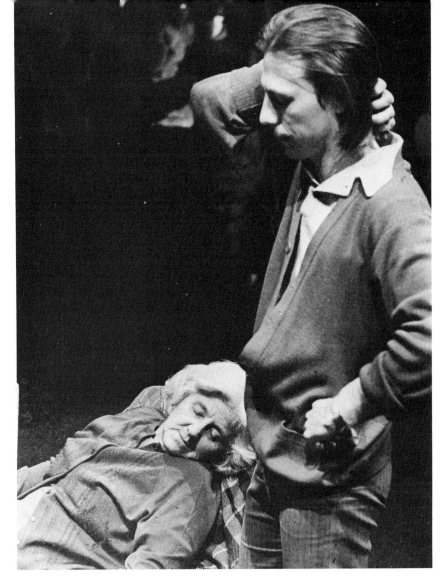

Owners, Upstairs, 1972. Eileen Devlin and Kenneth Cranham. Caryl Churchill's first play for the theatre: since 1972 six Churchill plays have been staged at the Court, and one – *Cloud Nine* – has been revived. (*Photograph: John Haynes*)

The plan was now to stay anonymous until I got at least an encouraging letter back, and then stun everyone at the Court with my unsuspected talent – a bit like the man whose friends laughed when he sat down to play the piano. I waited for weeks but nothing happened, so I rang Bill Gaskill and asked him for an interview.

Bill was, of all the people at the Court, the one I was most frightened of. But I went in and explained to him how much I wanted to work there, and he listened carefully and was totally sympathetic. I began to wonder if it wouldn't have been simpler to have gone to see him in the first place, rather than spending a year pushing sheep about and going to Greece. It was only when I revealed that I had written a play, and that the script was at this moment somewhere in his theatre, albeit in disguise, that he got edgy. He buzzed through to his secretary to find it, and then said he was fed up with *noms de plume*, they were a lot of nonsense and could it please stop. He had recently been one of the judges of a play competition, he said, and had

Paul Curran as Maxim Gorky in Nicholas Wright's third play, *The Gorky Brigade*, 1979. Set in the Russia of 1920, it marked the return of Bill Gaskill as a director to the Royal Court.
(*Photograph: John Haynes*)

given a prize to a playwright who had embarrassingly turned out to be his best friend Peter Gill. At this point my script was brought in, a pink report sheet fluttering from it. Bill read the report and gave it to me: it said that Mr Jefferson should definitely be encouraged. The interview was now back on course, everything was going according to plan, and it was time to ask Bill if I could have a job as an assistant director. He said, no. I was taken aback. Was he sure? Yes, quite sure. There wasn't a vacancy and none was expected. This was something I'd not thought of, and I left kicking myself.

Pauline Melville and I had become great friends on the movie. A month or so later she told me that Bill was looking for a casting director. He'd asked her if she was interested, but she had decided to go to university. Why didn't I put myself up for it? I asked what the job was like. She said: 'Unbelievably frightening. You keep thinking they're going to give you the sack.' When she'd started there she'd thought that Samuel Beckett, Oscar Lewenstein and the old man who

Was He Anyone?, Upstairs, 1972. Rowena Cooper, Stanley Lebor, Yvonne Antrobus and Geoffrey Chater in N.F. Simpson's first full-length play for seven years, the fifth to be staged at the Royal Court. The six members of the cast played 34 roles. (*Photograph: John Haynes*)

used to come in from the pub at lunchtimes to work the switchboard all looked confusingly alike. She lived in terror of buying the teetotal Oscar a double scotch or asking Beckett if he'd mind unblocking the drain. She also said, 'You'll find you learn a lot. When I have to fill out a form, and it says "Where educated?" I always think I ought to put down "Royal Court".'

It's never been very easy to define whatever it is that makes the Royal Court a theatre with a personality. The fact that people feel peculiarly loyal to it, and get terribly angry with it, is more easily observed than explained. By the time I started to work at the Court I'd been seeing plays there for years. Some plays had seemed much 'righter' than others; so had some actors, some productions. But what accounted for the distinction? I experienced it as merit: but merit on what terms? This was something I hoped to find out.

I don't know that I'd really expected to find a body of theory: I doubt it, and certainly nothing like that was apparent. People were very conscious of the fact that they worked at the Court rather than any other theatre (they still are) but what artistic implications this might have were never spelled out. A connection was often made, but it was done in an elliptical way: 'Not for us' or 'Is it right for the Court?' And when decisions were made, however 'artistic', their terms of reference were empiric and local.

This may be why so much of the working day and evening was dominated by conversation. It served, depending on how you look at it, either as a substitute for theory, or (as I now think) as a mediator between theory and practice. Mostly it took place in the casting office, which isn't to say that it was necessarily about casting. It might be sparked off by a casting problem, but once four or five more people had poked their heads round the door and joined in, it might be about blocking or set design. The next stage – Vakhtangov, the dance of Frederick Ashton, or food – would be a fascinating distraction as far as casting was concerned. I realized why Pauline had said I'd learn a lot; I wondered if this was what seminars were like. In the jargon of the period, my mind was being blown. The vocabulary was private; linear thinking was optional, insights were oblique and the paranoia quotient was on semi-permanent red alert. It seems to me now that the whole game, or course, or art-form, had the function of entrenching a shared aesthetic, modifying it and initiating newcomers. And that it was the sense of a shared aesthetic which *on the one hand* identified outsiders, defined solecisms and made the jokes work or fall flat, and *on the other* informed empiric decisions and gave them their style.

After six months I was moved up, as I had hoped, to be an assistant director. I was followed in time by one very brilliant casting director,

185

Gillian Diamond, who was in turn followed by another, Patsy Pollock. Conversation continued throughout their reigns, sometimes very sharply. People at the Royal Court are famous for disagreeing with each other on any number of subjects. The things they generally agree about are more revealing: here, at the points where opinions overlap, ideology is most explicit. One such point is the very aversion to theory I've mentioned. Another is combativeness in the face of attack from outside: the Lord Chamberlain, the critics and the Arts Council on the warpath have all in their time been champion buriers of hatchets.

The third point is, I think, central to the figurative nature of most of the Court's work, and relates to an approach to acting. The first time I'd seen a play there, I'd picked up a sense of the strength of a certain kind of playing. Over the years I'd developed a love of it. And when I got a job there I found that the people I was working with felt the same way. One thing you could always rely on everyone agreeing on was the quality of classic realistic acting: its humour, its temperament, its gift for placing profound emotion in a social perspective. And for my money these are qualities which the Court's best work has shared.

I left the Royal Court in 1976, after having been joint artistic director for a season with Bob Kidd. It was a painful break-up, and for a while I wanted to stay out of its way and not think about it. It felt like the end of a love affair; and writing now about my wooing of the Royal Court, and an early stage of my work there, was the problem of writing about a love affair. It's difficult to explain pleasure. To the listener it's just a couple of people drinking cocoa in bed.

There's also a narrative problem, since the story doesn't have a pay-off. A couple of years after the break-up one of my plays was directed at the Court by Bill Gaskill. At the same time I started and ran a group of young playwrights there. It was a useful and enjoyable time and again I learned a lot. I wasn't any longer obsessed by the Royal Court, and I don't work there now. But I still think of it as my theatre.

Nigel Williams

Nigel Williams. With his first full-length play, *Class Enemy*, he won the *Plays and Players* award as Most Promising Playwright of the year; with his first novel, *My Life Closed Twice*, he won a Somerset Maugham award. (*Photograph: Suzan Harrison*)

Natural Platform

For a start the auditorium is the right size. You can see the actors. They, were they so minded, could see you, but the place is large enough for them to be lost in their own world. In Peter Gill's *Small Change* – a triumph of intimate observation – I remember an argument between the two central characters that seemed close enough to touch, and yet as far away as Chekhov. In fact that tone of distantly authentic realism is, for me, the thing that makes the Royal Court such an attractive theatre. For any writer interested in making effects not through sound, light or press communiqués, but through language, the Royal Court is the natural platform. It is exactly what it claims to be – a writers' theatre. Which is why I like it so much.

I can recall that on my first visit there, clutching a highly obscure play improbably titled *Martin Swift Completely*, I was met by a man with a striped head and a very small behind, who rotated several feet above the chair in which I was sitting and said, apparently to the bookcase behind me, 'What do you think of Ford Madox Ford?' How extraordinary that a 'man of the theatre' (and I privately considered that all persons concerned with the theatre, apart from myself, were savages or fools) should have heard of the man who wrote *The Good Soldier*! And how even more extraordinary that he should care about what a comparative stranger should think of that book! The conviction was born in me – not totally dispelled by subsequent events – that people at Sloane Square thought that questions such as these were, in fact, the most important things in the world.

I was later to discover that the Royal Court, like all significant institutions, is a battle-ground: a fact which can be observed by studying the reports made by the assistant directors there on scripts currently under discussion. 'This is sexist crap!' is followed by 'Quite an interesting play about brothels.' Greatly to my joy I once discovered that these same assistant directors actually *marked* plays on a scale from A to D – a system of critical response I earnestly commend to the theatre critics of our national newspapers.

Within the walls of the theatre are Marxists, Showbiz Impresarios,

187

Class Enemy, Upstairs and Downstairs, 1978. Peter-Hugo Daly and Phil Daniels. Nigel Williams's play about a London comprehensive school was largely cast from the Anna Scher Drama School in Islington. (*Photograph: John Haynes*)

Gay Activists and Earnest Groupies. The current management often hates the last management and, outside, the last management snarls over current successes and whoops over spectacular failures. But in spite of the fact that it contains people who judge plays purely on their politics and, as well, people who suppose that plays can be judged without reference to such things, it is acknowledged that the first task is to get hold of a text that is not of interest simply because of what it is about or whether its author has a reputation but because of *what it is*; which is why, of course, debates in the theatre about which play to do are so public, so desperate and so frequently unpleasant for the writer.

The Royal Court plays host to an awkward, libertarian radicalism that is never happier than when screaming loudly at persons with whom it is supposed to collaborate. In the audience there you find people almost nightmarishly *à la mode* but you also find sports-jacketed Ph.D. students, madmen with orange hair and leather boots, and earnest groups of Americans. I remember on one occasion a fattish man in his late forties who, halfway through a particularly dreary scene in a particularly dreary play, announced: "Allelujah, I am fuckin' off.' And fuck off he did, with the underground trains rattling underneath Sloane Square, out into that weird reservoir at the end of the King's Road, with its fairy lights, soldiers, yobs, tourists and locals. And that, I suppose, is one reason why I and a lot of other people love the Royal Court – you can tell people to fuck off in it; people fuck off *from* it, with style; it often tells you to fuck off; but, most important of all, you can tell it – or its current artistic director and assistant directors – to fuck off, and there is never a thought that you should be behaving as if you were in that drab English substitute for church, the Proper Theatre. The Royal Court is Improper Theatre. Death to its enemies!

188

The Young Tradition

During the past five years the relative contraction in productivity by both upstairs and downstairs theatres at the Royal Court has been accompanied by a vigorous expansion in the output (and auxiliary labours) of the Young People's Theatre Scheme. Since 1976 more plays by and for teenagers have been staged than in the preceding 20 years, with the co-operation of a score of Court authors and artists and the help of special grants from charitable trusts and public bodies. This trend has provoked criticism – both inside and outside the Court – from those who see this flurry of activity as a dangerous diversion of talent, energy and resources from the prime functions of a severely beleaguered theatre: an acquiescence in the modish phenomena of theatrical politicization and youth-worship. But the YPTS may well claim that its unmistakeable social concern, like its search for new writers and new audiences, reflects traditional Court policies.

It is, in fact, rooted in the early history of the English Stage Company. The ideal of involving young people in the theatre has been a persistent element in the Company's theory, and a spasmodic factor in the Company's practice, during the past 25 years. In this field, as in others, the Court has often pointed others in the right direction, even when it has not been able to lead the way.

George Devine was an enthusiast for children's theatre. The Young Vic, of which he was director from 1946 to 1951, ran the first children's theatre company to operate on a national scale in Britain; but he saw it as theatre *for* children, not *by* them or about their lives. When he joined the English Stage Company he brought with him dreams of educating and mobilizing a vast new audience, recruited from the young. Support for young people's theatre came, at the start, from Edward Blacksell. It was on his insistence that the Company's 1955 manifesto announced, a year before the Court regime began, that one of its aims was 'to encourage children to develop a genuine enthusiasm for and critical appreciation of good theatre.' The Company promised to present seasons of plays intended for younger audiences, to be toured 'wherever educational authorities and schools offer facilities.' Blacksell and Duncannon formed a 'Children's Sub-Committee' on which the LCC Inspector of Drama agreed to serve. After the Court was occupied, special performances for children were given on Saturday mornings for a time. But this experiment was short-lived, and nothing more was done to implement the manifesto until the autumn of 1960. Then it was initiated, as often in Court history, as an improvised, empirical response. Two Hertfordshire teachers, who occasionally took parties of senior children to London theatres, wrote to Devine bemoaning the general lack of extramural facilities for young visitors. Devine sent his assistant John Blatchley to meet the teachers, and a plan for Court visits was worked out. The first group of 16 youngsters, between the ages of 16 and 18, came for five days that autumn, and during the following year they were followed, once a month, by other groups. They visited a London theatre at least once every day; went backstage and watched rehearsals; listened to the stage-manager, box office manager, front of house manager, as well as the director and actors; and took part in a discussion about what they had seen, at the end of their week. Encouraged by Helene Weigel, Devine aspired to establish this as a weekly, rather than a monthly event. 'If you're going to make the theatre a part of your life you need *formation* and that, I think, ought to start in schooldays.' A more ambitious Schools Scheme was planned in 1961. Neville Blond offered £1,000 to help in getting it started. Because of its demands on space, time and money, the scheme was put on the shelf. But Devine remained convinced, as he wrote in a 1962 letter, that the way to bridge the gap between the 'serious' theatre and the majority of the population lay in the schools and 'a radical reappraisal of the teaching of drama.'

In 1966 Bill Gaskill – who shared Devine's enthusiasm for the cause – restarted the Schools Scheme, with a grant of £5,000 from the Arts Council: in the following year children's theatre figured for the first time in the Arts Council's budget, and a Young People's Theatre Panel was established. As part of her job as an assistant director, Jane Howell took charge of the Scheme. Under its auspices the Company staged revivals of *Roots*, with matinees for schools only (every morning 100 children were introduced to the theatre); Brendan Behan's *The Hostage*; and *Live Like Pigs*. A morning 'demonstration' of *Julius Caesar* was presented, which ended by involving 17 children in the forum scene. Increasing participation now began to be the order of the day. Ann Jellicoe's *The Rising Generation* – written for a cast of 900 in the Empire Pool, Wembley – was presented in a truncated version with no more than 150 teenagers. *Dance of the Teletape*, 'a capsule history of the human race in 20 minutes,' was written and directed by a 14-year-old schoolboy, Charles Wood, and performed by fellow-pupils at Dulwich College. In 1969 Jane Howell organized an extraordinary event labelled *Revolution*. After two weeks of discussion and visits, with the general theme of 'revolution' as a background, 120 London schoolchildren were encouraged to act out their feelings and ideas about their lives and the world around them in a three-hour performance which was, in effect, all their own work. This was acclaimed by *The Times* as 'a splendid vindication of the Schools Scheme.' Jane Howell, and her successors, felt in frequent need of vindication because, they believed, this work with young

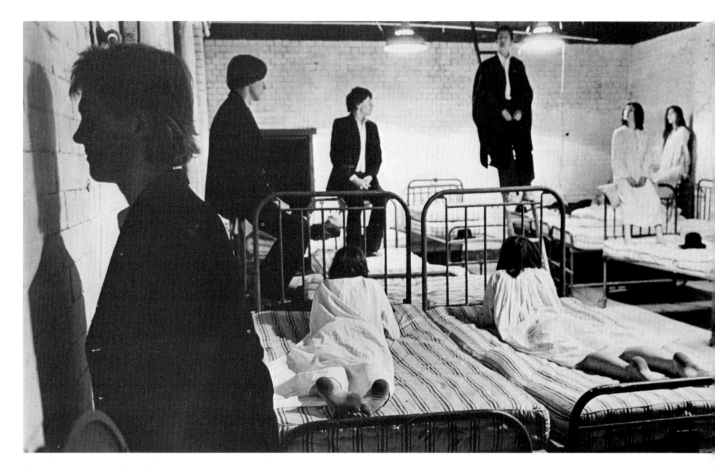

Spring Awakening, 1977. Wedekind's play staged by the Activists Youth Club in the Garage, their headquarters behind Sloane Square underground station. (*Photograph: Chris Davies*)

people came low in ESC priorities; but by 1970 it was claimed that 10,000 students a year came to the Court under the student card scheme, started in 1967 – 100 seats at five shillings each were reserved for authenticated students at every performance. To sell a quarter of the Court seats at cut-rate prices in this way may well have seemed to the Council an indication of their sympathy with the cause. Economic pressures later in the 1970's obliged them to withdraw this concession; but in 1980 it was still possible for a student who presented himself at the box office with a student card half an hour before curtain-up to get any seat left for £1.

Jane Howell was succeeded in 1970 by Pam Brighton, whose productions under the Young People's Theatre Scheme (as it was now significantly renamed, extending its range to school-leavers and post-school students) included revivals of *Live Like Pigs, Skyvers* (transferred to the Roundhouse) and *The Sport of My Mad Mother* with updated 'bad' language which shocked the Inner London Education Authority and even provoked questions in Parliament. She also produced *Show Me the Way to go Home*, 'a collective work about housing' staged Upstairs, adaptable for schools, community centres, pubs, etc; and Harald Mueller's war orphan play *Big Wolf*, which was first staged with an amateur cast Upstairs on a Saturday morning in 1971, and which Gaskill brought downstairs with professional actors

Activists' mask class, with Jennifer Carey, 1976. (*Photograph: Laurie Sparham, IFL*)

the following spring. In such ways the work of the Court writers of the 1950's was kept alive in its original home for a new generation, and the YPTS showed its continuing concern for making the theatre connect with contemporary social realities.

Under Joan Mills, who took over in 1972 as director, the YPTS organized 'drama workshops' in schools and ran a regular workshop at the Oval House in Kennington, with sessions of improvisational writing, in addition to touring productions to schools and introducing the young to theatres. In 1973 the first playwriting competition for under-18s was launched, limited to schools in the London area: the 'winning' plays were performed by amateur actors at the Oval House. In the following year it became a national competition, in conjunction with the *Observer Magazine*; and the winners were given professional productions in the Theatre Upstairs. This Young Writers' Festival became an annual landmark in the Royal Court year, acclaimed by newspapers which were not always ready to commend the theatre's work for older writers.

When Gerald Chapman became YPTS Director in 1976, he continued the policy of 'educating the audiences of the future' by encouraging young people to participate in the making of theatre, and of discovering and nurturing young writers. He obtained a Gulbenkian grant of nearly £10,000 over two years towards the cost of the latter activity. But he also aimed at helping young people to understand their environment, and to express their ideas and feelings about it. Prompted by his own experience in community theatre, he aimed in particular at giving a voice to urban minorities – Bengalis in the East End, Indians in Tooting, West Indians in the Portobello Road – and the problems of truants, unemployed school-leavers and other alienated young. 'Our aims are both social and artistic. They cannot be separated in practice.'

Chapman set up a youth club, for the 16 to 23 age-range – the Activists – whose membership rapidly rose from 50 to 200. He also established a close working relationship with London teachers, on

Hard Time Pressure, 1980. The author,
Michael MacMillan, an 18-year-old West
Indian from Bethnal Green
comprehensive, was a 'winner' in the
Young Writers' Festival two years
earlier with *The School Leaver*.
(*Photograph : Mark Rusher*)

which he put a high value, and he persuaded the ESC to lease a disused
garage round the corner from the Court in Holbein Place as a work-
shop-showplace for the YPTS and a headquarters for the Activists.
This soon acquired a reputation as 'The Garage', especially after the
much-praised performance there in 1977 by the Activists of Wedekind's *Spring Awakening*, directed by Tim Fywell and John Chapman.

A Young Writers' Group was set up at the suggestion of Nicholas
Wright, who was appointed tutor to it in 1979. (He was succeeded by
Caryl Churchill.) Local youth groups were invited to see perfor-
mances at the Court, and also to give performances in The Garage.
Several groups from all over the country took part in a 1977 Jubilee
Festival, with visitors from Poland, Canada and Italy. Chapman
enlisted the help of many writers whose plays had been staged at the
Court. He commissioned Heathcote Williams to write *Playpen*,
which was performed by Theatre Machine – a link with the Studio
tradition. Liane Aukin, Howard Brenton, Alan Brown, Alan Drury,

193

Robert Holman, Nigel Williams and Nicholas Wright were invited to collaborate with a director in setting up writers' workshops with young people in different parts of London. Caryl Churchill, Arnold Wesker, Christopher Hampton, Stephen Poliakoff, David Lan and Edward Bond have all given talks and joined in discussions. David Lan, Leigh Jackson and Dilip Hiro have worked on plays for minority and community theatre groups. Plays for the Activists have been written by Nigel Baldwin and Gilly Fraser (whose *Blame it on the Boogie* was identified by *The Times* as *Blame it on the Borgias*!). Works by two of the authors chosen for production in the annual Young Writers' Festival have been staged by the ESC – Lenka Janiurek's *In the Blood*, presented Upstairs in 1978, and *The Arbor*, by Andrea Dunbar, restaged Downstairs in 1980 in an expanded version after its Festival appearance Upstairs. Edward Bond directed the Activists in his play *The Worlds*, before its production by the Royal Shakespeare Company.

Controversy has flared up, from time to time, over the content of some YPTS plays – spotlighting the problems of young gays, blacks, and other victims of police harassment – and by such extra-curricular activities as seminars on Marxism, sexism and other aspects of answers to the question, 'What is it like to be young today?' which Gerald Chapman took as his guideline when he was appointed. Some champions of the older Court tradition – most notably John Osborne – view the YPTS as a disaster area. But Chapman described it, with justification, as 'the growth area of the Royal Court,' and it seems likely to remain an integral part of the English Stage Company's work. In July 1980 the directorship of the YPTS passed to David Sulkin. With the news that the Garage was to be demolished and the site redeveloped, it seemed to be time to take stock of the Scheme. The ESC's concern for the YPTS is a sign that, after 25 years, the ESC is still looking firmly into the future.

Richard Findlater

Max Stafford-Clark

Under the Microscope

It was during one of my school holidays that I saw *The Long and the Short and the Tall* by Willis Hall at the Royal Court and it was my second-ever formative theatre experience. The first had been *Babes in the Wood* at the Lewisham Hippodrome. I was also miserably jealous at Dinah Stabb's 21st birthday party, which was held in Clement Freud's nightclub, now the Theatre Upstairs. But apart from these two occasions I remained distant from events in Sloane Square until a successful Traverse production of Stanley Eveling's *Dear Janet Rosenberg, Dear Mr Kooning* moved to the freshly opened Theatre Upstairs.

Max Stafford-Clark. Artistic director of the English Stage Company since 1979 and co-founder of the Joint Stock Company. (*Photograph: John Haynes*)

The Glad Hand, 1978. Snoo Wilson's inventive fantasy about a South African fascist bound for the Bermuda Triangle on an oil tanker with a bizarrely assorted crew, in search of the Anti-Christ. Left to right: Julie Walters, Di Patrick, Will Knightley, Nick Le Prevost, Olivier Pierre, Julian Hough, Manning Redwood, Antony Sher, Alan Devlin, Rachel Bell, Gwyneth Strong, Tony Rohr. (*Photograph: John Haynes*)

Far right: The Arbor, Upstairs and Downstairs, 1980. Kathryn Pogson and Paul Barber in Andrea Dunbar's first play, written at 15 (*Photograph: John Haynes*)

Wheelchair Willie, 1978. Tony Rohr and Carrie Lee-Barker, in a peaceful moment among the horrors of Alan Brown's play about a cripple in a crippled society. 'Rape: unemployment: poverty: physical, social, psychological violence: sexual depravity. Handicapped Willie's homelife is far from idyllic,' said the Court's handout. (*Photograph: John Haynes*)

The production and the play had been attracting packed houses in Edinburgh for several months and had already received a lavish rave from Harold Hobson so I was not that apprehensive about the London opening. Not, that is, until about six o'clock on the evening of the first night, when a pale and haunted figure came into the Theatre Upstairs and anxiously enquired if everything was all right. I said everything was fine as far as I could tell.

'You see,' said David Hare, for it was he, 'I recommended this show to them so I hope it's going to be OK.'

David was the literary manager at the Court and 'them' was a looming inner circle of grown-ups who were rumoured to include Bill Gaskill, Lindsay Anderson and Anthony Page. This was my first taste of life at the Court, and of the importance that was given to the inner circle whose taste and judgement were anxiously monitored by the rest of the building.

Later I was invited to direct David Hare's *Slag* at the Court. Lindsay, Tony Page and Bill were all present at the first production meeting at which the poster was discussed. It was decided that this should feature a pair of female breasts. Now, on the post-*Hair*, pre-feminist fringe, a pair of tits was a pair of tits, and as such adorned many a fringe production. No Pip Simmons show was complete without several. This was not so at the Court, where they were perceived as an aesthetic feature of the production, which must be discussed in exhaustive detail. After 40 minutes' discussion on breasts, involving some of the keenest minds currently working in British theatre, Lindsay's suggestion of a pair of ceramic tits was agreed upon. The poster is on the wall in front of me now and, although I make the point frivolously, this was the first lesson that I learned from the Court: that the 'standard' of the 'work' was the important criterion and that this led to the meticulous examination of every detail of the production.

Slag was in 1971, and I directed Howard Brenton's *Magnificence* at the Court in 1973, but I didn't work there much after that; and

196

strangely I absorbed more of the Court's method working with Bill Gaskill in Joint Stock than I ever did by working at the Court itself. Bill constantly probed my imagination in the three productions we did together. He dug at what the final stage picture should look like, at how a prop should be handled, and at what stage pictures we intended to present. Even the question of the actors' involvement in budgetary responsibility was judged by whether this would make the standard of the work higher by increasing their commitment. It did.

I think this attention to detail derives partly from the rigorous demands made by the Royal Court's proscenium and size. The Court is a fine instrument – a microscope that examines and presents the detail of the work placed upon it and exposes the flaws. On the fringe we toured a lot. Each space was different, and usually the proximity of the audience warmed rather than distanced the experience. The exactness of the Court places a particular demand on the work.

At the moment, the Royal Court elsewhere than at the Royal Court seems unthinkable. This hasn't always been the case; at different times moves have been proposed to such diverse places as the Old Vic or to a warehouse in Covent Garden. But the one unifying factor of the English Stage Company's first 25 years is that it has all taken place in a proscenium theatre called the Royal Court, which seats over 400 people. This fact, too, has shaped the work. Producing new plays in a 400-seat theatre is hazardous and expensive. Indeed, George Devine declared as a matter of policy that the Royal Court should transfer a number of plays each year to the West End. Certainly he did not believe that new work alone was a viable policy. In the first five years of its operation the English Stage Company produced 24 world premieres in the main auditorium; of these, four were successful (75% business or more), nine were unsuccessful (30% business or less) and 11 fell between the two. For the past five years (up to 1980) the figures have been: 24 world premieres, of which four have been successful, eight unsuccessful and 12 between the two.

Some things remain astonishingly similar over 25 years. So probably do the two key factors that will determine our future: the selection of the plays and the standard of the work.

Afterpiece

During its 25 years at the Royal Court the English Stage Company has rarely succeeded in satisfying left, right and centre at the same time. Like all really live theatres the Court has generated rage as well as rapture and respect: it has, in its ESC time, offended a great many people, and we are confident that it will continue to do so. To the traditional Establishment the Court has sometimes appeared alarmingly as a nest of radicals. To radicals in the past decade it has often seemed a camouflaged blockhouse of the Establishment, defending the bourgeois, literary, apolitical theatre. Some critics have attacked the Court for excessive solemnity, emotional bleakness, half-baked politicization and obsessive preoccupation with social problems. Others have anathematized it for indulgence in high jinks, acquiescence in star worship, enjoyment of glamour, compromise with the theatre of comfort, and elitist perfectionism in maintaining production standards. Many have agreed at frequent intervals in the past quarter-century that the Court is not what it used to be, and that the golden days – of 1957, 1963, 1968, 1970 or 1974, according to nostalgic taste – will never return. Although John Osborne remains on the Council he has become one of the Company's severest judges. Some may even share Glenda Jackson's belief, expressed to the writer, that the Court is now 'an albatross round the neck of the British theatre.' It has never been short of critics, enemies and epitaph-writers.

It has, moreover, never been adequately supported by public funds for the work – of so many different kinds – that it has done since 1956. The inevitable gap between box office revenue and Arts Council subsidy has usually been filled, *somehow*, by profits from West End transfers, film rights, etc; by private patrons, fund-raising concerts, charity galas; and – least conspicuously but most persistently – by its own theatre writers, workers and artists. That it should have endured for so long and with such resilient vigour, despite the inevitable creative doldrums and financial catastrophes, is an astonishing feat of survival. The most accurate way of describing it would be to say that it is a miracle, were it not that such a concept is incompatible with at least two underlying Court traditions – the rational, sceptical verification of reality, and the rejection of magic and illusionism. But it is, nevertheless, near-miraculous that a theatre so often poised on the brink of disaster should outlive so many crises, so much competition, so many changes in fashion, so many apparently irrefutable explanations of why it is bound to die, and indeed *ought* to die; and that in this book we are not only celebrating its past but its *future*. There is, however, nothing supernatural about the Court's refusal to perish: the reason is, simply, that it still plays, uniquely well, a role that no other theatre can fill in quite the same way.

199

The difficulties of survival are manifestly even more acute in its 25th year. True, the Court's finances may *appear* to have improved immensely. In 1980 Arts Council grants and guarantees amounted to £385,000 compared with £8,000 in 1960. In 1980 the Greater London Council gave £17,000: no grant was made by its predecessors, the London County Council, until 1961/62. The maximum nightly take at the main theatre box office was £1,330 in 1980, compared with £340 in 1960. But in 1980 it cost an estimated £296,400 p.a. to run the building (compared with £86,450 in 1960), and between £15,000 and £24,000 to mount a production (compared with between £1,100 and £5,000 in 1960). Revenue from subsidies and seats has lagged far behind the inflationary increases in almost all the costs involved in keeping the Court alive as a home for new work. The scale of operations is far bigger now than in 1960, comprising, as it does, the Theatre Upstairs and the Young People's Theatre Scheme as well as the main theatre. Box office success is, of course, no more predictable than it was 20 years ago. No counterparts of Osborne have as yet emerged from whom the Court might optimistically expect a flow of supplementary revenue from film rights and so on. And the West End transfers on which the Court's survival has traditionally depended have become, inevitably, far less frequent, and far less dependably profitable, because of radical reductions in Shaftesbury Avenue margins for experiment.

With all its obvious merits, the Sloane Square building itself — whose lease expires in 1991 — has become dismayingly expensive to service and maintain. From the start of the ESC regime George Devine regarded it, in spite of his affection for the place, as too small and restricted, socially, economically and aesthetically, to be the ESC's only home. As we have seen, both he and Oscar Lewenstein aspired to rebuild it and link it to a bigger theatre. Among the writers, directors and actors who emerged in the late 1960's there was a growing demand — urgently expressed in the 1977 crisis — that the ESC should move to a much less costly, hierarchic centre (like a converted warehouse in Covent Garden). Many believed that, as Caryl Churchill put it, 'the work is more important than the place.' As they see it, far too big a proportion of the ESC's subsidies goes to the place instead of the work.

Yet it is surely premature to assume that the Royal Court must, necessarily, be abandoned by the ESC: the prime need is for an increase in subsidy, not a reduction in the size of its home and the scale of its operations. From the 1980 viewpoint, meanwhile, the place and its resources offer to writers, actors, directors and other theatre workers, in the words of the Willatt report, 'an independent full-scale theatre, both as a platform and a home,' with a studio stage, a young people's satellite – and a unique artistic tradition. The Royal Court remains a very special place, with a range of freedoms and opportunities, and a reputation for maintaining standards, that cannot be matched elsewhere.

True, there are worlds elsewhere that never existed in 1956, when the Court was virtually alone in the field as a writers' theatre. By 1980 there were scores of outlets for new talent of the kind for which the ESC may once have appeared to be the only possible platform. In London, apart from the five theatres of the National and Royal Shakespeare organizations, there are theatres in Greenwich, Shepherd's Bush, Hampstead, and Hammersmith, with several pub and studio stages. In the regions dozens of resident companies have been freed from the 1950's treadmill of weekly rep, many in new buildings with satellite studios. Scores of new plays are staged every year by alternative theatre companies, of which there are well over 100, half of them full-time. One might well think that the very success of the Court in its pioneering efforts to transform the theatre and the attitudes towards it of paymasters, patrons and potential customers has paralysed its progress, if not endangered its future. Yet, in fact, none of these apparent competitors – whatever their creativity and baits for authors and artists – can be said to have made the Royal Court and its policies redundant. Between the empires of the two national mammoths, the network of regional institutions and the trail of touring fringe teams, the English Stage Company provides a proper theatre – and one where, as Nigel Williams says here, improper theatre may still feel at home: a theatre which enjoys especial loyalties and unique advantages, in spite of its economic hazards.

As long as the need persists for an independent writers' theatre in the heart of London which links the majority and the minority stages, the classical tradition with contemporary experiment, the art theatre with community theatre, the world of show business with the world of young people's theatre; for a theatre which continues to unite the arts and crafts of the actor, designer, director and other theatre workers in the service of the writer, with the high standards of exact, concerned production that have won renown for the Court in the last 25 years; then the English Stage Company will persist – despite the mountainous difficulties ahead – in its traditional activity: doing the impossible.

Richard Findlater

Appendix I

This is a list of all dramatic productions presented by the English Stage Company at the Royal Court and elsewhere between April 1956 and November 1980. It does not include concerts, recitals, opera, ballet, music-hall, poetry readings or charity

	Date	Production	Author	Director	Design/Music
1956	2 April	**The Mulberry Bush**	**Angus Wilson**	George Devine	Motley
	9 April	**The Crucible**	**Arthur Miller**	George Devine	Stephen Doncaster Motley (costumes)
	8 May	**Look Back in Anger** (transf. Lyric Hammersmith 5.11.56)	**John Osborne**	Tony Richardson	Alan Tagg Thomas Eastwood (music)
	15 May	**Don Juan**	**Ronald Duncan**	George Devine	John Minton Richard Negri (costumes) Thomas Eastwood (music)
		The Death of Satan	**Ronald Duncan**	George Devine	John Minton Richard Negri (costumes) Thomas Eastwood (music)
	26 June	**Cards of Identity**	**Nigel Dennis**	Tony Richardson	Alan Tagg Motley (costumes) Thomas Eastwood (music)
	31 Oct	**The Good Woman of Setzuan**	**Bertolt Brecht** (transl. Eric Bentley)	George Devine	Teo Otto Paul Dessau (music)
	12 Dec	**The Country Wife** (transf. Adelphi 4.2.57)	**William Wycherley**	George Devine	Motley Thomas Eastwood (music)
1957	5 Feb	**The Member of the Wedding**	**Carson McCullers**	Tony Richardson	Alan Tagg Stephen Doncaster (costumes)
	11 March	**Look Back in Anger**	**John Osborne**	Tony Richardson	Alan Tagg
	3 April	**Fin de Partie**	**Samuel Beckett**	Roger Blin	Jacques Noel John Beckett (music)
		Acte Sans Paroles	**Samuel Beckett**	Deryk Mendel	Jacques Noel John Beckett (music)
	10 April	**The Entertainer** (transf. Palace 10.9.57)	**John Osborne**	Tony Richardson	Alan Tagg Clare Jeffery (costumes) John Addison (music)
	14 May	**The Apollo de Bellac**	**Jean Giraudoux** (transl. Ronald Duncan)	Tony Richardson	Carl Toms
		The Chairs	**Eugene Ionesco** (transl. Donald Watson)	Tony Richardson	Jocelyn Herbert John Addison (music)
	26 May	The Correspondence Course	Charles Robinson	Peter Coe	
	9 June	Yes – and After	Michael Hastings	John Dexter	
	25 June	**The Making of Moo**	**Nigel Dennis**	Tony Richardson	Audrey Cruddas
	22 July	**Purgatory** (Devon Festival)	**W. B. Yeats**	John Dexter	Jocelyn Herbert
	30 June	The Waiting of Lester Abbs	Kathleen Sully	Lindsay Anderson	
	5 Aug	**How Can We Save Father?**	**Oliver Marlow Wilkinson**	Peter Wood	Clare Jeffery
		The Chairs	**Eugene Ionesco** (transl. Donald Watson)	Tony Richardson	Jocelyn Herbert
	12 Aug	**Look Back in Anger**	**John Osborne**	Tony Richardson	Alan Tagg

performances. Performances in the main theatre are indicated in **bold** type, the Sunday night productions without decor in roman, and all productions in the Theatre Upstairs in *italic*.

Cast

Alan Bates, Stephen Dartnell, Nigel Davenport, Christopher Fettes, Gwen Ffrangcon-Davies, Kenneth Haigh, Helena Hughes, Rachel Kempson, Agnes Lauchlan, John Welsh

Alan Bates, Rosalie Crutchley, Stephen Dartnell, Nigel Davenport, George Devine, Christopher Fettes, Barbara Grimes, Michael Gwynn, Kenneth Haigh, Helena Hughes, Rachel Kempson, Agnes Lauchlan, Marcia Manolesceu, Joan Plowright, Josée Richard, George Selway, Connie Smith, Robert Stephens, Mary Ure, John Welsh

Alan Bates, Kenneth Haigh, Helena Hughes, Mary Ure, John Welsh

Rosalie Crutchley, Stephen Dartnell, Nigel Davenport, Christopher Fettes, Barbara Grimes, Agnes Lauchlan, Keith Michell, John Osborne, Joan Plowright, Josée Richard, George Selway, Geoffrey Sisley, Robert Stephens, John Welsh

Rosalie Crutchley, Stephen Dartnell, Nigel Davenport, Christopher Fettes, Michael Gwynn, Rachel Kempson, Keith Michell, John Osborne, Joan Plowright, George Selway, Robert Stephens, John Welsh

Sheila Ballantine, Alan Bates, Nigel Davenport, George Devine, Peter Duguid, Christopher Fettes, Joan Greenwood, Michael Gwynn, Kenneth Haigh, Colin Jeavons, Rachel Kempson, John Moffatt, John Osborne, Joan Plowright, George Selway, Robert Stephens, John Welsh

Peggy Ashcroft, Sheila Ballantine, Maurice Bennis, Margery Caldicott, Golda Casimir, Stephen Dartnell, Nigel Davenport, George Devine, Norman Foreman, Robert Gillespie, Frazer Hines, Colin Jeavons, Sean Kelly, Rachel Kempson, John Moffatt, Lilian Moubrey, Michael Murray, John Nettleton, John Osborne, Esmé Percy, Joan Plowright, Maureen Quinney, John Rae, Jill Showell, Robert Stephens, Peter Woodthorpe, Peter Wyngarde

Margaret Ashcroft, Sheila Ballantine, Alan Bates, Margery Caldicott, Diana Churchill, Stephen Dartnell, Nigel Davenport, George Devine, Moyra Fraser, Brian Hankins, Laurence Harvey, John Moffatt, Esmé Percy, Joan Plowright, Maureen Quinney, Robert Stephens

Ann Dickins, Vivienne Drummond, James Dyrenforth, John Hall, Neville Jacobsen, Errol John, Geraldine McEwan, Orlando Martins, Garry Nesbitt, Dudy Nimmo, Richard Pasco, Bertice Reading, Anthony Richmond, Connie Smith, Greta Watson, Susan Westerby

Alan Bates, Vivienne Drummond, Richard Pasco, Heather Sears, Deering Wells

Georges Adet, Roger Blin, Jean Martin, Christine Tsingos

Deryk Mendel

Brenda de Banzie, Aubrey Dexter, Vivienne Drummond, Stanley Meadows, Laurence Olivier, Richard Pasco, George Relph, Valentina Richmond, Dorothy Tutin

Margaret Ashcroft, Alan Bates, Anthony Creighton, Stephen Dartnell, Vivienne Drummond, John Moffatt, John Osborne, Richard Pasco, Esmé Percy, Heather Sears, Robert Stephens

George Devine, Richard Pasco, Joan Plowright

Carmen Blanch-Sickel, Sylvia Herklots, John Herrington, Tony Hill, David Jackson, Richard Rudd

Alan Bates, Anthony Carrick, Jimmy Carroll, Olivia Irving, Patricia Lawrence, Graham Pyle, Heather Sears, Robert Stephens

Nicholas Brady, Anthony Creighton, Stephen Dartnell, George Devine, Martin Miller, John Moffatt, John Osborne, Joan Plowright, Robert Stephens, James Villiers, John Wood

cast list not available

Ian Bannen, James Beatty, Geoffrey Bellman, Peter Bennett, Gerald Blake, Amos Brandstatter, Alfred Burke, Fanny Carby, Angela Crowe, John Dexter, Michael Hastings, Barbara Hicks, Robert Hollyman, Mary Manson, Alun Owen, Brigid Panet, Claire Pollock, Alistair Speed, Gladys Spencer, Anna Steele, Robert Stephens, Catherine Wilmer, Michael Wynne

Margaret Ashcroft, Jacqueline Forster, Mary Manson, John Moffatt, Richard Pasco, John Phillips, Maureen Quinney, Susan Richmond, Robert Stephens
as 14 May

Alan Bates, Vivienne Drummond, Richard Pasco, Deering Wells, Wendy Williams

Date	Production	Author	Director	Design/Music
17 Sept	**Nekrassov**	**Jean-Paul Sartre** (transl. Sylvia & George Leeson)	George Devine	Richard Negri Thomas Eastwood (music)
20 Oct	The Waters of Babylon	John Arden	Graham Evans	
28 Oct	**Look Back in Anger**	**John Osborne**	John Dexter	Alan Tagg
26 Nov	**Requiem for a Nun**	**William Faulkner**	Tony Richardson	Motley
1 Dec	A Resounding Tinkle	N. F. Simpson	William Gaskill	
26 Dec	**Lysistrata** (transf. Duke of York's 18.2.58)	**Aristophanes** (version Dudley Fitts)	Minos Volanakis	Nicholas Georgiadis Thomas Eastwood (music)

1958

Date	Production	Author	Director	Design/Music
11 Feb	**Epitaph for George Dillon** (transf. Comedy 29.5.58 as George Dillon)	**John Osborne &** **Anthony Creighton**	William Gaskill	Stephen Doncaster
16 Feb	Love from Margaret	Evelyn Ford	John Wood	
25 Feb	**The Sport of My Mad Mother**	**Ann Jellicoe**	George Devine & Ann Jellicoe	Jocelyn Herbert
9 March	The Tenth Chance	Stuart Holroyd	Anthony Creighton	
23 March	Each His Own Wilderness	Doris Lessing	John Dexter	
25 March	**The Catalyst** (at the Arts Theatre Club)	**Ronald Duncan**	Phil Brown	Stephen Doncaster
2 April	**A Resounding Tinkle**	**N. F. Simpson**	William Gaskill	Tazeena Firth Stephen Doncaster (costumes)
	The Hole	**N. F. Simpson**	William Gaskill	Stanley Rixon Stephen Doncaster (costumes)
21 May	**Flesh to a Tiger**	**Barry Reckord**	Tony Richardson	Loudon Sainthill Geoffrey Wright (music)
18 June	**The Lesson**	**Eugene Ionesco** (transl. Donald Watson)	Tony Richardson	Jocelyn Herbert
	The Chairs	**Eugene Ionesco** (transl. Donald Watson)	Tony Richardson	Jocelyn Herbert
22 June	Brixham Regatta For Children (at the Aldeburgh Festival)	Keith Johnstone Keith Johnstone	William Gaskill Ann Jellicoe	
7 July	**Gay Landscape** (Glasgow Citizens)	**George Munro**	Peter Duguid	David Jones
14 July	**Chicken Soup With Barley** (Belgrade Coventry)	**Arnold Wesker**	John Dexter	Michael Richardson
21 July	**The Private Prosecutor** (Salisbury Arts Theatre)	**Thomas Wiseman**	Derek Benfield	Jean Adams
28 July	**Dear Augustine** (Leatherhead Repertory)	**Alison Macleod**	Jordan Lawrence	Gillian Armitage
4 Aug	**The Lesson** **The Chairs**	**Eugene Ionesco** **Eugene Ionesco**	Tony Richardson Tony Richardson	Jocelyn Herbert Jocelyn Herbert
28 Aug	**Major Barbara**	**Bernard Shaw**	George Devine	Motley
14 Sept	Lady on the Barometer	Donald Howarth	Miriam Brickman & Donald Howarth	

Cast

Robert Aldous, Ronald Barker, George Benson, Nicholas Brady, Margery Caldicott, Percy Cartwright, Harry H. Corbett, Anthony Creighton, Margo Cunningham, Ann Davies, Jane Downs, Felix Felton, Robert Helpmann, Kerry Jordan, Bernard Kay, Roddy McMillan, George Merritt, Martin Miller, Kendrick Owen, Milo Sperber, Anna Steele, James Villiers, John Wood

Margaret Ashcroft, Donald Bradley, Peter Collingwood, Margaret Diamond, John Flexman, Kerry Jordan, Gertan Klauber, Phyllida Law, Lucille Mapp, Mark Shurland, Robert Stephens, George Tovey

Clare Austin, Willoughby Gray, Alec McCowen, Gary Raymond, Anna Steele

Mark Baker, John Crawford, Ruth Ford, David Gardner, John McCarthy, Bertice Reading, Zachary Scott

Patrick Barton, Fanny Carby, Wendy Craig, Graham Crowden, Nigel Davenport, Leslie Glazer, Marigold Sharman, Toke Townley, Rita Webb, John Wood

Margaret Ashcroft, Ronald Barker, George Benson, Patricia Burke, Isla Cameron, Robert Cartland, John Church, Margo Cunningham, Tessa Davies, James Donnelly, Joan Greenwood, James Grout, Alexander Harris, Maxine Holden, Phyllida Law, Neil McCarthy, John McDonald, Patricia Marmont, Ruth Morrison, Gillian Neason, Natasha Parry, Gary Raymond, David Ritch, Laura Sarti, Clare Walmsley

Paul Bailey, Wendy Craig, Nigel Davenport, Avril Elgar, Alison Leggatt, Philip Locke, Yvonne Mitchell, Robert Stephens, Toke Townley

Phyllis Calvert, Miranda Connell, Margaret Halstan, John Richmond, Gordon Whiting

Paul Bailey, Sheila Ballantine, Wendy Craig, Avril Elgar, Philip Locke, Jerry Stovin, Anthony Valentine

Nicholas Brady, David Butler, Donald Conlon, June Dawes, Ronald Fraser, John Gordon, Michael Hawkins, Bernard Kay, Patrick Newall, Henry Rayner, James Villiers

Philip Bond, Patricia Burke, Colin Jeavons, Ewen MacDuff, Sarah Preston, Vernon Smythe, Valerie Taylor

Renée Asherson, Phil Brown, Virginia Maskell

Sheila Ballantine, Wendy Craig, Nigel Davenport

Sheila Ballantine, Nigel Davenport, Avril Elgar, Philip Locke, Robert Stephens, Toke Townley

Tamba Allen, Ena Babb, Dorothy Blondel-Francis, Berril Briggs, Nadia Cattouse, James Clarke, Franciska Francis, Lloyd Innis, Cleo Laine, Edmundo Otero, Pearl Prescod, Lloyd Reckord, Maureen Seale, Johnny Sekka, Connie Smith, Edgar Wreford

Phyllis Morris, Joan Plowright, Edgar Wreford

George Devine, Jeremy Kemp, Joan Plowright

David Andrews, David Barron, Jerome Brehony, Dudley Foster, Tamara Hinchco, Jocelyne Page
Keith Crane, Geraldine Neyle

Annette Crosbie, Iain Cuthbertson, John Grieve, Edith Macarthur, Fulton Mackay, Colette O'Neil, Hilary Paterson, Irene Sunters, Harry Walker, Frank Wylie

Richard Briers, Patsy Byrne, Charmian Eyre, Frank Finlay, Alfred Lynch, Henry Manning, Richard Martin, Cherry Morris, Anthony Valentine, Jacqueline Wilson

Michael Atkinson, Nancie Herrod, Geoffrey Lumsden, Ronald Magill, Ian Mullins, Diana Scougall

Edmund Bailey, Terence Bayler, Anne Blake, Bernard Brown, Raymond Cooke, George Cooper, George Cormack, Gareth Davies, Sonia Graham, Maurice Hedley, Kerry Jordan, Derek Martinus, Kevin Miles, Basil Moss, Christine Pollon, Jocelyn Tawse, Frank Topping

as 18 June
as 18 June but with David Buck instead of Jeremy Kemp

Hilda Barry, Peter Birrel, Simon Carter, Paul Daneman, Alan Dobie, Robert Gillespie, Jacqueline Hussey, Lala Lloyd, Philip Locke, Alfred Lynch, Joan Plowright, Vanessa Redgrave, Frances Rowe, Toke Townley, Alan Webb

Ronald Barker, Hilda Barry, Anne Bishop, John Gatrill, Patricia Jessel, Alfred Lynch, Eric Thompson, Jeanne Watts. Keef West, Meurig Wyn-Jones

Date	Production	Author	Director	Design/Music
30 Sept	**Live Like Pigs**	**John Arden**	George Devine & Anthony Page	Alan Tagg A. L. Lloyd (music)
19 Oct	Actors' Workshop			
	Redbrick	Gillian Richards	Miriam Brickman	
	The Tent	John McGrath	Anthony Page	
	The Lodger	Frank Hatt	Anthony Page	
	Top Deck	John Arden	Anthony Page	
	The Signature in the Corner	Frank Hatt	Anthony Page	
	The Nigger Hunt	Keith Johnstone	Ann Jellicoe	
28 Oct	**Krapp's Last Tape**	**Samuel Beckett**	Donald McWhinnie & George Devine	Jocelyn Herbert
	Endgame	**Samuel Beckett**	Donald McWhinnie & George Devine	Jocelyn Herbert
30 Nov	More Like Strangers	George Hulme	Phil Brown	
4 Dec	**Moon on a Rainbow Shawl**	**Errol John**	Frith Banbury	Loudon Sainthill
1959 7 Jan	**The Long and the Short and the Tall** (transf. New 8.4.59)	**Willis Hall**	Lindsay Anderson	Alan Tagg
8 Feb	Progress to the Park	Alun Owen	Lindsay Anderson	The Temperance Seven (music)
15 March	A Resounding Tinkle (Cambridge ADC)	N. F. Simpson	John Bird	John Bird
9 April	**Sugar in the Morning** (Produced as Lady on the Barometer 14.9.58)	**Donald Howarth**	William Gaskill	Sean Kenny
19 April	Leonce and Lena	Georg Büchner	Michael Geliot	
26 April	The Trial of Cob and Leach	Christopher Logue	Lindsay Anderson	
	Jazzetry	Christopher Logue	Lindsay Anderson	Tony Kinsey & Bill Le Sage (music)
14 May	**Orpheus Descending**	**Tennessee Williams**	Tony Richardson	Loudon Sainthill
17 May	The Shameless Professor	Luigi Pirandello	Victor Rietti	
30 June	**Roots** (Belgrade Coventry, transf. Duke of York's 30.7.59)	**Arnold Wesker**	John Dexter	Jocelyn Herbert
19 July	Eleven Men Dead at Hola Camp	Keith Johnstone & William Gaskill	Keith Johnstone & William Gaskill	
29 July	**Look After Lulu** (transf. New 8.9.59)	**Noël Coward** (based on Georges Feydeau)	Tony Richardson	Roger Furse
6 Sept	The Kitchen	Arnold Wesker	John Dexter	Jocelyn Herbert
17 Sept	**Cock-a-Doodle Dandy**	**Sean O'Casey**	George Devine	Sean Kenny Geoffrey Wright (music)
22 Oct	**Serjeant Musgrave's Dance**	**John Arden**	Lindsay Anderson	Jocelyn Herbert Dudley Moore (music)
1 Nov	The Invention	Wole Soyinka	Wole Soyinka	

Cast

Anne Blake, Madge Brindley, Peggyann Clifford, Frances Cuka, Margaretta D'Arcy, Nigel Davenport, Alan Dobie, Daphne Foreman, Jacqueline Hussey, Stratford Johns, Wilfrid Lawson, Alfred Lynch, Anna Manahan, Robert Shaw

David Buck, Tamara Hinchco
David Andrews, David Buck
Peter Birrel, Margaretta D'Arcy, Johnny Sekka
Margaretta D'Arcy, Johnny Sekka
David Andrews, Peter Birrel, Tamara Hinchco, Johnny Sekka
David Andrews, Tamara Hinchco, Johnny Sekka

Patrick Magee

Frances Cuka, George Devine, Richard Goolden, Jack MacGowran

John Bay, Leo Ciceri, Gerry Jones, Roray MacDermott, Vivian Matalon, Kerrigan Prescott, Deirdre White, Valerie White, Pauline Yates

Barbara Assoon, John Bouie, Berril Briggs, Leo Carrera, Vinette Carroll, Jacqueline Chan, Leonard Davies, Earle Hyman, Robert Jackson, Clifton Jones, Lionel Ngakane, Soraya Rafat, Johnny Sekka

David Andrews, Ronald Fraser, Edward Judd, Alfred Lynch, Bryan Pringle, Peter O'Toole, Robert Shaw, Kenji Takaki

Tom Bell, Fanny Carby, Harry H. Corbett, Donal Donnelly, Bee Duffell, Gerard Dynevor, Donald Howarth, Joyce Latham, Margaret Tyzack

Penny Balchin, Timothy Birdsall, Eleanor Bron, Catharine Buckley, Peter Cook, James Cornford, Jill Daltry, Peter Forster, David Johnson, Geoff Pattie, Joyce Quinney, Freda Stratton, John Tydeman, Bill Wallis

Irvin Allen, Hilda Barry, Anne Bishop, Frank Finlay, John Fraser, Margaret Johnston, Ray Smith, Toke Townley, Jeanne Watts, Peter Wood

Laurence Asprey, Michael Davies, Bill Wallis

Zoe Caldwell, Peter Duguid, Murray Evans, Peter Fraser, Laurence Harrington, Peter Holmes, Hazel Hughes, Trevor Martin, Dickie Owen, Morris Perry, George Rose, Tony Selby, Mary Ure

Lindsay Anderson, Peter Collingwood, Charles Fox, Barbara Hicks, Christopher Logue, John Malcolm, Peter O'Toole, Shani Wallis

David Airey, Diana Beaumont, Maria Britneva, Robert Cawdron, Diane Cilento, Gary Cockrell, Bee Duffell, May Hallatt, John Harrison, Fred Johnson, Bessie Love, Isa Miranda, Ivor Salter, Michael Seaver, Richard Wilding

Antonietta Arden, Hilary Bamberger, David Campton, Dora Cooper, Gwen Lewis, David Lyn, Maureen O'Moor, Robert Rietti, Victor Rietti, Arnold Ridley

Patsy Byrne, Alan Howard, Charles Kay, Richard Martin, Gwen Nelson, Patrick O'Connell, Brenda Peters, Joan Plowright, Jack Rodney

Harry Baird, Ray Barnett, Aleksander Browne, Jan Carew, Andre Dakar, Nigel Davenport, Astley Harvey, Stanley Jack, Bloke Modisane, Neville Munro, Johnny Sekka, Wole Soyinka

Max Adrian, Michael Bates, Anne Bishop, Cecil Brock, Shirley Cameron, Fanny Carby, Lawrence Davidson, Meriel Forbes, John Gatrell, Richard Goolden, Barbara Hicks, Sean Kelly, Vivien Leigh, Elaine Millar, Anthony Quayle, David Ryder, Peter Stephens, Robert Stephens, Jeanne Watts, Peter Wyatt, Arnold Yarrow

Kenneth Adams, Tarn Bassett, Anne Bishop, James Bolam, John Briggs, Cecil Brock, Patsy Byrne, Anthony Carrick, James Culliford, Tenniel Evans, Peter Gill, Ida Goldapple, Alan Howard, Charles Kay, Ann King, Alfred Lynch, Gwen Nelson, Mary Miller, Sandra Miller, Patrick O'Connell, Brenda Peters, Jack Rodney, David Ryder, Christopher Sandford, Jennifer Wallace, Jeanne Watts

Robert Arnold, Colin Blakely, Stephen Dartnell, J. G. Devlin, Pauline Flanagan, Alex Farrell, Jeanne Hepple, Eamon Keane, Bill Keating, Wilfrid Lawson, Patrick Magee, Etain O'Dell, Joan O'Hara, Berto Pasuka, Charles Wade

Robert Aldous, Ian Bannen, Colin Blakely, James Bree, Patsy Byrne, Richard Caldicott, Harry Gwynn Davies, Shirley Dixon, Alan Dobie, Donal Donnelly, Frank Finlay, Clinton Greyn, Michael Hunt, Freda Jackson, Stratford Johns, Jack Smethurst, Barry Wilsher

Colin Blakely, Aleksander Browne, Graham Crowden, Ursula Franklin, Roy Hepworth, Barbara Hicks, Michael Hunt, Jeremy Longhurst, Bryan Pringle, David Ryder, Olu Sowande, Jeanne Watts, Barry Wilsher, Peter Wyatt

	Date	Production	Author	Director	Design/Music
	18 Nov	**Rosmersholm** (transf. Comedy 5.1.60)	**Henrik Ibsen** (transl. Ann Jellicoe)	George Devine	Motley
	22 Nov	The Naming of Murderer's Rock	Frederick Bland	John Bird	
	22 Dec	**One Way Pendulum** (transf. Criterion 23.2.60)	**N. F. Simpson**	William Gaskill	Stephen Doncaster Dudley Moore (music)
1960	24 Jan	Christopher Sly	Opera: Thomas Eastwood Libretto: Ronald Duncan	Colin Graham	
	27 Jan	**The Lily White Boys**	**Harry Cookson &** **Christopher Logue** (Lyrics)	Lindsay Anderson	Sean Kenny Tony Kinsey & Bill Le Sage (music)
	8 March	**The Dumb Waiter** **The Room**	**Harold Pinter** **Harold Pinter**	James Roose Evans Anthony Page	Michael Young Michael Young
	20 March	One Leg Over the Wrong Wall	Albert Bermel	John Blatchley	Thea Musgrave (music)
	30 March	**The Naming of Murderer's** **Rock**	**Frederick Bland**	John Bird	Motley
	10 April	Eleven Plus	Kon Fraser	Keith Johnstone	Marc Wilkinson (music)
	28 April	**Rhinoceros** (transf. Strand 8.6.60)	**Eugene Ionesco** (transl. Derek Prouse)	Orson Welles	Orson Welles Stuart Stallard (costumes)
	1 May	The Sport of My Mad Mother (Bristol Old Vic Theatre School)	Ann Jellicoe	Jane Howell	Kenneth Jones
	7 June	**Chicken Soup With Barley**	**Arnold Wesker**	John Dexter	Jocelyn Herbert
	28 June	**Roots**	**Arnold Wesker**	John Dexter	Jocelyn Herbert
	10 July	Sea at Dauphin (New Way Theatre Co)	Derek Walcott	Lloyd Reckord	Colin Garland
		Six in the Rain (New Way Theatre Co)	Derek Walcott	Lloyd Reckord	Colin Garland
	27 July	**I'm Talking About Jerusalem**	**Arnold Wesker**	John Dexter	Jocelyn Herbert
	7 Aug	The Keep	Gwyn Thomas	Graham Crowden	
	11 Sept	**The Happy Haven**	**John Arden**	William Gaskill	Michael Ackland Dudley Moore (music)
	13 Oct	**Platonov**	**Anton Chekhov** (Eng. version Dimitri Makaroff)	George Devine & John Blatchley	Richard Negri Dudley Moore (music)
	23 Oct	You in Your Small Corner (Cheltenham Theatre Co)	Barry Reckord	John Bird	Motley
	23 Nov	**Trials by Logue** **Antigone**	**Christopher Logue**	Lindsay Anderson	Jocelyn Herbert Bill Le Sage (music)
		Cob and Leach	**Christopher Logue**	Lindsay Anderson	Jocelyn Herbert Bill Le Sage (music)
	27 Nov	The Maimed	Bartho Smit	Keith Johnstone	
	11 Dec	On the Wall	Henry Chapman	Peter Duguid	Barbara Chapman (music)
	29 Dec	**The Lion in Love**	**Shelagh Delaney**	Clive Barker	Una Collins
1961	21 Feb	**The Changeling**	**Thomas Middleton &** **William Rowley**	Tony Richardson	Jocelyn Herbert David Walker (costumes) Raymond Leppard (music)

Cast

Peggy Ashcroft, John Blatchley, Mark Dignam, Bee Duffell, Patrick Magee, Eric Porter

Colin Blakely, Robin Chapman, Tony Church, Andrew Downie, Mark Eden, Dione Ewin, Terence Greenidge, Kenneth Mackintosh, Ruth Meyers, Anthony Page, Richard Pescud, Bryan Pringle, Jeanne Watts, Arnold Yarrow

Graham Armitage, George Benson, Patsy Byrne, Graham Crowden, Alan Gibson, John Horsley, Alison Leggatt, Robert Levis, Douglas Livingstone, Jeremy Longhurst, Roddy Maude-Roxby, Gwen Nelson, Patsy Rowlands, Douglas Wilmer

April Cantelo, Jacqueline Delman, John Kentish, Kevin Miller, Julian Moyle, Forbes Robinson, Joseph Ward

Georgia Brown, Shirley Ann Field, Albert Finney, Willoughby Goddard, James Grout, Geoffrey Hibbert, Barbara Hicks, Monty Landis, Philip Locke, Ann Lynn, Ronnie Stevens

Nicholas Selby, George Tovey
Thomas Baptiste, Anne Bishop, Michael Brennan, Michael Caine, John Cater, Vivien Merchant

Edward Bond, Christopher Burgess, Graham Crowden, Lorne Cosette, Nigel Davenport, Alan Dobie, Murray Gilmore, Stuart Hutchinson, Roger Kemp, Robert Lewis, Stephen Moore, Oliver Neville, Morris Perry, Edward Petherbridge, Jeffrey Segal, Tobi Weinberg, Margaret Worsley

Christopher Banks, Colin Blakely, Raf de la Torre, Dione Ewin, Edwin Finn, Wilfrid Grantham, Michael Hunt, Rob Inglis, Mary Jones, Kenneth Mackintosh, Nicholas Meredith, Ruth Meyers, Ralph Nossek, Richard Pescud, Stanley Price, John Rae, Hamish Roughead, Nicholas Selby, Roy Spencer, Arnold Yarrow

Barbara Bolton, Edwin Finn, Sheila Gill, Brian Gilmer, Wilfrid Grantham, Leonard Kingston, David Lander, Douglas Livingstone, Richard Martin, Viera Shelley, Mimi Whitford, Marie Wreford

Michael Bates, Geoffrey Dunn, Gladys Henson, Hazel Hughes, Duncan Macrae, Miles Malleson, Laurence Olivier, Joan Plowright, Peter Sallis, Alan Webb, Henry Woolf

Julia Blake, Grant Cowan, Graham D'Albert, Christopher Dunham, Ann Richards, Althea Stewart, Joachim Tillinger

Patsy Byrne, Mark Eden, Frank Finlay, Alan Howard, Charles Kay, Ruth Meyers, Kathleen Michael, Cherry Morris, David Saire

Patsy Byrne, John Colin, Frank Finlay, Anthony Hall, Alan Howard, Charles Kay, Cherry Morris, Joan Plowright

Leo Carrera, Olive Douglas, Mike Gambon, Mike Goddard, Clarina Harris, Mark Heath, Dudley Hunte, Jean Martin, Lionel Ngakane, Kathleen Roach, Carla Shackell, Jessie Stephens, Gordon Woolford

Barbara Assoon, Allister Bain, Jeffrey Biddeau, Leo Carrera, Mike Goddard, Mark Heath, Jeff Henry, Jean Martin, Lionel Ngakane, Lloyd Reckord, Keef West, Gordon Woolford

Mark Eden, Frank Finlay, Alan Howard, Charles Kay, Ruth Meyers, Kathleen Michael, Cherry Morris, Terry Palmer, Michael Phillips, Jessie Robins

Richard Davies, Jessie Evans, Denys Graham, Glyn Houston, Dudley Jones, Emrys Leyshon, Lane Meddick, Ken Wynne

James Bolam, Peter Bowles, Susan Engel, Frank Finlay, Edward Fox, Barrie Ingham, Rosalind Knight, Rachel Roberts, Nicholas Selby, Mary Watson

Ronald Barker, James Bolam, Peter Bowles, Graham Crowden, Peter Duguid, Susan Engel, Frank Finlay, Jeremy Geidt, Murray Gilmore, Elvi Hale, Thomas Hammerton, Rex Harrison, Rosalind Knight, George Murcell, Morris Perry, Norman Pitt, Rachel Roberts, Nicholas Selby, Mary Watson, Susan Westerby

Jeanne Hepple, Rachel Herbert, Allan Mitchell, Pearl Nunez, Lloyd Reckord, Margery Withers, Gordon Woolford

Zoe Caldwell, Peter Duguid, Murray Evans, Peter Fraser, Laurence Harrington, Peter Holmes, Trevor Martin, Dickie Owen, Morris Perry, George Rose, Tony Selby, Mary Ure

Zoe Caldwell, Peter Duguid, Murray Evans, Peter Fraser, Hazel Hughes, Trevor Martin, Dickie Owen, Morris Perry, George Rose, Tony Selby, Mary Ure

Nadia Cattouse, Edward Dentith, Tommy Eytle, Suzanne Fuller, Trevor Martin, Brian Phelan, Wensley Pithey

Donal Donnelly, Murray Evans, Gordon Gostelow, Peter Holmes, Bernard Kay, Morris Perry, Bryan Pringle, Norman Rossington, Hamish Roughead, Bernard Stone

Juliet Alliston, Anthony Beeston, Patricia Burke, Kenneth Cope, Diana Coupland, Brian Croft, Maureen Dormer, Peter Fraser, Howard Goorney, Patricia Healey, Jeanette Hider, Renny Lister, Margery Mason, Dermot McDowell, Garfield Morgan

John Blatchley, Jeremy Brett, Zoe Caldwell, Robin Chapman, Annette Crosbie, Roland Curram, Peter Duguid, Derek Fuke, Alan Howard, Charles Kay, Basil Moss, Derek Newark, Morris Perry, Robin Ray, Norman Rossington, Robert Shaw, Mary Ure, David William

Date	Production	Author	Director	Design/Music
22 March	**Jacques**	**Eugene Ionesco** (transl. Donald Watson)	R. D. Smith	Michael Young
19 April	**Altona** (transf. Saville 5.6.61)	**Jean-Paul Sartre** (adapt. Justin O'Brien)	John Berry	Sean Kenny
7 May	The Departures	Jacques Languirand (transl. Albert Bermel)	John Blatchley	
28 May	The Triple Alliance	J. A. Cuddon	Keith Johnstone	
30 May	**The Blacks**	**Jean Genet** (transl. Bernard Frechtman)	Roger Blin	André Acquart Patrick Cowen (music)
18 June	Empress With Teapot	R. B. Whiting	Nicholas Garland	
27 June	**The Kitchen**	**Arnold Wesker**	John Dexter	Jocelyn Herbert
27 July	**Luther** (transf. Phoenix 5.9.61)	**John Osborne**	Tony Richardson	Jocelyn Herbert John Addison (music)
13 Aug	Humphrey, Armand and the Artichoke	G. Roy Levin	Piers Haggard	
21 Aug	**The Kitchen**	**Arnold Wesker**	John Dexter	Jocelyn Herbert
12 Sept	**August for the People**	**Nigel Dennis**	George Devine	Stephen Doncaster
25 Sept	**The Kitchen**	**Arnold Wesker**	John Dexter	Jocelyn Herbert
24 Oct	**The Death of Bessie Smith** **The American Dream**	**Edward Albee** **Edward Albee**	Peter Yates Peter Yates	Alan Tagg Alan Tagg
13 Nov	**That's Us** (Cambridge Arts)	**Henry Chapman**	William Gaskill	Stephen Doncaster Barbara Chapman (music)
22 Nov	**The Keep**	**Gwyn Thomas**	John Dexter	Ken Calder Dudley Moore (music)
26 Nov	Orison	Fernando Arrabal (transl. Barbara Wright)	Nicholas Garland	
	Fando and Lis	Fernando Arrabal (transl. Barbara Wright)	Nicholas Garland	
3 Dec	The Scarecrow	Derek Marlowe	Corin Redgrave	
21 Dec	**Box and Cox**	**John Maddison Morton**	Lindsay Anderson	Alan Tagg Dudley Moore (music)
	The Fire Raisers	**Max Frisch** (transl. Michael Bullock)	Lindsay Anderson	Alan Tagg Dudley Moore (music)
1962 24 Jan	**A Midsummer Night's Dream**	**Shakespeare**	Tony Richardson	Jocelyn Herbert John Addison (music)
28 Jan	Sacred Cow	Kon Fraser	Keith Johnstone	
18 Feb	Twelfth Night	Shakespeare	George Devine	Anne Lockwood (music)
20 Feb	**The Keep** (transf. Piccadilly 27.3.62)	**Gwyn Thomas**	John Dexter	Ken Calder
27 March	**The Knack**	**Ann Jellicoe**	Ann Jellicoe & Keith Johnstone	Alan Tagg

Cast

Madge Brindley, Zoe Caldwell, Peter Duguid, Valerie Hanson, Denys Hawthorne, Mollie Maureen, George Merritt, John Moffatt, Selma Vaz Dias

Claire Bloom, Richard Butler, Diane Cilento, Julian Glover, Kenneth Haigh, Derek Newark, Nigel Stock, Basil Sydney

Sheila Ballantine, Catherine Clouzot, Diana Fairfax, Derek Godfrey, Roger Kemp, Jerome Willis

Caroline Blakiston, Richard Butler, Edwin Finn, Robert Gillespie, Grahame McPherson, Derek Newark, Derek Smith, Anna Wing

Harry Baird, Brunetta Bernstein, Vida Deghanar, Rodney Douglas, Joan Hooley, Joseph Layode, Bloke Modisane, Neville Monroe, Felicia Okoli, Rashidi Onikoyi, Lloyd Reckord, Neville Russell, Yolande

Jean Conroy, Derek Fowlds, Gerald James, Gerry Jones, Pamela Lane, Bloke Modisane, Nan Munro, Sebastian Shaw

Dimitri Andreas, Tarn Bassett, Alison Bayley, Martin Boddey, Andre Bolton, Shirley Cameron, Sandra Caron, Gladys Dawson, Tommy Eytle, Ida Goldapple, Reginald Green, Harry Landis, Andreas Lysandrou, Andreas Markos, Marcos Markou, Jane Morrow, Patrick O'Connell, Wolf Parr, Ken Parry, Mary Peach, Brian Phelan, Jessie Robins, Charlotte Selwyn, Robert Stephens, Rita Tushingham, Jeanne Watts, Arnold Yarrow

Peter Bull, James Cairncross, Stacey Davies, George Devine, Peter Duguid, Murray Evans, Albert Finney, Derek Fuke, Julian Glover, Meryl Gourley, Charles Kay, John Moffatt, Dan Meaden, Bill Owen, Malcolm Taylor

John Carney, Carolyn Gaye, Topsy Jane, Tucker McGuire, Ralph Nossek, Robert Nichols, Willie Payne, Bryan Stanyon

Dimitri Andreas, Mai Bacon, Tarn Bassett, Alison Bayley, Steven Berkoff, Jeremy Brett, Shirley Cameron, Sandra Caron, Gladys Dawson, Rodney Douglas, Ida Goldapple, Reginald Green, Glenda Jackson, Panayiotis Jacovou, Harry Landis, Andreas Lysandrou, Michael McKevitt, Andreas Markos, Jane Morrow, Patrick O'Connell, Wolf Parr, Ken Parry, Charlotte Selwyn, Martin Sterndale, Rita Tushingham, Jeanne Watts, Arnold Yarrow

Yemi Ajibade, Elizabeth Bell, George Benson, Terence Brook, Edric Connor, Douglas Ditta, Laura Graham, Rex Harrison, Caroline John, John Junkin, William Kendall, Kate Lansbury, Hugh Latimer, Constance Lorne, Kenneth McClellan, Arthur Mullard, Pauline Munro, Gwen Nelson, Paulette Preney, Priou Pritt, Cyril Raymond, Rachel Roberts, Donald Sutherland

as 21 Aug

Gene Anderson, Robert Ayres, Richard Easton, Tommy Eytle, Alexis Kanner, Neville Monroe, Mavis Villiers, Jeanne Watts, Robert Ayres, Avril Elgar, Alexis Kanner, Mavis Villiers, Jeanne Watts

Edwin Finn, Edward Fox, Douglas Ditta, James MacLoughlin, Trevor Martin, Ronald Pember, Nicholas Selby, Pauline Taylor, Nicol Williamson, Arnold Yarrow

Windsor Davies, Jessie Evans, David Garfield, Denys Graham, Mervyn Johns, Dudley Jones, Glyn Owen, Aubrey Richards, Graham Suter

Jacqueline Ellis, Daniel Moynihan

Graham Crowden, Stanley Daniels, Jacqueline Ellis, Daniel Moynihan, Geoffrey Wright

Eileen Atkins, Keith Barron, Jonathan Burn, Patrick Duggan, Eric Elliot, Derek Fuke, Colin Jeavons, Julian Glover, Mary Jones, John Levitt, Derek Marlowe, Mollie Maureen, Mandy Miller, Dudy Nimmo, Roy Patrick, Morgan Sheppard, Malcolm Taylor, Danvers Walker

Colin Blakely, James Booth, Doris Hare

Ann Beach, Colin Blakely, James Booth, Trevor Danby, Doris Hare, Norman Henry, David Jackson, Roger Kemp, Alfred Marks, Dickie Owen, Gordon Rollings, John Thaw, Catherine Wilmer, Henry Woolf

Ronnie Barker, Yolande Bavan, Colin Blakely, James Bolam, Carol Dilworth, Samantha Eggar, Pauline Foreman, Peter Froggatt, Stuart Harris, Gillian Hoyle, Colin Jeavons, Robert Lang, Alfred Lynch, Kenneth McReddie, Morris Perry, Corin Redgrave, Lynn Redgrave, Lesley Scoble, Teresa Scoble, Rita Tushingham, David Warner, Nicol Williamson

Charles Conabere, Susan Engel, Peter Madden, Mollie Maureen, Jessie Robins, Jeremy Young

Lorna Cosette, Samantha Eggar, Albert Finney, Derek Fuke, Julian Glover, Stuart Harris, Charles Kay, Robert Lang, Dan Meaden, Morris Perry, Corin Redgrave, Lynn Redgrave, Jane Storm, Rita Tushingham, David Warner, Nicol Williamson

Windsor Davies, Jessie Evans, Tenniel Evans, Denys Graham, David Garfield, Mervyn Johns, Dudley Jones, Glyn Owen, Aubrey Richards, Graham Suter

James Bolam, Julian Glover, Philip Locke, Rita Tushingham

Date	Production	Author	Director	Design/Music
27 April	**Chips With Everything** (transf. Vaudeville 13.6.62)	**Arnold Wesker**	John Dexter	Jocelyn Herbert Colin Farrell (music)
13 June	**Period of Adjustment** (transf. Wyndham's 10.7.62)	**Tennessee Williams**	Roger Graef	Seamus Flannery
1 July	The Captain's Hero	Claus Hubalek (transl. Derek Goldby)	Derek Goldby	
19 July	**Plays for England** **The Blood of the Bambergs**	**John Osborne**	John Dexter	Alan Tagg John Addison (music)
	Under Plain Cover	**John Osborne**	Jonathan Miller	Alan Tagg John Addison (music)
11 Sept	**Brecht on Brecht**	**George Tabori** (arranger)	John Bird	Kurt Weill, Hans Eisler, Paul Dessau and Bertolt Brecht (music)
16 Sept	Day of the Prince	Frank Hilton	Keith Johnstone	
1 Nov	**Happy Days**	**Samuel Beckett**	George Devine	Jocelyn Herbert
9 Dec	The Pope's Wedding	Edward Bond	Keith Johnstone	
18 Dec	**The Sponge Room**	**Keith Waterhouse & Willis Hall**	John Dexter	Ken Calder
	Squat Betty	**Keith Waterhouse & Willis Hall**	John Dexter	Ken Calder
1963 8 Jan	**Misalliance** (Oxford Playhouse: transf. Criterion 29.1.63)	**Bernard Shaw**	Frank Hauser	Desmond Heeley
1 Feb	**Jackie the Jumper**	**Gwyn Thomas**	John Dexter	Michael Annals Alun Hoddinott (music)
7 March	**The Diary of a Madman**	**Richard Harris & Lindsay Anderson** (from Gogol)	Lindsay Anderson	Voytek Carl Davis (music)
4 April	**Naked**	**Luigi Pirandello** (transl. Diane Cilento)	David William	Henry Bardon
7 April	Skyvers	Barry Reckord	Ann Jellicoe	
21 April	Spring Awakening	Frank Wedekind (transl. Thomas Osborn)	Desmond O'Donovan	
14 May	**Day of the Prince**	**Frank Hilton**	Keith Johnstone	Sally Jacobs
12 June	**Kelly's Eye**	**Henry Livings**	David Scase	Alan Tagg
23 July	**Skyvers**	**Barry Reckord**	Ann Jellicoe	Jocelyn Herbert & Suzanne Glanister
28 July	Wiley	Mary McCormick	Elaine Pransky	
15 Aug	**Chips With Everything**	**Arnold Wesker**	John Dexter	Jocelyn Herbert
12 Sept	**Exit the King**	**Eugene Ionesco** (transl. Donald Watson)	George Devine	Jocelyn Herbert

Cast

Laurie Asprey, Alexander Balfour, Michael Blackham, Martin Boddey, Robert Bruce, John Bull, Colin Campbell, Michael Craze, Colin Farrell, Frank Finlay, Hugh Futcher, Michael Goldie, Roger Heathcott, Bruce Heighley, George Innes, John Kelland, Peter Kelly, Ronald Lacey, Corin Redgrave, Alan Stevens

David Bauer, Bernard Braden, Neil McCullum, Betty McDowell, Tucker McGuire, Bill Mitchell, Carmen Munroe, Collin Wilcox

Alexander Balfour, Michael Craze, Peter Ellis, Tommy Eytle, Ronald Falk, Colin Farrell, Michael Goldie, Bruce Heighley, Donald Hoath, George Innes, Peter Kelly, John Kobol, Alison Morris, Godfrey Quigley, Brenda Saunders, John Stuart, David Weston, Arnold Yarrow

Norman Allen, Alan Bennett, Tony Caunter, Robin Chapman, James Cossins, Graham Crowden, Avril Elgar, Jimmy Gardner, Barbara Keogh, Charles Lewsen, Constance Lorne, John Maynard, John Meillon, Glyn Owen, Vivian Pickles, Anton Rodgers, Billy Russell
Norman Allen, Ann Beach, Tony Caunter, Robin Chapman, James Cossins, Robert Eastgate, Avril Elgar, Jimmy Gardner, Barbara Keogh, Charles Lewsen, Constance Lorne, John Maynard, Glyn Owen, Anton Rodgers, Billy Russell, Pauline Taylor, Donald Troedsen

George Devine, Barry Foster, Valerie Gearon, Lotte Lenya, Norman Rossington

Jean Conroy, Jimmy Gardner, Tamara Hinchco, George Innes, Bari Johnson, Gwen Nelson, Richard O'Sullivan

Brenda Bruce, Peter Duguid

Janie Booth, Julian Chagrin, Lawrence Craine, David Ellison, Harold Goodwin, Adrienne Hill, Philip Lowrie, George Ogilvie, Malcolm Patton, Michael Standing, Malcolm Taylor

Jill Bennett, George Cole, Robert Stephens

Jill Bennett, George Cole, Robert Stephens

Dennis Chinnery, Christopher Guinee, Patricia Healey, Robin Hawdon, Barbara Jefford, Alison Leggatt, Alan Macnaughton, John Normington, Campbell Singer

Graham Crowden, Graham Curnow, Frank Davies, Sian Davies, Anne Edwards, Peter Forest, David Garfield, John Gill, Michael Gough, Branwen Iorwerth, Dudley Jones, Anne Lakeman, Jeanne Le Bars, Ronald Lewis, Raymond Llewellyn, Judith Lloyd Thomas, William McAllister, Bernard Martin, Maureen Morelle, Vernon Morris, Arthur Parry, Gaynor Rees, Talfryn Thomas, Meg Wynn Owen

Richard Harris

Diane Cilento, Peter Cartwright, Murray Gilmore, Julian Glover, John Hollis, Freda Jackson, Toni Kanal, Mollie Maureen, Joseph Wiseman, John Woodvine

Dallas Cavell, Harriet Devine, Nicholas Edmett, John Hall, David Hemmings, Lance Kaufman, Annette Robertson, John Woodnutt

Chloe Ashcroft, Sydney Bromley, Maurice Browning, Edward Burrell, Tony Calvin, Wynne Clark, James Cossins, Wilfred Downing, David Duke, Barry Evans, Eric Gould, John Hall, Barry Justice, Annette Kerr, Jo Maxwell Muller, John H. Moore, Annette Robertson, Wendy Rosen, Peter Stephens, Derek Ware, Beresford Williams, Nicol Williamson

Angela Baddeley, Bernard Bresslaw, Pauline Boty, Jean Conroy, John East, Bari Jonson, Christopher Sandford, Arnold Yarrow

Richard Carpenter, Clive Graham, Rowena Gregory, Barry Jackson, Roger Kemp, Arthur Lowe, Sarah Miles, Barbara New, Richard Vernon, Nicol Williamson

as 7 April but with Chloe Ashcroft instead of Harriet Devine

Peter Birrel, Noel Collins, Alice Fraser, Hal Galili, Gordon Gostelow, Charles Hyatt, Hugh Janes, Frank Lieberman, Philip Newman, Graham Rowse, Georgina Ward, Bill Wiesener

Norman Allen, Gary Bond, Edward Burrell, Tony Caunter, Howard Marion Crawford, Alan Dobie, Patrick Ellis, Barry Evans, Derek Fowlds, Robert Hewitt, George Innes, Ronald Lacey, John Lane, George Layton, John Levitt, James Luck, Gerald McNally, John Noakes, Corin Redgrave, Michael Standing, Terence Taplin, Christopher Timothy, Frank Wylie

Eileen Atkins, Peter Baylis, Graham Crowden, Alec Guinness, Natasha Parry, Googie Withers

	Date	Production	Author	Director	Design/Music
	15 Dec	Edgware Road Blues (transf. as Travelling Light to Prince of Wales 8.4.64)	Leonard Kingston	Keith Johnstone	
1964	12 March	ESC at the Queen's: **The Seagull**	**Anton Chekhov** (transl. Ann Jellicoe)	Tony Richardson	Jocelyn Herbert John Addison (music)
	11 June	ESC at the Queen's: **Saint Joan of the Stockyards**	**Bertolt Brecht** (transl. Charlotte & A. L. Lloyd)	Tony Richardson	Jocelyn Herbert John Addison (music)
	9 Sept	**Inadmissible Evidence** (transf. Wyndham's 17.3.65)	**John Osborne**	Anthony Page	Jocelyn Herbert Marc Wilkinson (music)
	22 Oct	**Cuckoo in the Nest**	**Ben Travers**	Anthony Page	Alan Tagg Motley (costumes)
	26 Nov	**Julius Caesar**	**Shakespeare**	Lindsay Anderson	Jocelyn Herbert Marc Wilkinson (music)
	30 Dec	**Waiting for Godot**	**Samuel Beckett**	Anthony Page	Timothy O'Brien
1965	28 Feb	The Sleepers' Den	Peter Gill	Desmond O'Donovan	Brenda Bryant
	11 March	**Happy End**	**Dorothy Lane & Bertolt Brecht** (transl. Monica Shelley, adapt. Michael Geliot)	Michael Geliot	Ralph Koltai Nadine Baylis (costumes) Kurt Weill (music)
	19 April	**Spring Awakening**	**Frank Wedekind** (transl. Thomas Osborn)	Desmond O'Donovan	Dacre Punt Motley (costumes) Marc Wilkinson (music)
	25 April	Miniatures	David Cregan	Donald Howarth	
	19 May	**Meals on Wheels**	**Charles Wood**	John Osborne	Alan Tagg Jocelyn Rickards (costumes)
	30 June	**A Patriot for Me**	**John Osborne**	Anthony Page	Jocelyn Herbert John Addison (music)
	8 Aug	A Collier's Friday Night	D. H. Lawrence	Peter Gill	Ruth Myers (costumes)
	25 Aug	**The Professor**	**Hal Porter**	Robin Midgley	Alix Stone
	29 Aug	The World's Baby (at the Embassy Theatre)	Michael Hastings	Patrick Dromgoole	
	18 Oct	**Shelley**	**Ann Jellicoe**	Ann Jellicoe	John Gunter George Hall (music)
	27 Oct	**The Cresta Run**	**N. F. Simpson**	Keith Johnstone	John Gunter
	3 Nov	**Saved**	**Edward Bond**	William Gaskill	John Gunter
	9 Dec	**Serjeant Musgrave's Dance**	**John Arden**	Jane Howell	Paul Mayo Robert Long (music)
	20 Dec	**Clowning**	**The Group**	Keith Johnstone	

Cast

Hazel Coppen, Alfred Hoffman, Peter John, Leonard Kingston, Elizabeth Proud

Peggy Ashcroft, Ann Beach, Kate Binchy, George Devine, Mark Dignam, Peter Finch, Derek Fuke, Reginald Gillam, Rachel Kempson, Philip Locke, Peter McEnery, Vanessa Redgrave, Malcolm Taylor

Brian Anderson, Robert Ayres, Bruce Boa, Jean Boht, Kate Brown, Patricia Connolly, Mark Dignam, Clive Endersby, Katie Fitzroy, Victor Flattery, Hal Galili, Paddy Glyn, Alan Guiness, Bob Haddow, George Hancock, Brian Hewitt, Dudley Hunte, Caroline Jones, Penelope Keith, Rachel Kempson, Joan Kennedy, Bessie Love, Siobhan McKenna, Michael Medwin, John Moore, Roy Pattison, Richard Pescud, Denis Shaw, Nicholas Smith, Desmond Stokes, Paul Tamarin, Malcolm Taylor, Dervis Ward, Thick Wilson

Sheila Allen, Ann Beach, Lois Daine, Clare Kelly, Arthur Lowe, Natasha Parry, John Quentin, Nicol Williamson

Petronella Barker, David Battley, Ann Beach, Alan Bennett, Harry Hutchinson, Polly James, Rosalind Knight, Beatrix Lehmann, Arthur Lowe, Robert McBain, Nan Munro, John Osborne, Nicol Williamson

Sheila Allen, Ian Bannen, Petronella Barker, Peter Brett, Roger Cooper, Graham Crowden, Paul Curran, Douglas Ditta, Edwin Finn, Nicholas Grimshaw, John Dunn Hill, Anthony Hopkins, Harry Hutchinson, David Jackson, Milton Johns, Lew Luton, Daniel Massey, Robert McBain, T. P. McKenna, Stephen Moore, Nan Munro, Ronald Pickup, Ewan Proctor, Malcolm Reynolds, Rex Robinson, Henry Stamper

Paul Curran, Alfred Lynch, Jack MacGowran, Kirk Martin, Nicol Williamson

Eileen Atkins, Sonia Graham, Anthony Hall, Trevor Peacock, Kathleen Williams, Jean Woollard

David Bauer, Beth Boyd, Christina Currie, Otto Diamant, Ros Drinkwater, Sylvia Gray, Roy Hanlon, Alan Hockey, Elric Hooper, Bettina Jonic, Chuck Julian, Paul Kermack, Jennifer McNae, Marcella Markham, Joe Melia, Declan Mulholland, Jane Murdoch, Maria Warburg, Thick Wilson

Bernard Adams, Jean Anderson, Andrew Aynsley, Kenneth Benda, Richard Brooke, Patrick Ellis, Barry Evans, John Falconer, Edwin Finn, Vanessa Forsyth, Derek Fowlds, John Garrie, Anne Holloway, Peter Illing, Sidney Johnson, Lewis Jones, Fletcher Lightfoot, Julia McCarthy, Petra Markham, John H. Moore, Ambrosine Phillpotts, Norman Scace, Colin Spaull, Annette Whitley, Theodore Wilhelm

Lindsay Anderson, Jane Birkin, Miriam Brickman, Brian Boulton, Pamela Craig, Graham Crowden, Paul Curran, George Devine, Vernon Dobtcheff, Anna Gilchrist, Anne James, Richard James, Sidney Johnson, Brenda Kempner, John Laurimore, Mary Macleod, Julia McCarthy, Roddy Maude-Roxby, Stephen Moore, Jane Murdoch, Raul Ostos, Bryan Pringle, Irene Richmond, Anthony Roy, June Sylvaine, Anthony Watkin, Nicol Williamson

Peter Collingwood, Liz Fraser, Caron Gardner, Roy Kinnear, Lee Montague, Frank Thornton

Bryn Bartlett, Jill Bennett, Timothy Carlton, John Castle, Jackie Daryl, Franco Derosa, George Devine, Vernon Dobtcheff, Sanor Eles, Rio Fanning, John Forbes, Edward Fox, Hal Hamilton, Sandra Hampton, Frederick Jaeger, Jennifer Jayne, Peter John, Robert Kidd, Lew Luton, Dona Martyn, Laurel Mather, Ferdy Mayne, Richard Morgan, Clive Morton, George Murcell, Tim Pearce, Desmond Perry, Domy Reiter, Paul Robert, Anthony Roye, Maximilian Schell, David Schurman, Sebastian Shaw, Douglas Sheldon, Virginia Wetherell, Cyril Wheeler, Thick Wilson

Richard Butler, Lucy Fleming, Victor Henry, Clare Kelly, Rosemary McHale, John Normington, Kate Story, Anthony Watkins, Gwendolyn Watts

Joss Ackland, Chong Choy, Barbara Couper, Eric Flynn, Vanda Godsell, Michael Hamilton, Briony Hodge, Kristopher Kum, Jenny Robins, David Sumner, Oko Tani, Alan White, Barbara Yu Ling

Coral Atkins, Peter Bowles, Sebastian Breaks, Richard Carpenter, Richard Dane, Desmond Davis, Alan Dobie, Michael Elwick, Michael Farnsworth, Ian Frost, Hal Galili, Kenneth Ives, Ronnie Johnson, Freddie Jones, Jon Laurimore, Michael McKevitt, Elizabeth McLennan, Vanessa Redgrave, Anthony Roye, Joan Sanderson

Timothy Carlton, John Castle, Frances Cuka, Iain Cuthbertson, Avril Elgar, Lucy Fleming, Bernard Gallagher, Nerys Hughes, Kika Markham, Ronald Pickup, Sebastian Shaw, Frank Williams

Timothy Carlton, Avril Elgar, Bernard Gallagher, Nerys Hughes, Sebastian Shaw, Frank Williams

John Bull, Richard Butler, John Castle, Barbara Ferris, Alison Frazer, Gwen Nelson, Ronald Pickup, Tony Selby, William Stewart, Dennis Waterman

Christopher Benjamin, Roger Booth, Richard Butler, Timothy Carlton, John Castle, Frances Cuka, Iain Cuthbertson, Bernard Gallagher, Joseph Greig, Victor Henry, Gillian Martell, Ronald Pickup, Sebastian Shaw, Jack Shepherd, William Stewart

Benjamin Benison, Lucy Fleming, Roddy Maude-Roxby, Richard Morgan, John Muirhead, Tony Taylor

	Date	Production	Author	Director	Design/Music
1966	13 Jan	**A Chaste Maid in Cheapside**	**Thomas Middleton**	William Gaskill	John Gunter Robert Long (music)
	23 Jan	Transcending The Dancers	David Cregan David Cregan	Jane Howell Jane Howell	
	17 Feb	**The Knack**	**Ann Jellicoe**	Desmond O'Donovan	John Gunter
	3 March	**The Performing Giant** **Transcending**	**Keith Johnstone** **David Cregan**	William Gaskill & Keith Johnstone Jane Howell	Charles Knode Marc Wilkinson (music) Charles Knode
	27 March	Little Guy, Napoleon The Local Stigmatic	Leonard Pluta Heathcote Williams	Tom Osborn Peter Gill	
	11 April	**The Voysey Inheritance**	**Harley Granville Barker**	Jane Howell	John Gunter Charles Knode (costumes) Robert Long (music)
	19 May	**Their Very Own and Golden City**	**Arnold Wesker**	William Gaskill	Christopher Morley Annena Stubbs (costumes)
	5 June	When Did You Last See My Mother? (transf. Comedy 4.7.66)	Christopher Hampton	Robert Kidd	John Gunter
	26 June	Bartleby The Local Stigmatic	Massimo Manuelli (after Herman Melville) Heathcote Williams	Massimo Manuelli Peter Gill	
	21 July	**Ubu Roi**	**Alfred Jarry** (transl. & adapt. Iain Cuthbertson)	Iain Cuthbertson	David Hockney
	21 Aug	The Ruffian on the Stair It's My Criminal	Joe Orton Howard Brenton	Peter Gill Ian Watt-Smith	
	30 Aug	**Bartholomew Fair** (National Youth Theatre)	**Ben Jonson**	Paul Hill	
	12 Sept	**Little Malcolm and His Struggle Against the Eunuchs** (National Youth Theatre)	**David Halliwell**	Michael Croft	
	21 Sept	**Three Men for Colverton**	**David Cregan**	Desmond O'Donovan	Christopher Morley Richard Montgomery (costumes) Marc Wilkinson (music)
	20 Oct	**Macbeth**	**Shakespeare**	William Gaskill	Christopher Morley Richard Montgomery (costumes) Marc Wilkinson (music)
	30 Oct	A Provincial Life	Peter Gill (after Chekhov)	Peter Gill	
	12 Dec	**The Lion and the Jewel**	**Wole Soyinka**	Desmond O'Donovan	Jocelyn Herbert Marc Wilkinson & Sanya Dousanmu (music)
1967	12 Jan	**The Soldier's Fortune**	**Thomas Otway**	Peter Gill	John Gunter John Dankworth (music)
	23 Feb	**Roots**	**Arnold Wesker**	Jane Howell	Jocelyn Herbert Robin Fraser-Paye (costumes)
	5 March	A Touch of Brightness	Partap Sharma	Ian Watt-Smith	Diana Wisbey (costumes)
	16 March	**The Daughter-in-Law**	**D. H. Lawrence**	Peter Gill	John Gunter Deirdre Clancy (costumes)

Cast

Christopher Benjamin, Jean Boht, Roger Booth, Richard Butler, Timothy Carlton, John Castle, Frances Cuka, Avril Elgar, Barbara Ferris, Lucy Fleming, Bernard Gallagher, Joseph Greig, Victor Henry, Gillian Martell, Gwen Nelson, Ronald Pickup, Tony Selby, Sebastian Shaw, Jack Shepherd, William Stewart, Dennis Waterman

Jean Boht, Roger Booth, Barbara Ferris, Bernard Gallagher, Ronald Pickup
Frances Cuka, Joseph Greig, Davyd Harries, Gillian Martell, Peter Wyatt

Timothy Carlton, John Castle, Barbara Ferris, Victor Henry

Roger Booth, Lucy Fleming, Bernard Gallagher, Joseph Greig, David Leland, Roddy Maude-Roxby, Jack Shepherd, William Stewart, Dennis Waterman
as 23 Jan but with Roddy Maude-Roxby instead of Ronald Pickup

Valentine Ashley, Barbara Bolton, Ken Jones, David Leland, Simon Mead, Jack Shepherd, William Stewart, Dennis Waterman
Oliver Cotton, Peter Hill, William Hoyland, Toby Salaman

Jean Boht, Roger Booth, Timothy Carlton, John Castle, Janet Chappell, Rowena Cooper, Avril Elgar, Lucy Fleming, Bernard Gallagher, Joseph Greig, Jacqueline Harrison, Victor Henry, George Howe, Gillian Martell, Gwen Nelson, Sebastian Shaw, Jeffry Wickham

Roger Booth, Richard Butler, Janet Chappell, Kenneth Cranham, Ann Firbank, Bernard Gallagher, Joseph Greig, Jacqueline Harrison, George Howe, Janette Legge, David Leland, Ian McKellen, Gillian Martell, Sebastian Shaw, Jack Shepherd, William Stewart, Jeffry Wickham

Lucy Fleming, Victor Henry, Julian Holloway, Christopher Matthews, Gwen Watford

John Arnatt, Roger Booth, Derrick Gilbert, Victor Henry, Dennis Waterman

Oliver Cotton, Peter Harlowe, William Hoyland, Toby Salaman

Kent Baker, Timothy Carlton, Janet Chappell, Kenneth Cranham, Ronald Falk, Bernard Gallagher, Joseph Greig, Jacqueline Harrison, Janette Legge, David Leland, Elspeth MacNaughton, Richard O'Callaghan, Robert Powell, Jack Shepherd, William Stewart, Max Wall, Bill Wallis, Hugh Walters, Colin Welland, Glenn Williams, Peter Wyatt

Sheila Ballantine, Kenneth Cranham, Bernard Gallagher
Oliver Cotton, William Stewart

cast list not available

cast list not available

Jean Boht, Sylvia Coleridge, Julian Curry, Joseph Greig, Mary Macleod, Margery Mason, Richard O'Callaghan, Leonard Pearce, Natasha Pyne, Leonard Sachs, Jack Shepherd, Malcolm Tierney, Peter Wyatt

John Castle, Terence Davies, Jumoke Debayo, Sean Farrelly, Donald Gee, Alec Guinness, Gordon Jackson, David Kincaid, John McKelvey, Gillian Martell, Zakes Mokae, John Nettles, Richard O'Callaghan, Leonard Pearce, John Rae, Maurice Roeves, Toby Salaman, Jack Shepherd, Simone Signoret

Jean Boht, Pamela Buchner, Richard Butler, Oliver Cotton, Anne Dyson, Susan Engel, Bernard Gallagher, Jean Holness, Anthony Hopkins, John McKelvey, Gillian Martell, John Normington, Richard O'Callaghan, Shivaun O'Casey, Trevor Peacock, Jack Shepherd, Geoffrey Whitehead, Peter Wyatt

Abdi Abobaker, Taiwo Ajai, Tommy Ansah, Hannah Bright-Taylor, Trudi Coleman, Shauree Crooks, Jumoke Debayo, Femi Euba, Plinio Galfetti, Kwesi Kay, David Longdon, Lionel Ngakane, Rosetta Nwanzoke, Stella Oshalake, Ilarrio Pedro, Blossom Pegram, Veronica Wilson

Elizabeth Bell, Wallas Eaton, Roger Foss, Bernard Gallagher, Sheila Hancock, Peter John, Janette Legge, Arthur Lowe, John Nettles, Maurice Roeves, Toby Salaman, Jack Shepherd, Bridget Turner, Richard Vanstone, Peter Wyatt

Leslie Anderson, Anne Carroll, Robert Grange, Gwen Nelson, Trevor Peacock, Billy Russell, Jack Shepherd, Bridget Turner, Thelma Whiteley

Prem Bakshi, Manisha Bose, Gerson Da Cunha, Saeed Jaffrey, Padma Kumari, Leslie Leveroy, Bobby Naidoo, Chitra Neogy, Zohra Segal, Roshan Seth, Dino Shafeek, Shivendra Sinha, Zoe Starr

Gabrielle Day, Anne Dyson, Victor Henry, Judy Parfitt, Mike Pratt

Date	Production	Author	Director	Design/Music
2 April	A View to the Common	James Casey	Desmond O'Donovan	Tony Whelan
18 April	**Three Sisters**	**Anton Chekhov** (transl. Edward Bond)	William Gaskill	Abd' Elkader Farrah
6 June	**The Ruffian on the Stair** **The Erpingham Camp**	**Joe Orton** **Joe Orton**	Peter Gill Peter Gill	Deirdre Clancy Deirdre Clancy
20 June	**A View to the Common**	**James Casey**	Desmond O'Donovan	Harry Waistnage
4 July	**The Restoration of Arnold Middleton** (transf. Criterion 31.8.67)	**David Storey**	Robert Kidd	Bernard Culshaw
23 July	Dance of the Teletape (YPTS) The Rising Generation (YPTS)	Charles Hayward Ann Jellicoe	Charles Hayward Jane Howell	
24 July	**OGODIVELEFTTHEGASON**	**Donald Howarth**	Donald Howarth	Vanessa James Carl Davis (music)
2 Aug	**America Hurrah:** **Interview** **TV** **Motel** (Open Theatre)	**Jean-Claude van Itallie**	Joseph Chaikin Jacques Levy Jacques Levy	Tania Leontov (costumes) Marianne du Puvy (music)
11 Sept	**Fill the Stage With Happy Hours** (at the Vaudeville Theatre)	**Charles Wood**	William Gaskill	Harry Waistnage
8 Oct	The Journey of the Fifth Horse	Ronald Ribman	Bill Bryden	Harry Waistnage
19 Oct	**Marya**	**Isaac Babel** (version Christopher Hampton)	Robert Kidd	John Gunter Deirdre Clancy (costumes) Julien Dawes (music)
15 Nov	**Dingo**	**Charles Wood**	Geoffrey Reeves	Charles Wood & Bernard Culshaw
7 Dec	**The Dragon**	**Yevgeny Schwartz** (transl. Max Hayward & Harold Shukman)	Jane Howell	Abd' Elkader Farrah Colin Norman (music)
21 Dec	**The Paperbag Players**		Judith Martin	
1968 31 Jan	**Twelfth Night**	**Shakespeare**	Jane Howell	Patrick Procktor Derek Oldfield (music)
11 Feb	Backbone	Michael Rosen	Bill Bryden	
29 Feb	**A Collier's Friday Night**	**D. H. Lawrence**	Peter Gill	John Gunter Deirdre Clancy (costumes)
7 March	**The Daughter-in-Law**	**D. H. Lawrence**	Peter Gill	John Gunter Deirdre Clancy (costumes)
14 March	**The Widowing of Mrs Holroyd**	**D. H. Lawrence**	Peter Gill	John Gunter Deirdre Clancy (costumes)
31 March	Early Morning	Edward Bond	William Gaskill	Deirdre Clancy
28 April	A Lesson in a Dead Language Funnyhouse of a Negro	Adrienne Kennedy Adrienne Kennedy	Rob Knights Rob Knights	Peter Whiteman Peter Whiteman
8 May	**Backbone**	**Michael Rosen**	Bill Bryden	Kenneth Bridgeman Denise Heywood (costumes)

Cast

Brian Coburn, Bernard Gallagher, Victor Henry, Doreen Mantle, Mike Pratt, Malcolm Tierney

George Cole, Avril Elgar, Marianne Faithfull, Michael Gwynn, Glenda Jackson, Marjie Lawrence, Rosemary McHale, Roddy Maude-Roxby, Stuart Mungall, John Nettles, John Rae, Peter Russell, Toby Salaman, Jack Shepherd, Madoline Thomas, Alan Webb

Avril Elgar, Bernard Gallagher, Michael Standing
Yvonne Antrobus, Roger Booth, Josie Bradley, Pauline Collins, Andrée Evans, Bernard Gallagher, Peter John, Rosemary McHale, Roddy Maude-Roxby, Malcolm Reid, Michael Standing, Johnny Wade, Ken Wynne

as 2 April but with Thelma Ruby instead of Doreen Mantle and Cyril Wheeler instead of Mike Pratt

Eileen Atkins, Noel Dyson, Andrée Evans, Tenniel Evans, Gillian Hills, Jack Shepherd

Boys of Dulwich College

Stewart Baron, Yvonne D'Alpra, Philip Sayer

Harry Baird, Joan Heal, John Phillips, Tony Robinson, Dudley Sutton, George Tovey

Joyce Aaron, James Barbosa, Henry Calvert, Conrad Fowkes, Sharon Gans, Ronnie Gilbert, Cynthia Harris, John Kramer, William Macy, Brenda Smiley

Hylda Baker, Faith Brook, Harry H. Corbett, Helen Cotterill, Sheila Hancock, Stella Moray, John Trigger, Ken Wynne

David Ashton, Gabrielle Daye, Vernon Dobtcheff, Ronnie Gilbert, Peter Gilmore, James Hazeldine, Janet Kelly, Jill Kerman, James Locker, David McKail, Moira Redmond, Guy Ross, Jack Shepherd, Kevin Stoney, David Sumner, Adam Verney

Elizabeth Bell, Diane Cilento, Archie Duncan, Ruby Head, Arthur Lowe, Niall MacGinnis, Carol Mason, Shivaun O'Casey, Peter Russell, Toby Salaman, Walter Sparrow, Peter Sproule, Madoline Thomas, Malcolm Tierney, Francis Wallis, Marion Winton, Peter Wyatt, Ken Wynne

Eric Allan, Robert Booth, Ian Collier, Gareth Forwood, Michael Francis, Neville Hughes, John Hussey, Mark Jones, Tom Kempinski, Leon Lissek, Barry Stanton, Henry Woolf

Stanley Bates, Elizabeth Bell, Sandra Billington, Roger Booth, Roger Brierley, Paola Dionisotti, Richard Douglas, Diane Fletcher, Stephen Follet, Bernard Gallagher, Victor Henry, Cyril Jackson, Arthur Lowe, Harry Meacher, John Nolan, Deborah Norton, Edward Peel, Jack Shepherd, Peter Sproule, Malcolm Tierney, Kate Williams, Peter Wyatt

Irving Burton, Judith Martin, Gary Maxwell, Gary Osgood

Tom Chadbon, Fiannuala Flanagan, Paul Greenwood, Judy Liebert, Malcolm McDowell, Kika Markham, Harry Meacher, Patrick Mower, John Normington, Edward Peel, Jack Shepherd, Peter Sproule, John Steiner, Malcolm Tierney, Vickery Turner, Dennis Waterman

Faith Brook, Timothy Carlton, Tom Chadbon, Marty Cruickshank, Roy Holder, Edward Jewesbury, Gillian Martell, Harry Meacher, Deborah Norton, John Shrapnel, Harry Towb

Jennifer Armitage, John Barrett, Anthony Douse, Anne Dyson, Christine Hargreaves, Victor Henry, Mark Jones, Gwendolyn Watts, Susan Williamson

Michael Coles, Gabrielle Daye, Anne Dyson, Victor Henry, Judy Parfitt

John Barrett, Michael Coles, Anthony Douse, Anne Dyson, Joan Francis, Len Jones, Mark Jones, June Liversidge, Judy Parfitt, Edward Peel, Tony Rohr, Gwendolyn Watts

Hugh Armstrong, Roger Booth, Tom Chadbon, Norman Eshley, Peter Eyre, Marianne Faithfull, Nigel Hawthorne, Jane Howell, Harry Meacher, Moira Redmond, Gavin Reed, Bruce Robinson, Jack Shepherd, Malcolm Tierney, Dennis Waterman

Elizabeth Adare, Nina Baden-Semper, George Baisley, Brigid Brett, Marinechi-chi Enis, Geula Jeffet, Stefan Kalipha, Julia McCarthy, David Rhys-Anderson, Anne Thompson, Anthony Villarcel, Keith Walker, Sheila Wilkinson
as above

Ray Brooks, Timothy Carlton, Tom Chadbon, Marty Cruickshank, Roy Holder, Edward Jewesbury, Clare Kelly, Harry Meacher, Deborah Norton, Harry Towb, Thelma Whiteley

Date	Production	Author	Director	Design/Music
23 May	**Time Present** (transf. Duke of York's 11.7.68)	**John Osborne**	Anthony Page	Tony Abbott & Donald Taylor Ruth Myers (costumes)
3 July	**The Hotel in Amsterdam** (transf. New 5.9.68)	**John Osborne**	Anthony Page	Tony Abbott & Donald Taylor Ruth Myers (costumes)
6 July	Captain Oates' Left Sock	John Antrobus	Barry Hanson	
4 Aug	Changing Lines	Nicholas Wright	Nicholas Wright	
21 Aug	**Trixie and Baba**	**John Antrobus**	Jane Howell	Hayden Griffin Deirdre Clancy (costumes)
11 Sept	**Total Eclipse**	**Christopher Hampton**	Robert Kidd	Patrick Procktor
2 Oct	**The Houses by the Green**	**David Cregan**	Jane Howell	Deirdre Clancy
13 Oct	The Tutor	Jacob Lenz (adapt. Bertolt Brecht, transl. Richard Grunberger)	Barry Hanson	
29 Oct	**Look Back in Anger** (transf. Criterion 10.12.68)	**John Osborne**	Anthony Page	Tony Abbott & Donald Taylor Anne Gainsford (costumes)
11 Nov	**The Beard** (late night)	**Michael McClure**	Rip Torn	Tony Abbott & Donald Taylor Ann Roth (costumes)
11 Dec	**This Story of Yours**	**John Hopkins**	Christopher Morahan	Tony Abbott & Donald Taylor Denise Heywood (costumes)

1969

Date	Production	Author	Director	Design/Music
9 Jan	**Life Price**	**Michael O'Neill & Jeremy Seabrook**	Peter Gill	Jocelyn Herbert
7 Feb	**Saved**	**Edward Bond**	William Gaskill	John Gunter
19 Feb	**Narrow Road to the Deep North**	**Edward Bond**	Jane Howell	Hayden Griffin
24 Feb	A Comedy of the Changing Years	David Cregan	Michael Bogdanov	Alan Pleass
27 Feb	Dandelion (Paperbag Players) (late night)	Judith Martin	Judith Martin	
13 March	**Early Morning**	**Edward Bond**	William Gaskill	Deirdre Clancy
18 March	La Turista	Sam Shepard	Roger Hendricks-Simon	John Napier
2 April	Erogenous Zones	Mike Stott	Geoffrey Reeves	John Gunter
22 April	**In Celebration**	**David Storey**	Lindsay Anderson	Peter Docherty
26 April	The Enoch Show	Peter Gill, Christopher Hampton, Edward Bond, Dilip Hiro, Shirley Matthews, Michael O'Neill, Jeremy Seabrook, Mike Stott, Heathcote Williams	Barry Hanson	Hayden Griffin
23 June	**The Cry of the People for Meat** (The Bread and Puppet Theatre)		Peter Schumann	
15 July	Blim at School	Peter Tegel	Nicholas Wright	Robin Hirtenstein

Cast

Tom Adams, Jill Bennett, Katherine Blake, Geoffrey Frederick, Harry Landis, Kika Markham, Sarah Taunton, Valerie Taylor

Joss Ackland, David Burke, Clare Davidson, Isabel Dean, Anthony Douse, Susan Engel, Judy Parfitt, Paul Scofield, Ralph Watson

Yvonne Antrobus, Margaret Brady, June Brown, James Donnelly, Andre Evans, Ronald Forfar, Raymond Francis, Carol Gillies, Michael Gough, Michael McKevitt, Gwen Nelson, Rory North, Norma Shebbeare, Dudley Sutton, Daniel Thorndike

Gillian Fairchild, Bernard Gallagher, Kenneth Hendel, Malcolm Ingram, Joan Sanderson, Susan Williamson

Tom Chadbon, William Hoyland, Malcolm Ingram, Stephen Lewis, Gillian Martell, Anthony May, Joe Melia

Kathleen Byron, Michele Dotrice, John Grillo, Nigel Hawthorne, Victor Henry, William Hoyland, Malcolm Ingram, Stanley Lebor, Judy Liebert, Gillian Martell, Ursula Smith

Yvonne Antrobus, Tom Chadbon, Bob Grant, John Normington

Jill Allen, Paul Aston, John Berrard, Vivienne Burgess, Jeremy Clyde, Oliver Cotton, Rosalind Elliott, John Gill, Bob Grant, Nigel Hawthorne, William Hoyland, Judy Liebert, Michael Maskery, Jack Niles, Jack Raby, Mary Rutherford, Di Seaney, Rosalind Shanks, Malcolm Tierney, June Watson, Theresa Watson

Jane Asher, Victor Henry, Edward Jewesbury, Caroline Mortimer, Martin Shaw

Richard Bright, Billie Dixon

Steven Barnes, Michael Bryant, Aletha Charlton, Edward Clayton, Gordon Jackson, Oliver Maguire, John Phillips, Colin Pinney

Yvonne Antrobus, June Brown, Derek Carpenter, Edward Clayton, Diana Coupland, Anthony Douse, Patrick Godfrey, Christine Hargreaves, Julie Kennard, Mary Macleod, James Mellor, Allan Mitchell, Tina Packer, Alec Ross, Anthony Sagar, June Watson, Thelma Whiteley, Philip Woods

John Barrett, Peter Blythe, Tom Chadbon, Kenneth Cranham, Brian Croucher, Patricia Franklin, Billy Hamon, Don Hawkins, Adrienne Posta, Queenie Watts

Peter Blythe, Tom Chadbon, Kenneth Cranham, Brian Croucher, Patricia Franklin, Don Hawkins, Nigel Hawthorne, James Hazeldine, Tom Marshall, Gillian Martell, Peter Needham, Jack Shepherd, Peter Sproule, Anna Wing

Barry Jackson, David Jackson, Jonathan Lynn, Carol Macready, Allan Mitchell, Judith Paris

Donald Aswander, Irving Burton, Charles Leipart, Judith Martin, Betty Osgood

John Barrett, Peter Blythe, Tom Chadbon, Kenneth Cranham, Brian Croucher, Shirley Ann Field, Patricia Franklin, Billy Hamon, Don Hawkins, Nigel Hawthorne, James Hazeldine, Tom Marshall, Peter Needham, Moira Redmond, Jack Shepherd, Peter Sproule, Queenie Watts, Anna Wing, Henry Woolf

Christopher Cabot, Barry Dennen, Lelia Goldoni, Al Mancini, George Margo

Petronella Barker, Oliver Cotton, John Grillo, Tom Kempinski, Pauline Munro, Henry Woolf

Alan Bates, James Bolam, Constance Chapman, Brian Cox, Gabrielle Daye, Fulton Mackay, Bill Owen

Oliver Cotton, Malcolm Ingram, Deborah Norton, Jack Shepherd, Henry Woolf

Michael Appleby, Eric Berne, Maurice Blanc, William Dalrymple, Bruno Eckardt, Carol Grosling, Irene Le Herissier, Deborah Knight, Uwe Krieger, Barton Lane, Murray Levy, Arnold Lippin, Mary Lippin, Manuel Narciza, Sara Peattie, German Ramirez, Margo Sherman, Harvey Spevak

Robert Bernal, Peter Blythe, Paul Brooke, Andrew Dallmeyer, Lynn Farleigh, Geoffrey Hughes, Steven Lewis, Dorothy Primrose

Date	Production	Author	Director	Design/Music
15 July	*Poet of the Anemones*	*Peter Tegel*	Nicholas Wright	Derek Jarman
18 July	**The Double Dealer**	**William Congreve**	William Gaskill	John Gunter Annena Stubbs (costumes)
4 Aug	*Over Gardens Out*	*Peter Gill*	Peter Gill	Denise Heywood (costumes)
18 Aug	*The Beach Ball Show* (The People Show)			
1 Sept	**Saved**	**Edward Bond**	William Gaskill	John Gunter
2 Sept	*Revenge*	*Howard Brenton*	Chris Parr	Philip Jordan
8 Sept	**Narrow Road to the Deep North**	**Edward Bond**	Jane Howell	Hayden Griffin
17 Sept	*Dear Janet Rosenberg, Dear Mr Kooning* (Traverse)	*Stanley Eveling*	Max Stafford-Clark	
25 Sept	**Oh! Les beaux jours** (Compagnie Renaud-Barrault)	**Samuel Beckett**	Roger Blin	Matias
	L'amante anglaise (Compagnie Renaud-Barrault)	**Samuel Beckett**	Claude Regy	Jacques Lemarquet
20 Oct	**The Contractor** (transf. Fortune 6.4.70)	**David Storey**	Lindsay Anderson	John Gunter
9 Nov	Famine	Thomas Murphy	Clifford Williams	Malak Khazi
18 Nov	*The Sleepers' Den*	*Peter Gill*	Peter Gill	Deirdre Clancy
24 Nov	**Insideout**	**Frank Norman**	Ken Campbell	John Gunter
25 Nov	*Over Gardens Out* (late night)	*Peter Gill*	Peter Gill	Denise Heywood (costumes)
12 Dec	*Pit*	*Peter Dockley*		
24 Dec	**The Three Musketeers Ride Again**	**The Alberts & Bruce Lacey**	Eleanor Fazan	Ann Gray
28 Jan	**Three Months Gone** (transf. Duchess 4.3.70)	**Donald Howarth**	Ronald Eyre	Jocelyn Herbert
1 Feb	The Big Romance	Robert Thornton	Roger Williams	
24 Feb	**Uncle Vanya**	**Anton Chekhov** (transl. Nina Froud, version Christopher Hampton)	Anthony Page	Deirdre Clancy
10 March	*Christie in Love*	*Howard Brenton*	David Hare	
10 March	*A Who's Who of Flapland* (late night)	*David Halliwell*	Michael Wearing	Jean Ramsey
31 March	*Beckett/3*			
	Come and Go	*Samuel Beckett*	William Gaskill	Jocelyn Herbert
	Cascando	*Samuel Beckett*	Roger Croucher	Jocelyn Herbert
	Play	*Samuel Beckett*	William Gaskill	Jocelyn Herbert
14 April	**Widowers' Houses** (Nottingham Playhouse)	**Bernard Shaw**	Michael Blakemore	Patrick Robertson
20 April	*An Account of the Marriage of August Strindberg and Harriet Bosse*	*John Abulafia*	Shell Abulafia	
	Brain (Incubus Theatre)	*John Abulafia & the cast*	John Abulafia	

1970

Cast

Robert Bernal, Peter Blythe, Lynn Farleigh, Dorothy Primrose

Celia Bannerman, Richard Beckinsale, Michael Byrne, John Castle, Geoffrey Chater, Nigel Hawthorne, George Howe, Alison Leggatt, Gillian Martell, Alan Meadows, Patricia Michael, Judy Parfitt, Hugh Sullivan, Malcolm Tierney, John White

Anthony Douse, Don Hawkins, James Hazeldine, Pamela Miles, Roger Nott, June Watson

Laura Gilbert, Mark Long, Roland Miller

Margaret Brady, Richard Butler, Tom Chadbon, Kenneth Cranham, Brian Croucher, Patricia Franklin, Michael Graves, Billy Hamon, Malcolm Tierney, Queenie Watts

Timothy Block, Paul Brooke, Barry Linehan, Ursula Mohan, Pamela Moiseiwitsch, John Normington, Bill Stewart

Margaret Brady, Kenneth Cranham, Brian Croucher, Michael Graves, Billy Hamon, Nigel Hawthorne, James Hazeldine, Tom Marshall, Gillian Martell, Peter Needham, Edward Peel, Peter Sproule, Malcolm Tierney

Susan Carpenter, Anthony Haygarth

Michel Bertay, Madeleine Renaud

Michael Lonsdale, Madeleine Renaud, Jean Servais

John Antrobus, Constance Chapman, Christopher Coll, Norman Jones, Judy Liebert, T. P. McKenna, Jim Norton, Bill Owen, Billy Russell, Martin Shaw, Philip Stone, Adele Strong

Frankie Bennett, Frederick Bennett, Jane Brown, Constance Chapman, Warren Clarke, Donal Cox, Alan Dobie, Frank Dunne, Bernard Gallagher, Shay Gorman, Gerald James, John Keogh, Robert Lang, Graham Larkin, Juliet Lawson-Johnston, Bert Lena, John Leonard, Oliver Maguire, Fidelma Murphy, Terry Murphy, Wesley Murphy, John Nightingale, Allan Olsen, Sheila Whitmill

Eileen Atkins, Anthony Douse, Kimberly Iles, Margaret John, John Rees, Madoline Thomas

Alba, Maurice Bush, Tom Chadbon, Warren Clarke, Athol Coats, Brian Croucher, Terry Downes, Femi Euba, Patrick Godfrey, Laurence Harrington, Nigel Hawthorne, John Keogh, Harry Landis, C. Lethbridge Baker, Oliver Maguire, Christine Noonan, Bill Owen, Elisabeth Paget, Peter Rocca, Tony Rohr, Denis Shaw, Malcolm Terris, George Tovey, Glen Williams

Anthony Douse, Don Hawkins, James Hazeldine, Pamela Miles, Roger Nott, June Watson

cast list not available

Jill Bruce, Fiona Clow, Valentine Dyall, Lorraine Field, Anthony Gray, Douglas Gray, Alexei Javdokimov, Colin Phillips, Rachel Roberts, David Sands

Jill Bennett, Warren Clarke, Diana Dors, Alan Lake, Richard O'Callaghan, Kevin Stoney

Richard Butler, Anna Carteret, Brian Cox, Dudley Foster, Hilary Mason, Phyllis Mason, Phyllis Morris

Elizabeth Bell, Colin Blakely, Anna Calder-Marshall, Denis Carey, Gwen Ffrangcon-Davies, Oliver Maguire, Ralph Michael, Paul Scofield, Madoline Thomas

Brian Croucher, William Hoyland, Stanley Lebor

Colin Gordon, Clive Revill

Gillian Martell, Queenie Watts, Susan Williamson
Kenneth Cranham, Stanley Lebor
Kenneth Cranham, Gillian Martell, Susan Williamson

Stephen Bradley, Robin Ellis, William Fisher, Frank Middlemass, Larry Noble, Anthony Newlands, Nicola Paget, Penelope Wilton

Libby Butterworth, Michael Prescott

John Abulafia, Ian Butterworth, Libby Butterworth, Paddy Fletcher, Michael Prescott, Pat Redman, Oliver Williams

Date	Production	Author	Director	Design/Music
10 May	**Strip Jack Naked** (Sheffield Playhouse)	Christopher Wilkinson	Colin George	
14 May	*AC/DC*	*Heathcote Williams*	Nicholas Wright	John Gunter
19 May	**Café La Mama Season** **Ubu**	**Alfred Jarry**	Andres Sherban	C. J. Strawn
	Arden of Faversham	**anon**	Andres Sherban	C. J. Strawn
	Cinque	**Leonard Melfi**	Ching Yeh	C. J. Strawn
	Rats Mass	**Adrienne Kennedy**	Ching Yeh	C. J. Strawn
1 June	*The Sport of My Mad Mother* (YPTS)	*Ann Jellicoe*	Pam Brighton	
17 June	**Home** (transf. Apollo 29.7.70)	**David Storey**	Lindsay Anderson	Jocelyn Herbert Alan Price (music)
30 June	*Billy's Last Stand*	*Barry Hines*	Michael Wearing	Jean Ramsey
27 July	*Theatre Machine*		Keith Johnstone	
3 Aug	**The Philanthropist** (transf. Mayfair 7.9.70)	**Christopher Hampton**	Robert Kidd	John Gunter
11 Aug	*When Did You Last See My Mother?*	*Christopher Hampton*	Roger Williams	Hugh Durrant
31 Aug	*Inédits Ionesco*	*Eugene Ionesco*	Jean Rougerie	Jean Rougerie Company
10 Sept	*Cheek*	*Howard Barker*	William Gaskill	Di Seymour
14 Sept	**Cancer**	**Michael Weller**	Peter Gill	John Napier
28 Sept	*Fruit* (Portable Theatre)	*Howard Brenton*	David Hare	Jenny Gaskin
29 Sept	*What Happened to Blake* (Portable Theatre)	*David Hare*	Tony Bicat	Jenny Gaskin
11 Oct	Research (Teheran Theatre Workshop)	Arby Ovanessian	Abbas Naalbandjan	
21 Oct– 9 Nov	**Come Together Festival**			
11 Nov	**AC/DC**	**Heathcote Williams**	Nicholas Wright	John Gunter
18 Nov	*No One Was Saved* (YPTS)	*Howard Barker*	Pam Brighton	Di Seymour
8 Dec	**Lulu** (Nottingham Playhouse)	**Frank Wedekind** (transl. Charlotte Beck, adapt. Peter Barnes)	Peter Barnes & Stuart Burge	Patrick Robertson Rosemary Vercoe (costumes)
13 Dec	Pirates	Keith Dewhurst	Bill Bryden	
28 Dec	*The Hunchback and the Barber*		Keith Johnstone	John Hallé & George Fathers
	Professor Pleasant's Guest (Theatre Machine)		Keith Johnstone	John Hallé & George Fathers
1971 18 Jan	**The Duchess of Malfi**	**John Webster**	Peter Gill	William Dudley The Gentle Fire (music) Deirdre Clancy (costumes)
20 Jan	*Captain Jack's Revenge*	*Michael Smith*	Nicholas Wright	Charles Dunlop
31 Jan	Morality	Michael O'Neill & Jeremy Seabrook	Roger Croucher	Di Seymour

Cast

David Bradley, Nigel Hawthorne, David Howey, John Pickles, Michael St. John, Barrie Smith

Pat Hartley, Ian Hogg, Robert Lloyd, Patricia Quinn, Henry Woolf

Lamar Alford, Patrick Burke, Michele Collison, Sabin Epstein, Patricia Gaul, William Griffin Duffy, Arthur Hill, Barbara Montgomery, June Perz, Lou Zeldis

Lamar Alford, Patrick Burke, Michele Collison, Sabin Epstein, William Griffin Duffy, Arthur Hill, Barbara Montgomery, Mervyn Willis, Lou Zeldis

Patrick Burke, Patricia Gaul, William Griffin Duffy, Arthur Hill, June Perz, Mervyn Willis

Lamar Alford, Patrick Burke, Michele Collison, Sabin Epstein, Patricia Gaul, William Griffin Duffy, Arthur Hill, Barbara Montgomery, June Perz, Mervyn Willis, Lou Zeldis

Margaret Brady, Tim Curry, Stanley Lebor, Roy McArthur, Jill Richards, Tony Robinson, Tara Prem

Warren Clarke, John Gielgud, Dandy Nichols, Ralph Richardson, Mona Washbourne

John Barrett, Ian McKellen

Ben Benison, Petra Markham, Roddy Maude-Roxby, Ric Morgan, Tony Trent

Jane Asher, David Ashton, Charles Gray, Dinsdale Landen, Alec McCowen, Tamara Ustinov, Penelope Wilton

Robert Fox, Jan Francis, Richard Howard, Nikolas Simmonds, Barbara Shelley

Anne Alexandre, André Chaumeau, Suzy Hannier, André Paulin, Jean Rougerie

Richard Butler, Tom Chadbon, Ken Cranham, Liz Edmiston, Cheryl Hall, Diane Hart, Marshall Jones, Susan Littler

Seth Allen, Cara Duff-MacCormick, Mari Gorman, David Hall, David Healy, Chuck Jones, Karen Ludwig, Chris Malcolm, Al Mancini, George Margo, Andrew Neil, Richard Portnow, Martin Shaw, Ann Way

Paul Brooke, Hilary Charlton, Will Knightley, Colin McCormack, William Morgan

Peter Brenner, Paul Brooke, Hilary Charlton, Colin McCormack, William Morgan

cast list not available

cast lists not available

Victor Henry, Deborah Norton, Sheila Scott-Wilkinson, Tony Sher, Henry Woolf

Lincoln Brown, Alan Buckingham, Kevin Davis, Diane Fletcher, Mick Hart, Barbara Keogh, Maureen Lipman, Andrew Neil, Madhav Sharma, Peter Sproule, Phil Woods

Sheila Ballantine, Michael Byrne, Julia Foster, Marilyn Fridjon, Jo Garrity, John Grillo, Paul Hennen, John Justin, Leonard Kavanagh, Chris Malcolm, Maggy Maxwell, Tom Owen, Edward Petherbridge, John Phillips, Francis Thomas, John Turner, John Whiting

Hugh Armstrong, Celia Bannerman, John Bennett, Martin Carthy, John Cater, John Dearth, Marie Delsol, Alfred Fagon, Helen Francoise, Brian Glover, Abi Gouhad, William Hoyland, Gavin Jones, Peter Knight, Mark Long, Anthony Milner, Bloke Modisane, Derek Newark, Patrick O'Connell, Robert Powell, Siobhan Quinlan, John Rae, Jack Shepherd, Corinne Skinner, Desmond Thomson, Philip Woods

Ben Benison, Judith Ann Blake, Roddy Maude-Roxby, Ric Morgan, Richard Pendrey

as above

Derek Carpenter, Judith Copeland, Oliver Cotton, Anthony Douse, Desmond Gill, Christine Hargreaves, Victor Henry, Andrew Neil, Judy Parfitt, Brian Prothero, Sheila Scott-Wilkinson, Gregg Smith, Kevan Stocker, Donald Sumpter, Gareth Thomas, Malcolm Tierney, Anthony Trent, Eric Woofe, Henry Woolf

Anthony Corlan, Edward Jewesbury, Martin Matthews, Allan Mitchell, Michael Pennington, Patricia Quinn

Matthew Corbett, Bernard Gallagher, Billy Hamon, Diane Hart, Joan Hickson, Stanley Meadows, Edward Petherbridge, Leon Vitali, Marjorie Yates

Date	Production	Author	Director	Design/Music
9 Feb	*The Baby Elephant*	*Bertolt Brecht* (transl. Steve Gooch)	Bill Bryden	Di Seymour
23 Feb	*A Game Called Arthur* (Traverse)	*David Snodin*	Michael Rudman	
1 March	**Man is Man**	**Bertolt Brecht** (transl. Steve Gooch)	William Gaskill	William Dudley John Cameron (music)
17 March	*The Foursome* (transf. Fortune 4.5.71)	*E. A. Whitehead*	Jonathan Hales	John Napier
6 April	*Stone Age Capers*	*Ken Campbell & Bob Hoskins*		
13 April	**One at Night**	**Denis Cannan**	Roger Williams	Charles Dunlop Chuck Mallett (music)
28 April	*Anarchist*	*Michael Almaz*	Chris Parr	William Dudley
18 May	*Corunna!*	*Keith Dewhurst*	Bill Bryden	Di Seymour Steeleye Span (music)
24 May	**Slag**	**David Hare**	Max Stafford-Clark	John Gunter
2 June	*Our Sunday Times* (Traverse Workshop)	*Stanley Eveling*	Max Stafford-Clark	
4 June	*Amaryllis* (late night)	*David McNiven & Traverse Workshop*	Max Stafford-Clark	
24 June	*Skyvers* (YPTS) (transf. Roundhouse 8.9.71)	*Barry Reckord*	Pam Brighton	Charles Dunlop
25 June	*Sweet Alice* (Traverse Workshop) (late night)	*Stanley Eveling*	Max Stafford-Clark	
6 July	**The Lovers of Viorne**	**Marguerite Duras**	Jonathan Hales	John Napier
19 Aug	*Boesman and Lena* (transf. Young Vic 16.8.71)	*Athol Fugard*	Athol Fugard	Douglas Heap
17 Aug	**West of Suez** (transf. to Cambridge 6.10.71)	**John Osborne**	Anthony Page	John Gunter Ronald Patterson (costumes)
1 Sept	*Do It*	*Pip Simmons*	Pip Simmons	
14 Sept	*As Time Goes By* (Traverse)	*Mustapha Matura*	Roland Rees	Jenni Holland
26 Sept	Lay By (Portable Theatre/Traverse)	Howard Brenton, Brian Clark, Trevor Griffiths, David Hare, Stephen Poliakoff, Hugh Stoddart, Snoo Wilson	Snoo Wilson	
29 Sept	**Lear**	**Edward Bond**	William Gaskill	John Napier Deirdre Clancy (costumes)
3 Oct	The Front Room Boys	Alexander Buzo	Clive Donner	Jenni Holland
12 Oct	*AC/DC*	*Heathcote Williams*	Nicholas Wright	Douglas Heap
9 Nov	**The Changing Room** (transf. Globe 15.12.71)	**David Storey**	Lindsay Anderson	Jocelyn Herbert
23 Nov	*Friday*	*Hugo Claus* (transl. Christopher Logue)	Roger Croucher	Douglas Heap
28 Dec	*Sylveste*	*Ken Campbell Road Show*		
1972 26 Jan	**Alpha Beta** (transf. Apollo 16.3.72)	**E. A. Whitehead**	Anthony Page	Alan Tagg

Cast

Tim Curry, David Hill, Robert Hoskins, Mark McManus, Anthony Milner, Derek Newark

Timothy Dalton, Edward Jewesbury, Judy Loe

Georgia Brown, Oliver Cotton, Tim Curry, David Hill, Bob Hoskins, Mark McManus, Roddy Maude-Roxby, Anthony Milner, Derek Newark, Trevor Peacock, Barrie Rutter, Susan Williamson, Henry Woolf

Paul Angelis, Philip Donaghy, Sharon Duce, Clare Sutcliffe

Andy Andrews, Dave Hill, Bob Hoskins, Susan Littler, Christopher Martin, P. K. Smith, Jane Wood

Margaret Brooks, Rowena Cooper, Frances Cuka, Roy Dotrice, Jeannie Fisher, Peter Fontaine, Alan Hay, June Jago, Mary Macleod, Reginald Marsh, Lionel Murton, Ralph Nossek, Christine Paul, George Pravda, Roger Swaine, Rudolph Walker

Gillian Brown, Brian Croucher, Leonard Fenton, John Grillo, John Malcolm, Deborah Norton, Miles Reithermann, Jeffrey Shankley

Juliet Aykroyd, Brian Glover, Dave Hill, Mark McManus, Jack Shepherd

Barbara Ferris, Anna Massey, Lynn Redgrave

David McNiven, John Ramsey, Angie Rew, Tony Rohr

Hugh Fraser, Amaryllis Garnett, Tony Haygarth, Ann Holloway, David McNiven, John Ramsey, Angie Rew, Tony Rohr

Jonathan Bergman, Jo Blatchley, Leonard Fenton, Dallas Gavell, Mike Grady, Cheryl Hall, Billy Hamon, William Hoyland, Mike Kitchen, Pam Scotcher

Tony Haygarth, Ann Holloway

Peggy Ashcroft, Maurice Denham, Gordon Jackson

Yvonne Bryceland, Bloke Modisane, Zakes Mokae

Sheila Ballantine, Jill Bennett, Leon Berton, John Bloomfield, Peter Carlisle, Anthony Gardner, Willoughby Gray, Nigel Hawthorne, Patricia Lawrence, Bessie Love, Montgomery Matthew, Raul Neunie, Geoffrey Palmer, Ralph Richardson, Nicholas Selby, Jeffrey Shankley, Frank Wylie

Ben Bazell, Nicky Edmett, Warren Hooper, Lu Jeffrey, Chris Jordan, Eric Loeb, Paddy O'Hagan

Robert Atiko, Robert Coleby, Alfred Fagon, Mona Hammond, Carole Hayman, Oscar James, Stefan Kalipha, Patricia Moseley, Frank Singuineau, Corinne Skinner, T-Bone Wilson

Meg Davies, Catherine Kessler, Nicholas N. Nacht, Graham Simpson, James Warrior, Mark York

Eric Allen, Harry Andrews, Ray Barron, Derek Carpenter, Oliver Cotton, Anthony Douse, Matthew Guinness, Alec Heggie, Geoffrey Hinsliff, Bob Hoskins, Richard Howard, George Howe, William Hoyland, Gareth Hunt, Rosemary McHale, Mark McManus, Carmel McSharry, Anthony Milner, Ron Pember, Celestine Randall, Struan Rodger, Marjorie Yates

Kevin Brennan, Vivienne Cohen, Gareth Forbes, John Gregg, Linal Haft, Jonathan Hardy, Jenni Holland, Veronica Lang, Donald Macdonald, Henry Szeps

Jonathan Bergman, John Grillo, Claudette Houchen, Pat Quinn, Henry Woolf

Alun Armstrong, John Barrett, Peter Childs, Warren Clarke, David Daker, Paul Dawkins, Michael Elphick, Brian Glover, Matthew Guinness, David Hill, Geoffrey Hinsliff, Edward Judd, Barry Keegan, Brian Lawson, Don McKillop, Mark McManus, Frank Mills, Jim Norton, Edward Peel, John Rae, Peter Schofield

Diana Coupland, Tony Selby, John Thaw

cast list not available

Albert Finney, Rachel Roberts

Date	Production	Author	Director	Design/Music
4 Feb	*Live Like Pigs* (YPTS)	*John Arden*	Pam Brighton	William Dudley
1 March	*Mary Mary* (Freehold)	*Roy Kift*	Nancy Meckler	
9 March	**Veterans**	**Charles Wood**	Ronald Eyre	Voytek Daphne Dare (costumes)
26 March	The Centaur	Jonathan Hales	Jonathan Hales	Jenni Holland
12 April	*Within Two Shadows*	*Wilson John Haire*	Alfred Lynch	Douglas Heap
14 April	**Big Wolf**	**Harald Mueller** (transl. Steve Gooch)	William Gaskill & Pam Brighton	John Napier
16 May	*Show Me the Way to Go Home*	*Phil Woods & the company*	Pam Brighton	Mike Cook
24 May	**Crete and Sergeant Pepper**	**John Antrobus**	Peter Gill	Douglas Heap Deirdre Clancy (costumes)
20 May	*The Moon is East, the Sun is West*	*Tokyo Kid Brothers*		
4 June	Pretty Boy	Stephen Poliakoff	Colin Cook	
13 June	*Hitler Dances* (Traverse Workshop)	*Howard Brenton*	Max Stafford-Clark	
28 June	**Hedda Gabler**	**Henrik Ibsen** (adapt. John Osborne)	Anthony Page	Alan Tagg Deirdre Clancy (costumes)
4 July	*Was He Anyone?*	*N. F. Simpson*	Nicholas Wright	Harriet Geddes
4 Aug	*Dreams of Mrs Fraser*	*Gabriel Josipovici*	Roger Croucher	Harriet Geddes
8 Aug	**The Old Ones**	**Arnold Wesker**	John Dexter	Douglas Heap
6 Sept	*Brussels* (YPTS)	*Jonathan Hales*	Jonathan Hales	Harriet Geddes
19 Sept	**Richard's Cork Leg**	**Brendan Behan & Alan Simpson**	Alan Simpson	Wendy Shea The Dubliners (music)
1 Oct	England's Ireland	Tony Bicat, Howard Brenton, Brian Clark, David Edgar, Francis Fuchs, David Hare, Snoo Wilson	David Hare & Snoo Wilson	John Hallé
12 Oct	*Eye Winker, Tom Tinker*	*Tom MacIntyre*	Robert Kidd	John Bolton
2 Nov	**A Pagan Place**	**Edna O'Brien**	Ronald Eyre	Sean Kenny
7 Nov	*State of Emergency*	*David Edgar*	David Edgar	
22 Nov	*Owners*	*Caryl Churchill*	Nicholas Wright	Di Seymour
4 Dec	**A Sense of Detachment**	**John Osborne**	Frank Dunlop	Nadine Baylis
19 Dec	*State of Emergency*	*David Edgar*	David Edgar	
27 Dec	*Pilk's Madhouse*	*Ken Campbell Road Show*		
1973 9 Jan	*A Fart for Europe*	*Howard Brenton & David Edgar*	Chris Parr	Di Seymour
16 Jan	**Krapp's Last Tape** **Not I**	**Samuel Beckett** **Samuel Beckett**	Anthony Page Anthony Page	Jocelyn Herbert Jocelyn Herbert
22 Jan	*José Pigs/Cattle Show* (The People Show 48)			

Cast

Hugh Armstrong, Margaret Brady, Juliet Duncan, Leonard Fenton, Don Hawkins, Mary Healey, Philip Jackson, Godfrey James, Geoffrey Larner, Pam Scotcher, Gwyneth Strong, Queenie Watts, Jane Wood

Marty Cruickshank, Paola Dionisotti, Mike Harley, Neil Johnston, Wolf Kahler, Christopher Ravenscroft, Jennie Stoller, Ruth Tansey

Ann Bell, James Bolam, Jane Evers, John Gielgud, Frank Grimes, Bob Hoskins, Gordon Jackson, Ahmed Khalil, John Mills

Alfred Burke, Michael Byrne, Isabel Dean, Mark Kingston, Maureen Lipman

Eve Belton, Tom Cockerell, Brenda Fricker, Mary Larkin, Peggy Marshall, Garfield Morgan, Struan Rodger, Leslie Schofield, Shane Shelton, Patsy Smart, Frances Tomelty

David Atkinson, Mike Grady, Billy Hamon, Philip Jackson, Michael Kitchen, Patrick Murray, John Price, Reg Stewart, Nigel Terry, Leon Vitali

Glyn Grain, Billy Hamon, William Hoyland, Gareth Hunt, Philip Jackson, John Price, Pam Scotcher, Phil Woods

Jeremy Child, Peter Childs, Anthony Douse, Leonard Fenton, Raymond Francis, Bernard Gallagher, Brian Hall, Robert Hamilton, Don Hawkins, James Hazeldine, John McKelvey, Chris Malcolm, Bill Maynard, Stephen Rea, Nicholas Smith

cast list not available

Jill Meers, Michael Pennington, Elizabeth Sladen, Tony Steadman, George Sweeney, Nicholas Willatt

Kevin Costello, Amaryllis Garnett, Linda Goddard, Carole Hayman, Tony Rohr

Jill Bennett, Brian Cox, Anne Dyson, Denholm Elliott, Barbara Ferris, Ronald Hines, Mary Merrall

Yvonne Antrobus, June Brown, Geoffrey Chater, Rowena Cooper, Carol Gillies, Richard Kay, Stanley Lebor

Mark McManus, Rosemary Martin

Amelia Bayntun, Terry Burns, Patience Collier, Susan Engel, Leonard Fenton, Stephen Grives, James Hazeldine, Rose Hill, George Pravda, Wanda Rotha, Martin Skinner, George Tovey, Max Wall

Peter Armitage, Sylvia Carson, Lorraine Hill, John Ringham, Geoffrey Wearing

Ciaron Bourke, Eileen Colgan, Ronnie Drew, Olu Jacobs, Luke Kelly, Fionnuala Kenny, Barney MacKenna, Dearbhla Molloy, Angela Newman, Joan O'Hara, John Sheanan

Peter Adair, Tim Curry, Timothy Davies, Denis Lawson, Stanley McGeagh, Walter Monagle, Fidelma Murphy, Wesley Murphy, Dennis O'Neal, Fianuala O'Shannon, Jeremy Wilkin

Philip Donaghy, John Dunn-Hill, Donal McCann, John McKelvey, Oliver Maguire, Gerard Murphy, Frances Tomelty, Harry Webster

Dave Allen, David Burke, Donal Cox, Angela Crow, Sheelagh Cullen, David Daker, Patrick Dawson, Avril Elgar, Alex Farrell, Kitty Fitzgerald, Brenda Fricker, Diane Holland, Declan Mulholland, Colette O'Neil, Veronica Quilligan, Sally Travers, Dermot Tuohy

John Cudmore, Brian Hubbard, Alan Hulse, Janet Kelly, Michele Ryan

Stephanie Bidmead, Kenneth Cranham, Lucinda Curtis, Eileen Devlin, Richard O'Callaghan, Anne Raitt, David Swift

Jeni Barnett, Denise Coffey, Terence Frisby, Hugh Hastings, Nigel Hawthorne, David Hill, Peter Jolley, Rachel Kempson, Ralph Michael, John Standing

as 7 Nov

Bob Dermer, Andy Jones, Philip Schreibam, Jennifer Watts

Alun Armstrong, Jeremy Child, Louis Haslar, Hugh Hastings

Albert Finney
Brian Miller, Billie Whitelaw

Laura Gilbert, Mike Figgis, Mark Long, José Nava, Derek Wilson

Date	Production	Author	Director	Design/Music
30 Jan	*The George Jackson Black & White Minstrel Show* (Pip Simmons Theatre Group)			
12 Feb	*Wimbo the Wonder Dog* (Hull Truck)	*Mike Bradwell*	Mike Bradwell	
13 Feb	*The Weekend After Next* (Hull Truck)	*Mike Bradwell*	Mike Bradwell	
20 Feb	*Wholesome Glory*	*Mike Leigh*	Mike Leigh	
27 Feb	*Mothers and Others*	*Anne Raitt*	Anne Raitt	
27 Feb	**The Freedom of the City**	**Brian Friel**	Albert Finney	Douglas Heap Harriet Geddes (costumes)
11 March	The Fourth World	David Caute	Buzz Goodbody	
12 March	*The Unseen Hand*	*Sam Shepard*	Jim Sharman	Brian Thomson
2 April	*Beowulf* (Freehold)	*dramatized by Liane Aukin*	Nancy Meckler	
12 April	**Savages** (transf. Comedy 20.6.73)	**Christopher Hampton**	Robert Kidd	Jocelyn Herbert & Andrew Sanders
16 April	*Captain Oates' Left Sock*	*John Antrobus*	Nicholas Wright	Harriet Geddes
17 April	*Coming Attractions* (late night)	*Lizette Kocur, Neil Johnston & O Lan Shepard*		Marty Cruickshank (music)
27 April	*The Orange Balloon* (late night)	*Andy Phillips*	Robert Fox	
18 May	*Give the Gaffers Time to Love You*	*Barry Reckord*	Pam Brighton	John Hallé
22 May	**The Sea**	**Edward Bond**	William Gaskill	Deirdre Clancy
3 June	Millennium	Jeremy Seabrook & Michael O'Neill	Roger Croucher	Harriet Geddes
19 June	*The Rocky Horror Show* (transf. Chelsea Classic 14.8.73)	*Richard O'Brien*	Jim Sharman	Brian Thomson Richard O'Brien (music) Sue Blane (costumes)
28 June	**Magnificence**	**Howard Brenton**	Max Stafford-Clark	William Dudley
19 July	**The Removalists**	**David Williamson**	Jim Sharman	Brian Thomson
31 July	*Sweet Talk*	*Michael Abbensetts*	Stephen Frears	William Dudley
15 Aug	**Cromwell**	**David Storey**	Anthony Page	Jocelyn Herbert
28 Aug	*Bright Scene Fading*	*Tom Gallacher*	Nicholas Wright	John Macfarlane
20 Sept	*Sizwe Bansi is Dead*	*Athol Fugard, John Kani & Winston Ntshona*	Athol Fugard	Douglas Heap
26 Sept	**The Farm** (transf. Mayfair 1.11.73)	**David Storey**	Lindsay Anderson	Hayden Griffin Alan Price (music)
7 Oct	*The Porter's Play* (Sunday)	*Anton Gill*	Anton Gill	Keith Cheetham
31 Oct	*Elizabeth I*	*Paul Foster*	Walter Donohue	Robin Don
7 Nov	**The Merry Go Round**	**D. H. Lawrence**	Peter Gill	William Dudley Sue Plummer (costumes)
22 Nov	*The Pleasure Principle*	*Snoo Wilson*	David Hare	Harriet Geddes

Cast

cast list not available

Joolia Cappleman, Steve Halliman, Cass Patton, Alan Williams

as above

Geoffrey Hutchings, Roger Sloman, Alison Steadman
Amjula Harman, Rosamund Nelson, Cass Patton

Peter Adair, David Atkinson, Raymond Campbell, Basil Dignam, Peter Frye, Matthew Guinness, Catherine Harding,
Louis Haslar, Nicholas Llewellyn, Alex McCrindle, Carmel McSharry, Anthony Nash, Michael O'Hagan, Stephen Rea,
George Shane

Yvonne Antrobus, Lois Baxter, Ben Bazell, John Biggerstaff, Julian Curry, Norman Ettlinger, Richard Kane, Maureen Lipman,
John Shrapnel

Warren Clarke, Clive Endersby, Christopher Malcolm, Richard O'Brien, Tony Sibbald

Marty Cruickshank, Michael Harley, Dorinda Hulton, Neil Johnston, Wolf Kahler, Christopher Ravenscroft, Dinah Stabb,
Paddy Swanson, Rowan Wylie

Rona Anderson, George Baizley, A. J. Brown, Terence Burns, Tom Conti, Lynda Dagley, Glyn Grain, Leonard Kavanagh,
Thelma Kidger, Donna Louise, Eddi Nedari, Geoffrey Palmer, Michael Pennington, Paul Scofield, J. C. Shepherd,
Frank Singuineau, Gordon Sterne

Margaret Brady, Oliver Cotton, Gabrielle Daye, James Donnelly, Geoffrey Edwards, Matthew Guinness, Charles Kinross,
Carol Macready, Judith Paris, Stephen Rea, Jill Richards, Nicholas Selby, Martin Skinner, Jenny Tomasin, Janet Webb

Lizette Kocur, Neil Johnston, O Lan Shepard

Warren Clarke, Lois Daine

Jonathan Adams, Paul Angelis, Tim Curry, Alan Ford, David Leland, Petra Markham, Peter Straker

Coral Browne, Adrienne Byrne, Simon Cord, Ian Holm, Anthony Langdon, Margaret Lawley, Mark McManus, Gillian Martell,
Barbara Ogilvie, Diana Quick, Simon Rouse, Alan Webb, Susan Williamson, Jeremy Wilson

Betty Alberge, James Aubrey, June Brown, Anthony Douse, Diane Fletcher, Philip Jackson, Norman Jones,
Pamela Moiseiwitsch, Jill Richards, David Rintoul, Gwyneth Strong, Leon Vitali

Jonathan Adams, Rayner Bourton, Julie Covington, Tim Curry, Christopher Malcolm, Little Nell, Richard O'Brien,
Paddy O'Hagan, Patricia Quinn

James Aubrey, Geoffrey Chater, Kenneth Cranham, Robert Eddison, Leonard Fenton, Carole Hayman, Michael Kitchen,
Peter Postlethwaite, Nikolaj Ryjtkov, Dinah Stabb

Brian Croucher, Ed Devereaux, Darlene Johnson, Mark McManus, Carole Mowlam, Struan Rodger

Alister Bain, Lee Davies, Mona Hammond, Joan-Ann Maynard, Don Warrington, Sally Watts

Alun Armstrong, Conrad Asquith, John Barrett, Colin Bennett, Kenneth Colley, Forbes Collins, Jarlath Conroy, Brian Cox,
Colin Douglass, Anne Dyson, Albert Finney, Alan Ford, Mark McManus, Michael Melia, Peter Postlethwaite, Diana Rayworth,
Martin Read

Rod Beacham, Adrienne Hill, Roderic Leigh, Andrew McCulloch, Paul Seed, Robert Trotter

John Kani, Winston Ntshona

Lewis Collins, Meg Davies, Prunella Gee, Frank Grimes, Patricia Healey, Bernard Lee, Doreen Mantle

Rod Beacham, Brian Croucher, Derek Deadman, Arthur English, John Fahey, Roderic Leigh, Andrew McCulloch,
Don McKillop, Stanley Meadows, Anthony Nash, George Shane

Charlotte Cornwell, Michael Feast, Carole Hayman, Paul Moriarty, Peter Postlethwaite, David Sands, Stuart Wilson

Anthony Baird, David Daker, Gabrielle Daye, Patricia Doyle, Anne Dyson, George Howe, Margaret Lawley, Alex McCrindle,
Oliver Maguire, George Malpas, Michael Melia, Mary Miller, Derrick O'Connor, Susan Traby, Marjorie Yates

Julie Covington, George Fenton, Ann Firbank, Neil Fitzwilliam, Brenda Fricker, Stewart Harwood, Dinsdale Landen,
Bob Sherman

	Date	Production	Author	Director	Design/Music
	26 Dec	*Dick Whittington*	*Mike Leigh*	Mike Leigh	
1974	2 Jan	**The Island** (transf. Ambassadors 10.4.74)	**Athol Fugard, John Kani & Winston Ntshona**	Athol Fugard	Douglas Heap
	8 Jan	**Sizwe Bansi is Dead** (transf. Ambassadors 10.4.74)	**Athol Fugard, John Kani & Winston Ntshona**	Athol Fugard	Douglas Heap
	22 Jan	**Statements After an Arrest Under the Immorality Act**	**Athol Fugard**	Athol Fugard	Douglas Heap
	29 Jan	*Two Jelliplays* (YPTS)			
		Clever Elsie, Smiling John, Silent Peter	*Ann Jellicoe*	Ann Jellicoe	David Short
		A Good Thing or a Bad Thing	*Ann Jellicoe*	Ann Jellicoe	David Short
	21 Feb	*Geography of a Horse Dreamer*	*Sam Shepard*	Sam Shepard	Bettina Reeves
	11 March	**Runaway**	**Peter Ransley**	Alfred Lynch	Hayden Griffin
	2 April	*Six of the Best* (YPTS)			
		Liberation City	*Michael Belbin*	Joan Mills	Bettina Reeves
		Errand	*Jim Irvin*	John Barlow	Bettina Reeves
		Big Business	*Mark Edwards*	Joan Mills	Bettina Reeves
		Maggie's Fortune	*Sheila Wright*	Ann Jellicoe	Bettina Reeves
		Fireman's Ball	*Stephen Frost*	Ann Jellicoe	Bettina Reeves
		Event	*James Clarke*	John Barlow	Bettina Reeves
		Zoological Palace	*Conrad Mullineaux*	Joan Mills	Bettina Reeves
	9 April	**Life Class**	**David Storey**	Lindsay Anderson	Jocelyn Herbert
	24 April	*Bird Child*	*David Lan*	Nicholas Wright	David Short
	28 April	Johnny	Robert Thornton	John Tydeman	
	14 May	*Shivvers* (Joint Stock)	*Stanley Eveling*	Max Stafford-Clark	Poppy Mitchell
	5 June	**Tooth of Crime**	**Sam Shepard**	Jim Sharman	Brian Thomson Sue Blane (costumes) Richard Hartley (music)
	10 June	*A Worthy Guest*	*Paul Bailey*	Ann Jellicoe	David Short
	16 June	The Watergate Tapes	Sam Wanamaker (editor)		
	11 July	*The Sea Anchor*	*E. A. Whitehead*	Jonathan Hales	Sue Plummer
	16 July	**Play Mas** (transf. Phoenix 21.8.74)	**Mustapha Matura**	Donald Howarth	Douglas Heap Peter Minshall (costumes)
	14 Aug	**Bingo**	**Edward Bond**	Jane Howell & John Dove	Hayden Griffin Martin Duncan (music)
	19 Aug	*X* (Joint Stock)	*Barry Reckord*	Max Stafford-Clark	Douglas Heap
	25 Aug	Taking Stock	Robert Holman	Chris Parr	
	17 Sept	*Action*	*Sam Shepard*	Nancy Meckler	David Short
	9 Oct	**The Great Caper**	**Ken Campbell**	Nicholas Wright	Bob Ringwood
	13 Oct	In Celebration	David Storey	Lindsay Anderson	Jocelyn Herbert
	16 Oct	*Lord Nelson Lives in Liverpool 8*	*Philip Martin*	Joan Mills	John Macfarlane

Cast

Lavinia Bertram, Paul Copley, Julia Coppleman, Peter Godfrey, Philip Jackson, Roger Sloman, Tim Stern

John Kani, Winston Ntshona

John Kani, Winston Ntshona

Yvonne Bryceland, Wilson Dunster, Ben Kingsley

Colin Bennett, Judy Buxton, Janette Legge, Stephen Mackenna, Tony Robinson

as above

Bill Bailey, Kenneth Cranham, Alfred Hoffman, Bob Hoskins, Neil Johnston, Stephen Rea, Raymond Skipp, George Silver

Bill Dean, Kim Moreton, Cherry Morris, Bill Owen, Peter Robinson, Simon Rouse, Susan Tracy

John Dicks, Michael Harbour, Guy Standeven, Maggie Wells
Patrick Murray, Guy Standeven
Angela Crow, Michael Harbour
Angela Crow, John Dicks, Michael Harbour, Maggie Wells
John Dicks, Michael Harbour
Michael Harbour, Patrick Murray, Guy Standeven
John Dicks, Patrick Murray, Guy Standeven, Maggie Wells

Alan Bates, Stephen Bent, Brenda Cavendish, Brian Glover, Frank Grimes, Gerald James, Paul Kelly, David Lincoln, Gabrielle Lloyd, Rosemary Martin, Bob Peck, Stuart Rayner, Sally Watts

James Aubrey, Geoffrey Bateman, Jumoke Debayo, Nigel Hawthorne, Douglas Heard, Marjie Lawrence, Janette Legge, Jacqueline Stanbury

John Biggerstaff, Adrienne Byrne, Ronald Forfar, Gabrielle Hamilton, Terence Hillyer, Robert Keegan, Paul Rosebury, David Sterne

Deirdre Costello, Tony Haygarth, Bill Stewart

Jonathan Adams, Kenneth Cranham, Paul Freeman, Diane Langton, Christopher Malcolm, Richard O'Brien, Mike Pratt

Tom Durham, Martin Fisk, Jimmy Gardner, Gordon Gostelow, Pat Keen, Eve Pearce, William Russell, Robin Summers, Angela Thorne, Jean Warren

Larry Adler, Frank Dux, Weston Gavin, Bill Hootkins, Bob Sherman, Sam Wanamaker

Peter Armitage, David Daker, Alison Steadman, Marjorie Yates

Norman Beaton, Ed Bishop, Tommy Eytle, Mona Hammond, Stefan Kalipha, Robert La Bossier, Lucita Lijertwood, Mercia Mansfield, Charles Pemberton, Frank Singuineau, Trevor Thomas, Rudolph Walker

John Barrett, Hilda Barry, Oliver Cotton, Yvonne Edgell, Derek Fuke, John Gielgud, Ewan Hooper, Paul Jesson, Arthur Lowe, Gillian Martell, Joanna Tope

Margaret Burnett, Libba Davies, Terence Frisby, Roderic Leigh

Susan Blake, Brian Deacon, Gerald James, Ian Marter, John Normington

Stephen Moore, Stephen Rea, Jill Richards, Jennie Stoller

Katie Allan, Judith Blake, Ken Campbell, Simon Coady, Eddie Davies, Lisa Harrow, Aharon Ipalé, Mark Jones, Richard O'Callaghan, Warren Mitchell

Alan Bates, James Bolam, Constance Chapman, Brian Cox, Gabrielle Daye, Bill Owen

Jane Anthony, James Broadbent, Chris Cregan, Brinsley Ford, Richard Forde, Stephen Pacey, Gordon Reid, Guy Standeven

Date	Production	Author	Director	Design/Music
6 Nov	*Fourth Day Like Four Long Months of Absence* (Joint Stock)	*Colin Bennett*	Max Stafford-Clark	Diana Greenwood
12 Nov	**The City** (Tokyo Kid Brothers)	**Yutaka Higashi**	Yutaka Higashi	Yutaka Higashi
13 Dec	*Remember the Truth Dentist*	*Heathcote Williams*	Ken Campbell	William Dudley Bob Flag (music)

1975

Date	Production	Author	Director	Design/Music
2 Jan	**Objections to Sex and Violence**	**Caryl Churchill**	John Tydeman	David Short
5 Jan	*Innocent Bystanders* (Sunday)	*Gordon Graham*	Denise Coffey	
19 Jan	Sand			
	Moments on Jaffa Beach	*Michael Almaz*	Peter Stevenson	Rita Fuzzey
	The Port Said Performance	*Michael Almaz*	Peter Stevenson	Rita Fuzzey
29 Jan	**Statements After an Arrest Under the Immorality Act**	**Athol Fugard**	Athol Fugard	Douglas Heap
	Not I	**Samuel Beckett**	Anthony Page	Jocelyn Herbert
11 Feb	*Mrs Grabowski's Academy*	*John Antrobus*	Jonathan Hales	Sue Plummer
16 Feb	Number One Rooster	David Throsby	William Alexander	
4 March	**Don's Party**	**David Williamson**	Michael Blakemore	Alan Pickford
10 March	*Loud Reports*	*John Burrows, John Harding & Peter Skellern*	Mark Wing-Davey	Peter Skellern (music)
25 March	*The Doomduckers' Ball* (Joint Stock)	*Carole Hayman, Neil Johnston, Mary Maddox, Dinah Stabb & Jeff Teare*		Free Money (music)
17 April	**Entertaining Mr Sloane** (transf. Duke of York's 2.6.75)	**Joe Orton**	Roger Croucher	John Gunter
28 April	*Paradise*	*David Lan*	Tessa Marwick & Nicholas Wright	William Dudley
28 May	*Echoes from a Concrete Canyon*	*Wilson John Haire*	Roger Croucher	Anne-Marie Schöne
3 June	**Loot**	**Joe Orton**	Albert Finney	Douglas Heap Harriet Geddes (costumes)
4 June	*Homage to Bean Soup* (lunchtime & late night)	*David Lan*	Tessa Marwick	
15 June	*Moving Clocks Go Slow* (Sunday)	*Caryl Churchill*	John Ford	Chris Bowler (costumes)
1 July	*Heroes*	*Stephen Poliakoff*	Tim Fywell	John Macfarlane
7 July	*Black Slaves, White Chains* (lunchtime & late night)	*Mustapha Matura*	Rufus Collins	
13 July	*A 'Nevolent Society* (Sunday)	*Mary O'Malley*	Henry Woolf	
16 July	**What the Butler Saw** (transf. Whitehall 19.8.75)	**Joe Orton**	Lindsay Anderson	Jocelyn Herbert
28 July	*Sex and Kinship in a Savage Society*	*Jeremy Seabrook & Michael O'Neill*	William Alexander	David Short
31 July	*Mean Time* (lunchtime)	*Richard Crane*	Richard Crane	
3 Aug	Soul of the Nation	Sebastian Clarke	Donald Howarth	

Cast

Mike Griggs, Carole Hayman, William Hoyland, Caroline Hutchison, Malcolm Ingram, Tony Rohr, Toby Salaman

Mitsko Fukami & Baby, Tsutomu Hori, Toshiko Inoue, Fumiko Kuniya, Hidehiko Okazaki, Shoichi Saito, Megumi Shimanuki, Ryusako Shinsui, Sansho Shinsui, Paul Waki

Paola Dionisotti, Philip Donaghy, David Hill, Roy Martin, John Prior, Demelza Val Baker

Anna Calder-Marshall, Sylvia Coleridge, Michael Harrigan, Rose Hill, Rosemary McHale, Stephen Moore, Ivor Roberts, Paul Seed

Sam Kelly, Nicholas Loukes, Paul Nicholas, Deborah Norton, Max Phipps

Jack Chissick, Phil Emanuel, Jon Flanagan, Philip Jackson, Patricia Leventon
David Arthur, Jack Chissick, Richard Crane, Tim Davis, Michael Deacon, Dominic Jepcott, Lesley Joseph, Harry Landis, Timothy Peters

Yvonne Bryceland, Wilson Dunster, Ben Kingsley

Melvyn Hastings, Billie Whitelaw

Richard Beckinsale, Simon Callow, Ian Charleson, Patience Collier, Cheryl Hall, Denis Lawson, Beth Morris, Philip Stone

Barbara Angell, Michael Balfour, Ed Bishop, Joan Bolken, Bob Hornery, Stephen Moore, Raymond O'Reilly, John Pine, Ken Shorter, Michael Staniforth

Ray Barrett, Barry Creyton, Barbara Ewing, John Gregg, Tony Haygarth, Briony Hodge, Veronica Lang, Ginette Macdonald, Carol Macready, Stephen O'Rourke, Max Phipps

John Burrows, John Harding, Peter Skellern

Carole Hayman, Neil Johnston, Mary Maddox, Dinah Stabb, Jeff Teare

Ronald Fraser, Malcolm McDowell, James Ottaway, Beryl Reid

Scott Antony, Jonathan Bergman, Jean Boht, Derek Carpenter, Robert Gillespie, Roger Lloyd Pack, Angela Phillips, Roger Rees

Nicholas Ball, James Grant, Judy Parfitt, Leslie Sarony, Gwyneth Strong

James Aubrey, Jill Bennett, Michael O'Hagan, Arthur O'Sullivan, Philip Stone, David Troughton

Jean Boht, Emma Williams

Nicholas Ball, Diana Barrett, Ronald Fraser, Aviva Goldkorn, Rose Hill, David Howey, Roger Rees, Paul Roylance, Jennie Stoller, Nigel Wilson

Lynsey Baxter, Peter Bennett, Phil Daniels, David Dixon, Christine Noonan, Jonathan Pryce

Eddy Grant, Mark Heath, Olu Jacobs, Saul Reichlin, Jean Warren

Leonard Fenton, Patricia Franklin, Edward Kelsey, Mary O'Malley, Henry Woolf

Jane Carr, Valentine Dyall, Brian Glover, Kevin Lloyd, Betty Marsden, Michael Medwin

Tom Bell, Lynn Farleigh, Doreen Mantle, Robert Putt

Amanda Reiss, Margaretta Scott

Caroline Burt, Michael Graham Cox, Frank Gatliff, Pat Hartley, Oscar James, Stefan Kalipha, Archie Pool, Ewan Roberts, T-Bone Wilson

Date	Production	Author	Director	Design/Music
2 Sept	**Teeth 'n' Smiles** (transf. Wyndham's 24.5.76)	**David Hare**	David Hare	Jocelyn Herbert Nick Bicat (music)
28 Sept	*Asleep at the Wheel* (Sunday)	*David Coulter*	John Ford	Eve Ritscher
14 Oct	**Stripwell**	**Howard Barker**	Chris Parr	Bob Ringwood
16 Oct	*Young Writers' Festival* *Travel Sickness*	*Matilda Hartwell*	John Ford	Jane Riply
	Stepping Stone	*James Bradley*	Joan Mills	Jane Riply
	Watercress Sandwiches	*Zoe Tamsyn & Sophia Everest-Phillips*	Joan Mills	Jane Riply
	St George and his Dragon	*Tanya Meadows*	John Ford	Jane Riply
	Interval	*Jim Irvin & Tim Whelan*	Joan Mills	Jane Riply
	How do You Clean a Sunflower? (West Indian Drama Group)		John Ford	Jane Riply
26 Oct	Under the Clock	Gordon Porterfield	William Alexander	
18 Nov	**The Fool**	**Edward Bond**	Peter Gill	William Dudley
14 Dec	A Tale of Three Cities	Gebre Yohanse Asefaw	Nicholas Wright	
1976 19 Jan	**Judgement** (National Theatre)	**Barry Collins**	Peter Hall	
3 Feb	**Treats** (transf. Mayfair 6.3.75)	**Christopher Hampton**	Robert Kidd	Andrew Sanders
16 March	**Parcel Post**	**Yemi Ajibade**	Donald Howarth	David Short
22 April	**Waiting for Godot** (in German: Schiller Theatre, Berlin)	**Samuel Beckett**	Samuel Beckett	Mateas
6 May	**Endgame**	**Samuel Beckett**	Donald McWhinnie	Andrew Sanders
11 May	*Yesterday's News* (Joint Stock)	*the actors & Jeremy Seabrook*	William Gaskill & Max Stafford-Clark	Hayden Griffin
20 May	**Play** **That Time** **Footfalls**	**Samuel Beckett** **Samuel Beckett** **Samuel Beckett**	Donald McWhinnie Donald McWhinnie Samuel Beckett	Jocelyn Herbert Jocelyn Herbert Jocelyn Herbert
30 June	*Amy and the Price of Cotton*	*Michael McGrath*	William Alexander	Polly Barlow
8 July	**Small Change**	**Peter Gill**	Peter Gill	William Dudley
29 July	*The Only Way Out*	*George Thatcher*	David Halliwell	
10 Aug	**T-Zee**	**Richard O'Brien**	Nicholas Wright	Brian Thomson Sue Blane (costumes) Richard Hartley (music)
25 Aug	*Just a Little Bit Less than Normal*	*Nigel Baldwin*	John Ashford	Mary Moore
22 Sept	**Mother's Day**	**David Storey**	Robert Kidd	Harry Waistnage Robert Dein (costumes)
27 Sept	*Light Shining in Buckinghamshire* (Joint Stock)	*Caryl Churchill*	Max Stafford-Clark	Sue Plummer
20 Oct	*An' Me Wi' a Bad Leg Tae* (Borderline Company)	*Billy Connolly*	Stuart Mungall	
3 Nov	**Rum an' Coca-Cola**	**Mustapha Matura**	Donald Howarth	Jocelyn Herbert
7 Dec	**Dracula** (Pip Simmons Group)	**Pip Simmons**		

Cast

Rene Augustus, David Charkham, Andrew Dickson, Ian Elliott, Mick Ford, Hugh Fraser, Heinz, Karl Howman, Rober Hume, Dave King, Cherie Lunghi, Helen Mirren, Jack Shepherd, Antony Sher

David Charkham, David Cross, Andy Hellerby, Kit Jackson, Raad Rawi, Diana Rowan

Peter Attard, Constance Cummings, Alan Foss, Michael Hordern, Jennifer Piercey, Patricia Quinn, Roger Sloman, Tim Woodward

Liz Bagley, Stephanie Fayerman, Lally Percy
Liz Bagley, Arthur Kelly, William Relton, Ted Richards, Jim Sweeney
Liz Bagley, Stephanie Fayerman, Arthur Kelly, Lally Percy, William Relton, Ted Richards, Jim Sweeney

Arthur Kelly, Lally Percy, William Relton, Ted Richards, Jim Sweeney
as above
members of the West Indian Drama Group

Ed Bishop, Frank Dodson, Kate Harper, Pat Hartley, Elaine Ives Cameron, Eiji Kusuhara, Antony Morton, Anthony Nash, Stephen O'Rourke, Joe Praml, Gordon Sterne, Ned Vanzandt

John Boswall, Tom Courtenay, Isabel Dean, David Ellison, Mick Ford, Bill Fraser, Brian Hall, Roger Hume, Caroline Hutchison, Malcolm Ingram, Sheila Kelley, Robert Lloyd, Avril Marsh, Gillian Martell, Peter Myers, John Normington, Tony Rohr, Nicholas Selby, Roderick Smith, Nigel Terry, David Troughton, Bridget Turner

William Alexander, Alun Armstrong, Ian Charleson, Jeremy Child, Peter Childs, Joanna Cooper, Peter-Hugo Daly, Lee Davis, Linda Goddard, Hugh Hastings, Carole Hayman, Paula Jacobs, Michael Joyce, Gorden Kaye, Catherine Kessler, Jeffrey Kissoon, Gwen Nelson, Pauline Quirke, George Raistrick, Renu Setna, Sally Watts

Colin Blakely

Jane Asher, James Bolam, Stephen Moore

Taiwo Ajai, Yemi Ajibade, Christopher Asante, Johnny Briggs, Gordon Case, Glenna Forster Jones, Muriel Odunton, Willie Payne, Ilarrio Bisi Pedro, Stuart Rayner, Rudolph Walker

Horst Bollmann, Klaus Herm, Carl Raddatz, Torsten Sense, Stefan Wigger

Rose Hill, Patrick Magee, Stephen Rea, Leslie Sarony

Gillian Barge, Linda Goddard, Paul Kember, Will Knightley, Philip McGough, Tony Mathews, David Rintoul

Anna Massey, Ronald Pickup, Penelope Wilton
Patrick Magee
Rose Hill, Billie Whitelaw

James Aubrey, Ian Cullen, Celia Gregory, Lydia Lisle, David Ryall

James Hazeldine, Phillip Joseph, June Watson, Marjorie Yates

Noel Collins, Brian Croucher, Steve Halliwell, Hugh McKenzie-Bailey, John Oxley, Oliver Smith, Derek West

Warren Clarke, Arthur Dignam, Gilyan Jones, Diane Langton, Julian Littman, Paul Nicholas, Charles Nowosielski, Jim Sweeney, Kimi Wong

June Brown, Karl Johnson, Alun Lewis, Steve McDonald, Judy Riley, David Sinclair

Alun Armstrong, Jane Carr, Colin Farrell, Patricia Healey, Gorden Kaye, Betty Marsden, Peter Myers, Dorothea Phillips, Susan Porrett, Bryan Pringle, David Ryan

Jan Chappell, Linda Goddard, Robert Hamilton, Will Knightley, Colin McCormack, Nigel Terry

Sarah Ballantyne, Margot Gillies, James Kennedy, Alex Norton, Bill Paterson, David Sands, Carey Wilson

Norman Beaton, Trevor Thomas

Ben Bazell, Rod Beddall, Sheila Burnett, Meirav Cary, Peter Jonfield, Chris Jordan, Roderic Leigh, Peter Oliver, Emil Wolk

	Date	Production	Author	Director	Design/Music
1977	5 Jan	*Uhlanga*	*Mshengu & James Mthoba*	James Mthoba	
	13 Jan	**Sizwe Bansi is Dead**	**Athol Fugard, John Kani & Winston Ntshona**	Athol Fugard	Douglas Heap
	27 Jan	*Traps*	*Caryl Churchill*	John Ashford	Terry Jacobs
	23 Feb	*Short Sleeves in Summer*	*Tunde Ikoli*	Michael Joyce	Douglas Heap
	24 Feb	**Devil's Island** (Joint Stock)	**Tony Bicat**	David Hare	Hayden Griffin
	17 March	*Young Writers' Festival* *Walking*	*Lenka Janiurek*	Tim Fywell	Jim Clay
		To Err is Human	*Liz Bellamy*	Gerald Chapman	Jim Clay
		West Side Bovver	*Shirley McKay & Christina Martin*	Gerald Chapman	Jim Clay
		Fishing	*Alexander Matthews*	Gerald Chapman	Jim Clay
	23 March	**Gimme Shelter** (The Network, Soho Poly)	**Barrie Keeffe**	Keith Washington	Mary Moore
	4 April	*For All Those Who Get Despondent* (cabaret)	*Bertolt Brecht & Frank Wedekind*	Peter Barnes	
	12 April	**Out of Our Heads** (7:84 Scotland)	**John McGrath**	Dave Anderson	
	14 April	*I Made it Ma Top of the World*	*devised by John Chapman & Tim Fywell*	John Chapman & Tim Fywell	
	21 April	**Curse of the Starving Class**	**Sam Shepard**	Nancy Meckler	Sue Plummer
	11 May	*For the West* (transf. Cottesloe 14.8.77)	*Michael Hastings*	Nicholas Wright	Anne-Marie Schöne
	13 June	**Fair Slaughter**	**Howard Barker**	Stuart Burge	Patrick Robertson Rosemary Vercoe (costume)
	15 June	*The Winter Dancers*	*David Lan*	Ian Kellgren	Gillian Daniell
	20 July	**Sleak!**	**C. P. Lee**	Charles Hanson	
	10 Aug	**Once a Catholic** (transf. Wyndham's 4.10.77)	**Mary O'Malley**	Mike Ockrent	Poppy Mitchell
	17 Aug	*Sudlow's Dawn*	*Nigel Baldwin*	Tim Fywell	Caroline Beaver
	12 Sept	**Sleak!**	**C. P. Lee**	Charles Hanson	
	27 Sept	*'tufff'*	*Bille Brown*	Diane Cilento	Jim Clay
	10 Oct	**The Good Woman of Setzuan** (Newcastle Theatre Tyneside Co)	**Bertolt Brecht**	Keith Hack	Sally Gardner
	17 Oct	*No Pasaran* (YPTS) (Free Form Roadshow '77)	*David Holman*	Sean Cunningham	
	21 Oct	*Skoolplay*	*Alan Brown*	Ian Kellgren	Rodger Parker
	31 Oct	*Return to My Native Land*	*Aimé Cesaire* (transl. John Berger & Anna Bostock)	John Russell Brown	Jim Clay
	22 Nov	*Playpen*	*Heathcote Williams*	Gerald Chapman	Ariane Gastambide & Jennifer Carey
	23 Nov	**Talbot's Box** (Abbey Theatre)	**Thomas Kilroy**	Patrick Mason	Wendy Shea
	20 Dec	**The Trembling Giant** (7:84 Scotland)	**John McGrath**	John McGrath	Allan Ross
1978	2 Jan	*The Kreutzer Sonata* (Birmingham Rep)	*Leo Tolstoy* (adapt. Peter Farago)	Peter Farago	Geoffrey Scott
	9 Jan	*Our Own People* (Pirate Jenny)	*David Edgar*	Walter Donohue	Di Seymour

Cast

James Mthoba

John Kani, Winston Ntshona

Hugh Fraser, Catherine Kessler, Anthony Milner, Catherine Neilson, Tim Pigott-Smith, Nigel Terry

Joseph Charles, Charles Cork, David Howe, Gregory Munroe, Anna Nygh, Barry Reckord, Sharon Rosita

Gillian Barge, Suzanne Bertish, Simon Callow, Philip Donaghy, David Rintoul, Jane Wood

Kay Adshead, Glenn Cunningham, Anthony Douse, Tony Mathews, Kate Saunders, Jim Sweeney
as above
as above

Kay Adshead, Anthony Douse, Tony Mathews, Jim Sweeney

Philip Davis, Peter Hughes, Phillip Joseph, Roger Leach, Sharman MacDonald, Ian Sharp

Anna Calder-Marshall, Maurice Colbourne, Terry Dougherty, Dilys Laye, Myra Love

Neil Gammack, James Grant, Elizabeth MacLennan, Terry Neason, Bill Riddoch, Allan Ross

Alan Butler, Caroline Embling, Brian Hall, Mike Kemp, Johanna Kirby, Albert Welling

Annette Crosbie, Brian Deacon, Michael Ensign, Ray Hassett, Patti Love, John Ratzenberger, Tony Sibbold, Dudley Sutton, Michael Walker

Basil Henson, Roger Milner, Renu Setna, Rudolph Walker

Jan Chappell, Nick Edmett, Robert Gary, Tony Halfpenny, David Jackson, Judy Liebert, Tony Mathews, Robin Meredith, John Thaw, Max Wall

Betty Hardy, Mary Larkin, Alex McCrindle, John McEnery, Fred Pearson, Sean Scanlan, Jack Shepherd, Stassia Stakis

Michael Deeks, Gorden Kaye, Arthur Kelly, Shelagh Stephenson, and Alberto y Los Trios Paranoias

John Boswall, Jane Carr, Kim Clifford, Daniel Gerroll, Mike Grady, Pat Heywood, Anna Keaveney, Doreen Keogh, June Page, Rowena Roberts, Lillian Rostkowska, John Rogan, Sally Watkins, Jeanne Watts

Roger Booth, Caroline Hutchison, Karl Johnson, Merdelle Jordine, Irene Sutcliffe, Peter Wigat

as 20 July but with Judy Lloyd instead of Shelagh Stephenson

Jeremy Chance, John Mangan, Raphael West

Constantin de Goguel, Renee Goddard, Richard Ireson, Jonathan Kent, Philip McGough, Gillian Martell, Fred Pearson, Mary Sheen, Janet Suzman, Frank Vincent

Liz Brailsford, Rod Brookes, Graham Downes, John Martin, Karen Merkel, John Say

Joan Geary, Richard Henry, Dave Hill, Leslie Pitt, Susan Porrett, Chloe Salaman, Peter Sproule

Cy Grant

Ben Benison, Roddy Maude-Roxby, Ric Morgan, John Muirhead

Stephen Brennan, Eileen Colgan, Ingrid Craigie, Clive Geraghty, John Molloy

Chas Ambler, David Anderson, Jackie Farrell, James Grant, Sean McCarthy, Elizabeth MacLennan, David McNiven, Terry Neason, Angie Rew, Ann Louise Ross

David Suchet

Chrissie Cotteril, John Gillett, Sue Glanville, Indira Joshi, Malcolm Raeburn, Reggee Ranjha, Tariq Yunus

Date	Production	Author	Director	Design/Music
18 Jan	*Says I, Says He* (Sheffield Crucible)	*Ron Hutchinson*	David Leland	Roger Glossop
24 Jan	**Laughter**	**Peter Barnes**	Charles Marowitz	Patrick Robertson Rosemary Vercoe (costumes)
13 Feb	*In the Blood*	*Lenka Janiurek*	Tim Fywell	David McHenry
19 Feb	*Procreation* (Sunday)	*Anthony Trent*	David Halliwell	
21 Feb	**The Bear**	**Anton Chekhov** (adapt. N. F. Simpson)	Stuart Burge	Pippy Bradshaw
	The Kreutzer Sonata	**Leo Tolstoy** (adapt. Peter Farago)	Peter Farago	Geoffrey Scott
26 Feb	*Bad Dream in an Old Hotel* (Sunday)	*James Pettifer*	Jonathan Holloway	
9 March	*Class Enemy*	*Nigel Williams*	William Alexander	Mary Moore
12 March	*Black Slaves, White Chains* *More, More* (Sunday)	*Mustapha Matura* *Mustapha Matura*	Charles Hanson Charles Hanson	
14 March	**A Bed of Roses** (Hull Truck)	**Mike Bradwell**	Mike Bradwell	Gemma Jackson
4 April	**Class Enemy**	**Nigel Williams**	William Alexander	
4 April	*Bleak House* (Shared Experience)	*Charles Dickens*	Mike Alfreds	
11 May	**The Glad Hand**	**Snoo Wilson**	Max Stafford-Clark	Peter Hartwell
17 May	*Young Writers' Festival* *From Cockneys to Toffs* *Artificial Living*	*Joanne Caffell* *Stephen Rowe*	John Dale Gerald Chapman & Tim Fywell	David Fielding & Kate Owen
	The School Leaver	*Michael McMillan*	Gerald Chapman	
	Covehithe	*Anna Wheatley*	Tim Fywell	
5 June	**I was Sitting on My Patio This Guy Appeared I Thought I was Hallucinating**	**Robert Wilson**	Robert Wilson	
20 June	**Flying Blind**	**Bill Morrison**	Alan Dossor	John Gunter Terry Canning (music)
12 July	*Irish Eyes and English Tears*	*Nigel Baldwin*	Ian Kellgren	Pippy Bradshaw & Andrew Sanders
2 Aug	**Eclipse**	**Leigh Jackson**	Stuart Burge	Nadine Baylis
11 Aug	*Bukharin* (rehearsed reading)	*Andy McSmith*	Les Waters	
18 Aug	*The Guise* (rehearsed reading)	*David Mowat*	Les Waters	
24 Aug	*Prayer for My Daughter*	*Thomas Babe*	Max Stafford-Clark	John Gunter
12 Sept	**Inadmissible Evidence**	**John Osborne**	John Osborne	John Gunter
18 Sept	*Emigrants* (Pirate Jenny)	*Peter Sheridan*	Jim Sheridan	Wendy Shea
2 Oct	*Nightfall* (Lumiere & Son)	*David Gale*	Hilary Westlake	
18 Oct	*The Slab Boys* (Traverse Theatre)	*John Byrne*	David Hayman	Grant Hicks

Cast

Raymond Campbell, James Duggan, Stephanie Fayerman, Christopher Hancock, Andrew Norton, Sean Scanlan, Maggie Shevlin, Ken Shorter, Ann Windsor

Paul Bentall, Neil Boorman, Patrick Connor, Frances de la Tour, Derek Francis, Roger Kemp, Patricia Leach, Stuart Rayner, Barry Stanton, David Suchet, Timothy West

Jean Boht, Anthony Douse, Carol Frazer, Shirley King, Toby Salaman, Sean Scanlan, Gwyneth Strong

Geoffrey Freshwater, Julie Newbert

Pauline Collins, Leslie Sarony, David Suchet

David Suchet

Patrick Duggan, Nick Gecks, Roland Macleod, Bryan Murray, John Say, Christine Schofield, Frank Vincent

Perry Benson, Brian Croucher, Peter-Hugo Daly, Phil Daniels, Michael Deeks, Tony London, Herbert Norville

Iain Armstrong, Malcolm Fredricks, Mark Heath, Hugh Quarshie, Carrie Segrave
Malcolm Fredricks, Mark Heath

Colin Goddard, Kathy Iddon, Robin Soans, Mia Soteriou, David Threlfall, Alan Williams

as 9 March

John Dicks, Pam Ferris, Jonathan Hackett, Eliza Hunt, Christopher Ryan, James Smith, Holly Wilson

Thomas Baptiste, Rachel Bell, Alan Devlin, Julian Hough, Will Knightley, Nick Le Prevost, Di Patrick, Olivier Pierre, Manning Redwood, Tony Rohr, Antony Sher, Gwyneth Strong, Julie Walters

David Ellison, Isabelle Lucas, Herbert Norville, Stephen Petcher, Veronica Quilligan
Mustafa Djemal, David Ellison, John Fowler, Trevor Laird, Stephen Petcher, Jane Wood

Alister Bain, Mustafa Djemal, David Ellison, John Fowler, Trevor Laird, Isabelle Lucas, Beverley Michaels, Stephen Petcher, Veronica Quilligan, Jane Wood
Stephen Petcher, Veronica Quilligan, Jane Wood

Lucinda Childs, Robert Wilson

Rachel Bell, Andrew Byatt, Simon Callow, Alan Devlin, Patrick Drury, James Duggan, Valerie Lilley, Sid Livingstone, Sharman MacDonald, Walter McMonagle, Peter Postlethwaite, Maggie Shevlin, Ewan Stewart, Christopher Whitehouse

Chris Fairbank, Jamie Foreman, Annie Hayes, Brian Hayes, Karl Johnson, Alfred Molina, Lesley Nightingale, Ian Redford

Ann Bell, Peter Bowles, James Cossins, Leonard Fenton, Paul Rogers

Paul Bentall, Kenneth Colley, James Duggan, Bob Hamilton, Annie Hayes, Robert Hickson, Ian Hogg, Godfrey Jackman, Philip Marchant, Alfred Molina, Peter Sproule

Paul Bentall, Sam Dale, Bob Hamilton, Annie Hayes, Carole Hayman, Kate Saunders, Robert Whelan

John Dicks, Donal McCann, Kevin McNally, Antony Sher

Elizabeth Bell, Paul Greenwood, Deborah Norton, Julie Peasgood, Rowena Roberts, Clive Swift, Nicol Williamson, Marjorie Yates

Shane Connaughton, Nora Connolly, Peter Cox, Alan Devlin, Gerard Mannix Flynn, Tom Jordan, Michael McKevitt, Peter MacNeill, Laurie Morton, Tim Munro, Lynda Rooke, Desmond Stokes, Russell Waters

Barbie Coles, David Gale, Brian Lipson, Julianne Mason, Trevor Stuart

Freddie Boardley, Jim Byars, Elaine Collins, Jake D'Arcy, Pat Doyle, Julia McCarthy, Billy McColl, Carey Wilson

Date	Production	Author	Director	Design/Music
14 Nov	**Prayer for My Daughter**	**Thomas Babe**	Max Stafford-Clark	John Gunter
27 Nov	Masada (Keskedee Workshop)	Edgar White	Rufus Collins	Henry Muttoo
6 Dec	**Wheelchair Willie**	**Alan Brown**	Max Stafford-Clark	Peter Hartwell

1979

Date	Production	Author	Director	Design/Music
9 Jan	Anchorman (CVI Theatre Co)	Ron Hutchinson	John Dove	Quentin Thomas
10 Jan	**Mary Barnes** (Birmingham Rep)	**David Edgar**	Peter Farago	Christopher Morley
1 Feb	On Top	Liane Aukin	Ann Pennington	
13 Feb	Full Frontal	Michael Hastings	Rufus Collins	Jim Clay
19 Feb	The Archangel Michael (rehearsed reading)	Georgi Markov	Roger Michell	
27 Feb	**The London Cuckolds**	**Edward Ravenscroft**	Stuart Burge	Robin Archer
8 March	A Question of Habit (rehearsed reading)	Jacki Holborough	Rio Fanning	
	The Irish Soldier (rehearsed reading)	David Stevens	Antonia Bird	
	Old Ed'll Fix It (rehearsed reading)	David Stevens	Antonia Bird	
15 March	The Dentist (rehearsed reading)	Jonathan Gems	Ian Kellgren	
23 March	Young Writers' Festival			
	Miracles Do Happen	Douglas Parkin	Philip Hedley	Monica Frawley, Sue Pearce & Chris Townsend
	Island	Paul Lister	Mervyn Willis	
	Me, I'd Like to Catch Miss Kerry	Julia James	Mervyn Willis	
	I'm Just Trying to Convince Myself that Vampires Don't Exist	Mark Power	Mervyn Willis	
	Humbug	A group of 13 children	Philip Hedley	
29 March	**Cloud Nine** (Joint Stock)	**Caryl Churchill**	Max Stafford-Clark	Peter Hartwell Andy Roberts (music)
26 April	Psy-Warriors	David Leland	David Leland	Jim Clay
3 May	**Bent** (transf. Criterion 4.7.79)	**Martin Sherman**	Robert Chetwyn	Alan Tagg
5 June	An Empty Desk	Alan Drury	Keith Washington	Peter Hartwell
7 June	**Happy Days**	**Samuel Beckett**	Samuel Beckett	Jocelyn Herbert
25 June	The Smell of Fantasy (rehearsed reading)	K. W. Ross	Antonia Bird	
28 June	Through the Kaleidoscope (rehearsed reading)	John Stevenson	Roger Michell	
9 July	**Reggae Britannia**	**Leigh Jackson**	Keith Washington	Richard Brown
13 July	Marie and Bruce	Wallace Shawn	Les Waters	Peter Hartwell
17 Aug	Carnival War a Go Hot	Michael Hastings	Antonia Bird	Roger Glossop
5 Sept	**The Gorky Brigade**	**Nicholas Wright**	William Gaskill	Eamon D'Arcy Pippy Bradshaw (costumes)
19 Sept	Gogol	Richard Crane	Faynia Williams	Faynia Williams
5 Oct	Sus (Soho Poly)	Barrie Keeffe	Ann Mitchell	Inigo Espejel

Cast

Kamillia Blanche, Roylyn Cohen, Witty Forde, Malcolm Fredricks, David Haynes, Millie Kiarie, Ellen Thomas, Trevor Ward

Frances de la Tour, Carole Hayman, Carrie Lee-Baker, Alfred Molina, Tony Rohr, Robert Walker

Jack Chissick, Caroline Hunt, Will Knightley, Joe Murcell, John Nightingale

Roger Allam, Colin Bennett, Simon Callow, David Gant, Tim Hardy, Judith Harte, Teddy Kempner, Katherine Kitovitz, Patti Love, Ann Mitchell, Judy Monahan, Timothy Spall, Donald Sumpter

Brian Cox, Steve Fletcher, Christine Hargreaves, Sean Scanlan

Winston Ntshona

Joseph Blatchley, Will Knightley

Stephanie Beacham, David Claridge, Kenneth Cranham, Alan Dobie, Ann Dyson, Michael Elphick, Roger Frost, Christopher Hancock, Annie Hulley, Roger Kemp, Cherith Mellor, Deborah Norton, Susan Porrett, Brian Protheroe, James Saxon, Reynold Silva, Barry Stanton, Nina Thomas

Gaye Brown, Jeananne Crowley, Souad Faress, Stacey Tendeter, Ann Windsor

Raymond Campbell, Warren Clarke, Sam Kydd, Eric Richard, Keith Varnier

Raymond Campbell, Warren Clarke, Jeananne Crowley, Sam Kydd, Jeff Rawle, Eric Richard, Harold Saks, Keith Varnier

Ron Berglas, William Hootkins, Matthew Kelly, Joe Melia, June Page, Patsy Rowlands

Brian Attree, Yvonne D'Alpra, Anita Dobson, Derek Fuke, Catherine Hall, Diana Rayworth, Laurance Rudic, Trevor T. Smith

Brian Attree, Catherine Hall, Laurance Rudic
Yvonne D'Alpra, Anita Dobson, Derek Fuke, Catherine Hall, Diana Rayworth, Trevor T. Smith
Brian Attree, Laurance Rudic

Brian Attree, Yvonne D'Alpra, Anita Dobson, Derek Fuke, Catherine Hall, Diana Rayworth, Laurance Rudic, Trevor T. Smith

Julie Covington, Carole Hayman, Jim Hooper, William Hoyland, Miriam Margolyes, Tony Rohr, Antony Sher

Peter Acre, Rio Fanning, Barbara Giles, Julian Hough, David Howey, Michael Irving, Eric Richard, Matthew Scurfield, Kevin Stoney

Jeremy Arnold, Tom Bell, Peter Cellier, Roger Dean, John Francis, Richard Gale, Ian McKellen, Gregory Martyn, Jeff Rawle, Simon Shepherd, Ken Shorter, Haydn Wood

Peter Acre, Stephen Boxer, Michael Cronin, Peter Hughes, Donald Pelmear, Natasha Pyne, Sian Thomas, Philip York

Leonard Fenton, Billie Whitelaw

Nigel Bradshaw, Daniel Gerroll, Alec Linstead, Michele Newell, David Yelland

Sean Barrett, Noel Collins, Michael Cronin, Gordon Hammersley, Malcolm Hayes, Will Knightley, Sheila Reid, Struan Rodger, Harold Saks, Fiona Walker

George Bell, Debby Bishop, James Coyle, Janet Dale, Jimmy Findley, Barry Ford, Simon Hall, Brian Hayes, Ram John Holder, Kelvin Omard, Tim Thomas, William Vanderpuye

Philip Donaghy, Stephanie Fayerman, Robert Hamilton, Annie Hayes, Paul Jesson, Paul Kember, Robin Pappas

Burt Caesar, Bernard Gallagher, Sue Lynne, Patrick Murray, Stephen Petcher, Harold Saks, Kate Saunders, Claire Walker, Daniel Webb

Paul Curran, Peter-Hugo Daly, Philip Davis, Elizabeth Estensen, Richard Mayes, Jonathan Moore, Gary Olsen, June Page, Daniel Peacock, Stuart Wilde, Jane Wood

Richard Crane

Paul Barber, Stuart Barren, Christopher Driscoll

Date	Production	Author	Director	Design/Music
23 Oct	**Sergeant Ola and His Followers**	**David Lan**	Max Stafford-Clark	Peter Hartwell
25 Oct	*The Key Tag* (rehearsed reading)	*Michael McGrath*	Roger Michell	
31 Oct	*The Guise* (Foco Novo)	*David Mowat*	Roland Rees	Adrian Vaux
11 Nov	Touch and Go (Oxford Playhouse)	D. H. Lawrence	Gordon McDougall	
21 Nov	*The Worlds* (YPTS)	*Edward Bond*	Edward Bond	Eamon D'Arcy
1980 14 Jan	**Love of a Good Man** (Oxford Playhouse)	**Howard Barker**	Nicolas Kent	Stephanie Howard
22 Jan	**Trees in the Wind** (7:84 England)	**John McGrath**	Penny Cherns	Jenny Tiramani
5 Feb	**People Show No. 84**			
7 Feb	*The Key Tag*	*Michael McGrath*	Roger Michell	Grant Hicks
28 Feb	**The Liberty Suit** (Project Arts Dublin)	**Peter Sheridan & Gerard Mannix Flynn**	Jim Sheridan	Wendy Shea
11 March	*Young Writers' Festival* *The Arbor* *The Morning Show* *The Personal Effects* *Waking Dreams* (rehearsed reading)	*Andrea Dunbar* *Daniel Goldberg* *Lucy Anderson Jones* *Richard Boswell*	Max Stafford-Clark Roger Michell Nicholas Wright Alby James	Gemma Jackson
2 April	**Hamlet**	**Shakespeare**	Richard Eyre	William Dudley Sue Plummer (costumes)
16 May	*Seduced*	*Sam Shepard*	Les Waters	Peter Hartwell
17 June	*Rutherford and Son* (Mrs Worthington's Daughters)	*Githa Sowerby*	Julie Holledge	Mary Moore
24 June	**The Arbor**	**Andrea Dunbar**	Max Stafford-Clark	Peter Hartwell
4 July	*In and Out the Union Jacks* (rehearsed reading)	*Ginnie Hole*	Antonia Bird	
11 July	*Wednesday Night Action* (RSC rehearsed reading)	*Johnny Quarrell*	John Chapman	
16 July	**A Short Sharp Shock**	**Howard Brenton & Tony Howard**	Rob Walker	Sue Blane
18 July	*Fear of the Dark* (RSC rehearsed reading)	*Doug Lucie*	Walter Donohue	
25 July	*Not Quite Jerusalem* (rehearsed reading)	*Paul Kember*	Les Waters	
5 Aug	*Three More Sleepless Nights* (Soho Poly)	*Caryl Churchill*	Les Waters	Di Seymour
4 Sept	**Cloud Nine**	**Caryl Churchill**	Max Stafford-Clark & Les Waters	Peter Hartwell
6 Sept	*Glasshouses* (rehearsed reading)	*Stephen Lowe*	Richard Wilson	
11 Sept	*Submariners*	*Tom McClenaghan*	Antonia Bird	Mary Moore
13 Oct	**Sugar and Spice**	**Nigel Williams**	Bill Alexander	Mary Moore

Cast

Bruce Alexander, Norman Beaton, Burt Caesar, Joseph Charles, Jimmy Findley, Paul Kember, Will Knightley, Sarah Lam, David Rintoul, Mia Soteriou, Ben Thomas

Patrick Drury, Bernard Gallagher, Diana Patrick, Veronica Quilligan, Mary Sheen

Andrew Berezowski, Cliff Burnett, Carl Davies, Ken Drury, Caroline Hutchison, Neil Johnston, Michael McVey, Tom Marshall

Robert Ashby, Steven Benton, Richard Durden, John Flanagan, Tenniel Evans, Philip Franks, David Haig, Guy Hibbert, Ian Hurley, Anthony Hyde, Godfrey Jackman, Louise Jameson, Karin MacCarthy, Robert Mill, David Plaut, June Redman, Jamie Roberts, Alyson Spiro

Patrick Bailey, Belinda Blanchard, Caroline Cook, Geoff Church, Mark French, Jessica Hawkesly, Dan Hildebrand, Tom Hodgkins, Diana Judd, Fiona McAlpine, Peter Malan, Bart Peel, Matthew Purves, Faith Tingle, Dave Toneri, Julie Wallace, Gordon Warren, Peter Watson, Lindsay Joe Wesker

Kevin Costello, Laura Davenport, Diane Fletcher, Daniel Gerroll, Nigel Gregory, Peter Howell, Edward Jewesbury, Peter Jonfield, Peter Kinley, Graham Lines, Ian McDiarmid, Anthony Pedley

Philip Donaghy, Annie Hayes, Cecily Hobbs, Tina Marian

Linda Hoyle, George Khan, Joy Lemoine, Mark Long, José Nava, Emil Wolk

Noel Collins, Patricia Drury, Marina McConnell, Diana Patrick, Veronica Quilligan

Paul Bennett, Gabriel Byrne, Peter Gaffrey, Ciaran Hind, Annie Kilmartin, Sean Lawlor, Vincent McCabe, Noel McGee, Frank Melia, John Murphy, Larry Murphy, Noel O'Donovan, Peter O'Donovan, Charlie Roberts, Robert Somerset, Eddie Stapleton

David Bamber, Ron Cook, Stephanie Fayerman, Patrick Field, David Haig, Kathryn Pogson, Jeff Rawle, Mia Soteriou
David Bamber, Ron Cook, Stephanie Fayerman, Kathryn Pogson, Jeff Rawle, Mia Soteriou
David Bamber, Ron Cook, Stephanie Fayerman, Patrick Field, Jeff Rawle, Mia Soteriou
David Bamber, Ron Cook, Patrick Field, David Haig, Kathryn Pogson, Jeff Rawle, Mia Soteriou

Judith Alderson, John Barrett, Jill Bennett, Simon Chandler, Geoffrey Chater, Jarlath Conroy, Richard Cottan, Michael Elphick, Colum Gullivan, Magnus Hastings, Will Knightley, Christopher Logue, David Neville, Jonathan Pryce, Kevin Quarmby, Harriet Walter

Kate Fahy, Celia Imrie, Larry Lamb, Ian McDiarmid

Geof Atwell, Stuart Barren, Stacey Charlesworth, Anne Engel, Peter Glancy, Stephen Ley, Maggie Wilkinson

Paul Barber, Ron Cook, David Haig, Dave Hill, Kathryn Pogson, Jeff Rawle, Lynda Rooke, Mia Soteriou, Jane Wood

John Challis, David Howey, Anne Raitt, Dikran Tulaine, Tilly Vosburgh

John Fowler, Irene Handl, Stuart Harwood, Nicky Henson, Julian Hough, Howard Lew Lewis, Desmond McNamara, Cindy O'Callaghan, Ron Pember, Bernard Spear, Susan Tracy

Gil Brailey, Alan Ford, Godfrey Jackman, Darlene Johnson, Alfred Molina, Mary Sheen, Linda Spurrier, Maggie Steed, Gwen Taylor, Joanna Van Gyseghem, Jane Wymark

Jill Baker, Bill Buffery, Burt Caesar, Anthony Head, Edward Jewesbury, Nicholas Le Prevost, David Lyon, Tim McInnerny, Lesley Manville, Lola Young

Mick Ford, Annie Hayes, Marcia Kash, Chris Ryan, Bernard Strother, Ray Winstone

Jan Chappell, Kevin McNally, Fred Pearson, Harriet Walter

Ron Cook, Hugh Fraser, Graeme Garden, Anna Nygh, Anthony O'Donnell, Maggie Steed, Harriet Walter

Leonard Fenton, Sarah Kenyon, Margaret Lawley, Marjie Lawrence, Graham Owens, Mike Packer, Julie Shipley, Allan Surtees

David Beames, Philip Davis, Andrew McCulloch, Donald McKillop, George Sweeney

John Fowler, Carole Hayman, Tammi Jacobs, Tony London, Caroline Quentin, Leroi Samuels, Gwyneth Strong, Toyah Willcox

Appendix 2 Financial Tables

Year ended 31 March 1957   Arts Council grant: £7,000

Production	Performances	Seats %	Box Office %	Production Costs	Box Office Takings
The Mulberry Bush	30	45·0	35·6 ⎫		2,757
The Crucible	32	45·0	39·0 ⎪		3,239
Look Back in Anger	151	67·8	59·8 ⎬	5,164*	23,089
Don Juan/The Death of Satan	8	18·0	22·0 ⎪		367
Cards of Identity	40	57·7	46·0 ⎭		4,836
The Good Woman of Setzuan	46	55·3	59·0	2,421	6,687
The Country Wife	60	94·8	90·0	1,274	13,962
The Member of the Wedding	37	41·4	39·0	1,728	3,743
	404	64·0	56·0	10,587	58,680
Overheads, running costs				65,160	
Transfers, rights, etc.					8,505

* No individual figures kept.

Year ended 31 March 1958   Arts Council grant: £5,000

Production	Performances	Seats %	Box Office %	Production Costs	Box Office Takings
Fin de Partie/Acte Sans Paroles	6	65	69	723	
The Entertainer	36	98	100	1,509	
The Apollo de Bellac/The Chairs	30	42	33	1,418	
The Making of Moo	30	49	40	1,755	
Look Back in Anger (first revival)	104	78	68	—	
The Chairs (revival)/How Can We Save Father?	8	40	31	857	
Nekrassov	46	58	50	2,260	
Requiem for a Nun	30	89	86	1,311	
Lysistrata	53	98	90	2,925	
Epitaph for George Dillon	38	52	46	1,144	
The Sport of My Mad Mother	14	35	23	872	
	395	70	63·8	14,774	65,289
Overheads, running costs				77,293	
Transfers, rights, etc.					39,631

Year ended 31 March 1959   Arts Council grant: £5,500

Production	Performances	Seats %	Box Office %	Production Costs	Box Office Takings
A Resounding Tinkle/The Hole	28	51	41	679	3,105
Epitaph for George Dillon	24	53	41	N.A.	2,710
Flesh to a Tiger	29	22	15	2,783	1,196
The Chairs/The Lesson	45	72	53	548	7,408
Gay Landscape ⎫ Guest	8	17	12	N.A.	268
Chicken Soup With Barley ⎬ Rep	8	40	26	N.A.	565
The Private Prosecutor ⎭ Season	8	18	31	N.A.	290
Dear Augustine	8	26	19	N.A.	410
Major Barbara	36	58	49	1,699	4,810
Live Like Pigs	22	34	25	1,778	1,486
Endgame/Krapp's Last Tape	38	40	28	529	2,853
Moon on a Rainbow Shawl	35	48	37	—	3,538
The Long and the Short and the Tall	94	70	59	2,270	14,952
	383	53	42		43,591
Overheads, running costs				78,447	
Transfers, rights, etc.					18,507

N.A. Not Available

Year ended 31 March 1960   Arts Council grant: £5,000

Production	Performances	Seats %	Box Office %	Production Costs	Box Office Takings
Sugar in the Morning	28	36	28	1,153	2,104
Orpheus Descending	52	64	53	2,728	7,461
Roots	31	74	66	831	5,543
Look After Lulu	45	97	93	4,381	12,603
Cock-a-Doodle Dandy	36	60	49	2,316	4,747
Serjeant Musgrave's Dance	28	30	21	2,088	1,578
Rosmersholm	37	100	93	2,150	9,343
One Way Pendulum	37	93	87	2,042	8,700
The Lily White Boys	45	68	59	2,620	7,222
The Room/The Dumb Waiter	22	40	30	785	1,818
The Naming of Murderer's Rock	2	22	19	1,952	106
	363	69	61	23,046	61,225
Overheads, running costs				83,261	
Transfers, rights, etc					19,653

Year ended 31 March 1961   Arts Council grant: £8,000

Production	Performances	Seats %	Box Office %	Production Costs	Box Office Takings
The Naming of Murderer's Rock	18	12·0	8·0	—	399
Rhinoceros	44	100·0	99·0	4,953	16,372
Chicken Soup With Barley	22	90·0	82·5	1,509	4,917
Roots	30	100·0	93·0	1,120	7,553
I'm Talking About Jerusalem	29	71·4	63·0	1,138	4,966
The Wesker Trilogy (the three plays in repertory)	24	83·6	75·0	—	4,870
The Happy Haven	21	18·0	12·0	1,720	706
Platonov	44	91·0	84·5	3,624	13,986
Trials by Logue	21	30·0	22·0	2,206	1,260
The Lion in Love	28	49·0	40·0	1,318	3,049
The Importance of Being Oscar	32	98·7	90·0	—	10,877
The Changeling	30	60·0	47·7	N.A.	5,386
Jacques	10	28·0	19·7	N.A.	614
	353	72·4	67·4		74,955
Overheads, running costs				86,449	
Transfers, rights, etc					7,888

Year ended 31 March 1962   Arts Council grant: £8,000   London County Council grant: £2,500

Production	Performances	Seats %	Box Office %	Production Costs	Box Office Takings
Altona	45	89·0	80·0	4,024	11,225
Jacques	18	24·6	15·0	—	847
The Blacks	30	41·0	30·0	3,690	2,806
The Kitchen	86	70·6	60·7	2,051	16,226
Luther	28	100·0	96·0	6,421	10,089
August for the People	15	89·0	82·0	4,227	4,632
The American Dream/The Death of Bessie Smith	22	46·4	35·4	2,256	2,423
That's Us	7	13·7	9·9	—	216
The Keep (first run)	29	80·5	72·0	2,093	6,496
The Fire Raisers/Box and Cox	36	57·2	46·6	3,288	5,216
A Midsummer Night's Dream	29	40·5	22·7	4,201	2,408
The Keep (second run)	38	77·6	70·0	—	8,263
The Knack	6	56·5	45·0	1,518	841
	389	67·0	57·0	33,769	71,688
Overheads, running costs				97,989	
Transfers, rights, etc					33,355

Year ended 31 March 1963   Arts Council grant: £20,000   London County Council grant: £2,500

Production	Performances	Seats %	Box Office %	Production Costs	Box Office Takings
The Knack	23	64	49	—	3,526
Chips With Everything	51	94	85	4,158	13,452
Period of Adjustment	29	74	66	2,937	5,962
Plays for England	60	71	58	6,007	13,193
Brecht on Brecht	54	73	64	2,189	10,734
Happy Days	35	49	36	1,769	3,905
The Sponge Room/Squat Betty	20	16	12	2,627	752
Misalliance	21	47	36	N.A.	2,364
Jackie the Jumper	27	28	17	4,921	1,704
The Diary of a Madman	28	35	24	2,935	2,067
	348	61	51		57,659
Naked				3,136	
Overheads, running costs				80,433	
Transfers, rights, etc					20,038

Year ended 31 March 1964   Arts Council grant: £20,000   London County Council grant: £2,500

Production	Performances	Seats %	Box Office %	Production Costs	Box Office Takings
Day of the Prince	28	25·0	18·1	2,370	1,748
Naked	37	38·0	28·7	—	3,665
Kelly's Eye	20	24·0	17·0	3,096	1,178
Skyvers	22	33·5	22·5	1,422	1,710
Exit the King	60	100·0	93·2	2,908	12,295
The Milk Train Doesn't Stop Here Anymore†	—	—	—	2,072	—
Chips With Everything‡	28	76·4	66·8		6,462
	195	59·3	50·6	11,868	27,058
Overheads, running costs				69,269	
Transfers, rights, etc					16,801

† Production abandoned.
‡ Pre-U.S.A. production. The entire cost was borne by the U.S. presenter.

Year ended 27 March 1965*   Arts Council grant: £32,500   London County Council grant: £2,500

Production	Performances	Seats %	Box Office %	Production Costs	Box Office Takings
Inadmissible Evidence	40	98	95·4	3,003	11,890
Cuckoo in the Nest	36	45	42	3,629	4,727
Julius Caesar	28	71	53·4	5,055	4,387
Waiting for Godot	69	81	73	2,164	14,856
Happy End	20	68·6	65	4,874	4,608
	193	74·7	68·4	18,725	40,468
Overheads, running costs				65,637	
Transfers, rights, etc					12,076

* The Royal Court was closed for redecoration until 9 September 1964.

28 March to 2 October 1965   Arts Council grant: £50,555   Greater London Council grant: £2,500

Production	Performances	Seats %	Box Office %	Production Costs	Box Office Takings
Happy End	16	61	52	—	2,952
Spring Awakening	32	60	52	4,279	4,892
Meals on Wheels	19	17	17	3,485	1,021
A Patriot for Me	53	92·5	94·4	12,506	17,516
	120	69	66·8	20,270	26,381

4 October 1965 to 2 April 1966
(Gaskill Season)

Production	Performances	Seats %	Box Office %	Production Costs	Box Office Takings
Shelley	19	44	28·1	1,799	1,799
The Cresta Run	19	41	26·5	2,118	1,689
Saved	24	50	36·7	1,180	3,051
Serjeant Musgrave's Dance	32	61	49·0	1,602	5,259
Clowning	15	22	9·7	454	507
A Chaste Maid in Cheapside	25	52	39·7	2,122	3,325
The Knack	19	43	29·8	1,230	1,907
The Performing Giant/Transcending	19	22	11·3	1,328	421
	172	42	32	11,833	17,958
Dress rehearsals	15				1,608
Overheads, running costs				117,896	
Transfers, rights, etc					26,537

Year ended 1 April 1967   Arts Council grant: £88,650   Greater London Council grant: £2,500

Production	Performances	Seats %	Box Office %	Production Costs	Box Office Takings
Serjeant Musgrave's Dance	13	45·4	34·8	—	1,512
The Voysey Inheritance	55	46·4	41·2	3,024	7,588
Their Very Own and Golden City	26	52·8	40·1	2,861	3,590
Ubu Roi	39	45·4	38·3	4,565	4,616
Three Men for Colverton	26	35·7	27·1	3,721	2,372
Macbeth (Guinness & Signoret)	32	97·7	98·1	6,181	12,098
Macbeth (Maurice Roeves & Susan Engel)	16	71·0	42·9	—	2,308
The Lion and the Jewel	27	57·5	48·9	4,624	4,398
The Soldier's Fortune	39	62·4	52·3	5,160	6,846
Roots	18	86·0	63·5	2,967	3,828
Roots (school matinées)	6	88·0	82·7	—	646
The Daughter-in-Law	17	58·5	46·0	2,426	2,622
	314	59·0	50·0	35,529	52,424
Overheads, running costs				110,198	
Transfers, rights, etc					714

Year ended 30 March 1968   Arts Council grant: £100,000   Greater London Council grant: £2,500

Production	Performances	Seats %	Box Office %	Production Costs	Box Office Takings
The Daughter-in-Law	8	67·7	51·5	—	1,388
Three Sisters	53	90·6	75·2	5,061	13,542
Crimes of Passion	15	41·3	28·3	1,683	1,428
A View to the Common	15	22·8	14·3	1,084	707
The Restoration of Arnold Middleton	22	71·2	59·6	1,287	4,373
OGODIVELEFTTHEGASON	8	46·6	33·2	2,120	889
Fill the Stage With Happy Hours†	32	36·1	44·9	3,543	4,817
Marya	25	64·1	54·3	3,429	4,615
Dingo	19	32·5	25·6	2,541	1,634
The Dragon	38	38·5	31·5	6,099	3,977
Twelfth Night	26	90·9	66·8	5,515	5,819
Twelfth Night (school matinées)	5	—	—		577
A Collier's Friday Night	9	72·5	57·0	8,408 ⎫	1,740
The Daughter-in-Law	8	79·8	63·0	⎬	1,689
The Widowing of Mrs Holroyd	10	87·7	74·3	⎭	2,481
	293	61·6	50·1	40,770	49,676
Dress rehearsal					1,811
Overheads, running costs				108,849	
Transfers, rights, etc					2,115

† Played at the Vaudeville.

Year ended 31 March 1969 — Arts Council grant: £94,000 — Greater London Council grant: £2,500

Production	Performances	Seats %	Box Office %	Production Costs	Box Office Takings
D. H. Lawrence Season	34	88·9	76·3	—	8,683
Backbone	12	51·6	41·6	2,182	1,685
Time Present	39	82·5	75·5	4,708	11,371
The Hotel in Amsterdam	47	98·4	96·2	5,204	17,495
Trixie and Baba	19	30·2	22·5	2,059	1,608
Total Eclipse	19	59·9	45·0	2,270	3,241
The Houses by the Green	19	26·0	18·6	2,666	1,343
Look Back in Anger	52	89·5	66·9	3,944	13,114
This Story of Yours	24	51·8	43·1	3,500	3,909
Life Price	11	22·0	14·4	5,588	596
Life Price – free seats	14	—	—	—	135
Saved	18	62·5	43·0	5,248	2,929
Narrow Road to the Deep North	19	44·2	28·6	7,493	2,032
Early Morning	13	52·0	35·6	5,832	1,746
	340	69·1	57·2	50,694	69,887
Overheads, running costs				123,801	
Transfers, rights, etc					13,615

Year ended 4 April 1970 — Arts Council grant: £94,000 — Greater London Council grant: £2,500

Production	Performances	Seats %	Box Office %	Production Costs	Box Office Takings
Saved	13	41·7	25·2	—	1,248
In Celebration	67	75·0	62·0	3,423	15,692
The Double Dealer	37	48·2	37·0	6,969	5,190
Bread and Puppet Theatre	17	53·2	30·0	385	1,925
Saved } Prior to European tour	7	53·5	35·1	—	931
Narrow Road } Prior to European tour	7	38·2	26·0	—	668
Madeleine Renaud Season	11	83·0	65·3	—	2,726
The Contractor	33	72·7	57·6	4,788	7,192
Insideout	26	40·7	28·0	4,681	2,773
The Three Musketeers Ride Again	28	30·7	23·7	4,751	2,507
Three Months Gone	25	79·5	69·9	4,235	6,590
Uncle Vanya	45	98·1	96·5	7,398	21,440
	316	64·9	57·6	36,630	68,882
Overheads, running costs				141,656	
Transfers, rights, etc					2,609

Year ended 3 April 1971 — Arts Council grant: £89,000* — Greater London Council grant: £2,500

Production	Performances	Seats %	Box Office %	Production Costs	Box Office Takings
Widowers' Houses	39	61·3	50·5	2,387	7,593
Café La Mama Season	19	51·0	33·9	812	2,465
Home	40	92·7	94·0	3,923	16,559
The Philanthropist	39	88·8	82·0	4,139	14,036
Cancer	36	42·2	29·7	4,425	4,722
Come Together Festival	19	76·0	31·0	5,357	2,446
AC/DC	16	32·0	20·0	1,326	1,378
Lulu	35	86·0	79·0	4,751	12,217
The Duchess of Malfi	38	60·7	39·5	5,749	6,618
Man is Man	38	55·0	40·0	4,807	6,752
	319	67·7	54·3	37,676	74,786
Overheads, running costs				144,806	
Transfers, rights, etc					40,372

* There was a £7,000 guarantee against loss which was not claimable as a surplus was made.

Year ended 3 April 1972   Arts Council grant: £91,250*   Greater London Council grant: £2,500

Production	Performances	Seats %	Box Office %	Production Costs	Box Office Takings
One At Night	33	39·0	28·2	4,779	4,090
Slag	39	92·0	82·0	5,240	14,087
The Lovers of Viorne	38	50·2	41·0	2,627	6,862
West of Suez	32	97·0	92·0	8,365	13,870
Lear	37	60·0	45·0	10,819	7,873
The Changing Room	39	94·0	89·0	7,943	16,041
Alpha Beta	39	96·7	88·0	5,963	16,368
Veterans	31	94·5	86·0	7,798	12,564
	288	78·2	68·8	53,534	91,755
Overheads, running costs				158,544	
Transfers, rights, etc					39,599

* There was a £8,750 guarantee against loss which was not claimable as a surplus was made.

Year ended 31 March 1973   Arts Council grant: £112,000   Greater London Council grant: £2,500

Production	Performances	Seats %	Box Office %	Production Costs	Box Office Takings
Veterans	7	98	95·8	—	3,197
Big Wolf	29	26	15·7	6,002	2,203
Crete and Sergeant Pepper	33	33	27·7	7,202	3,996
Hedda Gabler	40	88	69·3	6,667	13,333
The Old Ones	38	76	49·0	8,571	8,910
Richard's Cork Leg	40	72	57·0	5,610	11,830
A Pagan Place	33	82	73·0	7,405	12,432
A Sense of Detachment	39	80	74·0	5,713	15,114
Not I/Krapp's Last Tape	40	97	87·0	5,162	18,167
The Freedom of the City	33	45	32·5	7,564	5,643
	332	68	57·5	59,896	94,825
Overheads, running costs				184,775	
Transfers, rights, etc					47,330

Year ended 31 March 1974   Arts Council grant: £135,000   Greater London Council grant: £2,500

Production	Performances	Seats %	Box Office %	Production Costs	Box Office Takings
Savages	39	97	89	12,309	18,313
The Sea	40	65	60	12,507	12,676
Magnificence	20	36	26	5,664	2,931
The Removalists	20	53	43	4,865	4,527
Cromwell	39	90	83	10,797	16,881
The Farm	40	78	69	8,863	14,445
The Merry Go Round	40	75	53	13,055	11,139
South African Season	71	93	82	7,605	30,639
Runaway	24	50	18	8,204	2,253
	333	77	65	83,869	113,804
Overheads, running costs				216,647	
Transfers, rights, etc					55,937

Year ended 29 March 1975 Arts Council grant: £170,000 Greater London Council grant: £5,000

Production	Performances	Seats %	Box Office %	Production Costs	Box Office Takings
Life Class	54	96	88	10,122	25,052
Tooth of Crime	39	53	43	12,067	8,687
Play Mas	26	77	48	6,790	6,598
Bingo	54	97	89	12,844	29,203
The Great Caper	25	29	20	7,789	3,028
The City	40	42	30	2,426	7,371
Objections to Sex and Violence	27	29	21	5,555	3,607
Statements After an Arrest Under the Immorality Act/Not I	27	64	54	4,057	8,941
Don's Party*	33	51	42	—	8,385
	325	65	54	61,650	100,872
Overheads, running costs				248,398	
Transfers, rights, etc					36,913

*The production costs of *Don's Party* were borne by an outside management.

Year ended 27 March 1976 Arts Council grant: £172,500 Greater London Council grant: £10,000

Production	Performances	Seats %	Box Office %	Production Costs	Box Office Takings
Don's Party	7	61	55	—	2,332
Entertaining Mr Sloane	41	95	91	8,162	22,679
Loot	40	73	63	7,483	15,521
What the Butler Saw	40	83	75	11,755	18,329
Teeth 'n' Smiles	39	87	77	12,379	23,845
Stripwell	33	54	46	13,226	11,917
The Fool	38	69	53	18,649	15,993
Treats	34	72	61	8,321	16,351
Parcel Post	15	24	17	8,097	2,023
	287	74	63	88,072	128,990
Overheads, running costs				264,572	
Transfers, rights, etc					43,476

Year ended 2 April 1977 Arts Council grant: £220,000 Greater London Council grant: £11,500

Production	Performances	Seats %	Box Office %	Production Costs	Box Office Takings
Parcel Post	14	30	22	—	2,417
Waiting for Godot	13	53	44	1,340	4,510
Endgame/Triple Bill	61	48	63	15,439	23,369
Small Change	23	26	34	7,651	4,739
T-Zee	39	52	42	15,706	15,688
Mother's Day	39	28	33	11,894	10,303
Rum an' Coca-Cola	34	42	29	6,024	9,324
Dracula	16	45	43	933	3,679
Sizwe Bansi is Dead	41	72	66	3,651	23,075
Devil's Island	28	17	14	1,431	3,381
Gimme Shelter	13	40	26	1,607	2,951
	321	43	42	65,676	103,436
Overheads, running costs				280,566	
Transfers, rights, etc					16,773

Year ended 1 April 1978 Arts Council grant: £247,000 Greater London Council grant: £12,500

Production	Performances	Seats %	Box Office %	Production Costs	Box Office Takings
Gimme Shelter	6	58	48	—	2,503
Out of Our Heads	6	78	65	591	3,093
Curse of the Starving Class	41	27	18	9,985	6,750
Fair Slaughter	38	22	17	9,447	5,569
Once a Catholic	38	90	88	11,411	28,036
Sleak!	22	99	99	—	14,088
The Good Woman of Setzuan	46	78	69	8,802	30,722
Talbot's Box	27	28	22	—	5,163
The Trembling Giant	21	29	17	—	2,914
Laughter	23	26	18	16,103	3,186
The Bear/The Kreutzer Sonata	21	32	26	3,418	4,511
A Bed of Roses	12	59	55	—	4,035
	301	51	45	59,757	110,570
Overheads, running costs				288,700	
Transfers, rights, etc					17,899

Year ended 31 March 1979 Arts Council grant (including supplementary grant): £305,000
Greater London Council grant: nil

Production	Performances	Seats %	Box Office %	Production Costs	Box Office Takings
Class Enemy	27	66	61	3,158	10,181
The Glad Hand	27	35	33	14,667	5,652
Flying Blind	35	39	36	18,597	10,880
Eclipse	28	17	17	10,897	3,719
Inadmissible Evidence	60	98	94	17,911	58,529
Prayer for My Daughter	18	47	38	6,010	6,966
Wheelchair Willie	16	34	28	9,756	4,083
Mary Barnes	42	91	82	11,880	34,035
The London Cuckolds	31	81	75	21,186	23,211
Cloud Nine	6	79	67	—	3,520
	290	64	59	114,062	160,776
Overheads, running costs				341,272	
Transfers, rights, etc					59,952

Year ended 31 March 1980* Arts Council grant: £350,000 Greater London Council grant: £15,000

Production	Performances	Seats %	Box Office %	Production Costs	Box Office Takings
Cloud Nine	20	92	87	—	17,629
Bent	38	95	90	26,582	33,553
Happy Days	27	94	88	10,782	22,727
Reggae Britannia	38	49	28	20,305	10,816
The Gorky Brigade	27	22	15	18,395	3,828
Sergeant Ola and His Followers	27	28	19	16,854	5,182
Love of a Good Man	8	75	58	—	5,125
Trees in the Wind	6	78	54	—	3,515
People Show No. 84	13	69	65	—	5,490
The Liberty Suit	19	41	28	—	5,899
Hamlet †	4	91	69	29,426	3,879
	227	62	53	122,344	117,643
Overheads, running costs				351,950	
Transfers, rights, etc					46,352

*Closed for redecoration from 17 November 1979 to 8 January 1980.
† Hamlet completed a run of 69 performances in 1980/81 (98% seats; Box Office £90,807: 93%).

Index to Persons

Figures in italics refer to captions

Index to Plays

LOOK BACK IN ANGER

ROYAL COURT THEATRE
OCTOBER 24th – DECEMBER 7th

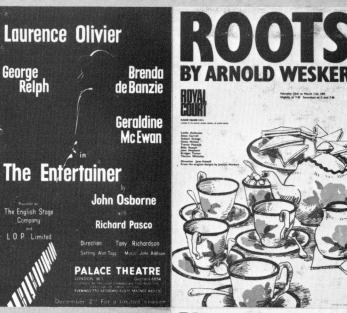

Laurence Olivier

George Relph   Brenda de Banzie

Geraldine McEwan

in

The Entertainer

by

John Osborne

with

Richard Pasco

Presented by
The English Stage Company
and
L O P Limited

Direction   Tony Richardson
Setting   Alan Tagg   Music   John Addison

PALACE THEATRE
LONDON, W.1.   Gerrard 6834

December 2nd For a limited season

ROOTS
BY ARNOLD WESKER

ROYAL COURT

the knack by ann jelli

james bolam
julian glover
philip locke
rita tushingham

directed by ann jellicoe and keith johnstone designed by alan tagg
nightly at 7.30 matinees thursdays 2.30 saturdays 5 and 8.15 slo 1745

"Come Together"
at The Royal Court

October 21 – November 9

ROYAL COURT THEATRE
SLOANE SQUARE SW1 01-730 1745

Once a Catholic

A Comedy by Mary O'Malley

John Boswall, Jane Carr, Kim Clifford
Daniel Gerroll, Mike Grady, Pat Heywood
Anna Keaveney, Doreen Keogh, June Page
Rowena Roberts, John Rogan
Lilian Rostkowska, Sally Watkins
Jeanne Watts
directed by Mike Ockrent
designed by Poppy Mitchell
lighting by Jack Raby

Sizwe Bansi is dead

The Royal Court Theatre Upstairs presents
Sizwe Bansi is dead, a new play devised by
Athol Fugard, John Kani, Winston Ntshona.
Directed by Athol Fugard.
Designed by Douglas Heap.

Lynn Redgrave   Barbara Ferris

Anna Massey

S.L.A.G

by David Hare

directed by Max Stafford-Clark
designed by John Gunter

Royal Court Theatre

FEBRUARY 6 UNTIL MARCH 29

BOND
AT THE
ROYAL COURT

EARLY MORNING, LEAR, AND
THE NARROW ROAD
TO THE DEEP NORTH

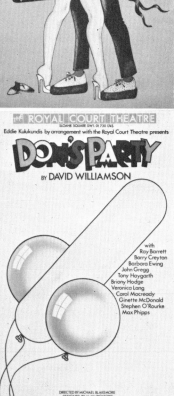

ROYAL COURT THEATRE
SLOANE SQUARE SW1 01 730 1745

Eddie Kulukundis by arrangement with the Royal Court Theatre presents

Don's Party
BY DAVID WILLIAMSON

with
Ray Barrett
Barry Creyton
Barbara Ewing
John Gregg
Tony Haygarth
Briony Hodge
Veronica Lang
Carol Macready
Ginette McDonald
Stephen O'Rourke
Max Phipps

DIRECTED BY MICHAEL BLAKEMORE
DESIGNED BY ALAN PICKFORD
LIGHTING BY LEONARD TUCKER

The Royal Court Theatre
Sloane Square SW1 01-730-1745

OBJECTIONS TO
Sex & Violence
by
Caryl Churchill

with Anna Calder-Marshall   Sylvia Coleridge
Michael Harrigan   Rose Hill   Rosemary McHale
Stephen Moore   Ivor Roberts   Paul Seed

Directed by John Tydeman
Designed by David Short
Lighting by Jack Raby

2 – 25 January

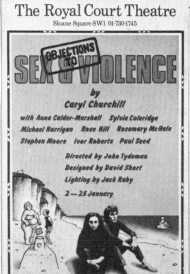

ROYAL COURT THEATRE

WITH
JANE CARR
VALENTINE DYALL
BRIAN GLOVER
KEVIN LLOYD
BETTY MARSDEN
MICHAEL MEDWIN

directed by
Lindsay Anderson

designed by
Jocelyn Herbert
lighting by
Nick Chelton
music by
Alan Price